Between Rationality & Irrationality

Between Rationality & Irrationality

The Jewish Psychotherapeutic System

Mordechai Rotenberg

With a new introduction and appendix by the author

Routledge
Taylor & Francis Group
LONDON AND NEW YORK

Originally published in 1991 by Praeger.

Published 2005 by Transaction Publishers

Published 2017 by Routledge
2 Park Square, Milton Park, Abingdon, Oxon OX14 4RN
711 Third Avenue, New York, NY 10017, USA

Routledge is an imprint of the Taylor & Francis Group, an informa business

Library of Congress Catalog Number: 2004041264

Library of Congress Cataloging-in-Publication Data

Rotenberg, Mordechai.
[Dia-logo therapy]
Between rationality and irrationality : the Jewish psychotherapeutic system / Mordechai Rotenberg ; with a new introduction and appendix by the author, p. cm.
Previously published: Dia-logo therapy. New York: Praeger, 1991.
Includes bibliographical references and index.
ISBN 0-7658-0583-9 (pbk.: alk. paper)
1. Logotherapy. 2. Bible O.T.—Criticism, interpretation, etc., Jewish. 3. Buber, Martin, 1878-1965. I. Title.

RC489.L6R67 2004
616.89'14—dc22 2004041264

ISBN 13: 978-0-7658-0583-6 (pbk)

Copyright Acknowledgments

The author gratefully acknowledges permission to use extracts from the following publications:

Evelyne Albrecht Schwaber, "Interpretation and the Therapeutic Action of Psycho-Analysis," International Journal of Psycho-Analysis 71, part 2 (1990): 229-40. Copyright © Institute of Psycho-Analysis. Reprinted by permission of the author and the Institute of Psycho-Analysis.

John Spiegel, Transactions (New York: Science House, 1971), pp. 318-23. Reprinted by permission of Jason Aronson Inc.

Contents

Introduction to the Transaction Edition

After Daniel Kahneman received the Nobel Prize in economics for demonstrating how intuitive-irrational factors predominate economic decisions, a radio commentator in Israel asked the following humorous rhetorical question: "For proving that people don't use their brains, Kahneman received the Nobel Prize...?"

It appears that Kahneman, who at the time taught psychology at the Hebrew University in Jerusalem, achieved his recognition in Western academic circles because he was able to use rational methods to show how people's economic calculations (or miscalculations) are irrationally derived from superstitious beliefs and intuitive emotionalism. It is no secret that since the rise of Protestantism in the sixteenth century, we have witnessed a systematic banning of irrational thinking in the West, as Max Weber, Michel Foucault, and others posited.

It has thus been convenient to divide people according to an "either/or" dichotomy, between those who are mastered by irrational superstitious fears of the unknown and those who are capable of calculating their movements via rational methodic steps. Should we then conclude that in the Western "money-theistic" world, the irrationalists (the mentally *unhealthy* and the uncalculating *wealthy*) should from now on be segregated on a "ship of fools"? Or may we admit that in our precarious cosmos, people will be forever doomed to communicate with the unknown world due to their unpredictable unreal and corporeal fears and losses?

While Kahneman demonstrated that it is futile to keep exorcising the demons of irrational superstition and intuition from Weber's methodic rational-bureaucratic salvation system, I attempted to extract and construct a bridge between the material-rational and the mystic-irrational worlds that is available in the Jewish hermeneutic tradition known as *PaRDeS* (an acronym of the Hebrew words *peshat*, *remez*, *derash*, and *sod*, which will be discussed in the book). By using psychotherapeutic case studies, I thus showed how people may communicate with the material-rational world of *peshat* (literal) that predominates in the West, while their simultaneous crossing of the bridge to handle their fears and hopes in the mystic-transcendental world of *sod* (hidden) does not precipitate excommunication from the normative social systems. To demonstrate how this back and forth crossing of the bridge must not lead to a one-way crucifying exile to the "ship of fools," I introduced the psychologist as a mediating "bridge" because he uses reason to decipher "unreason" in his psychotherapeutic dialogues with people who seek his guidance. By introducing the psychotherapeutic dialogue as a bridging device between the rational and the irrational languages, I claimed, in fact, that the dialogically committed psychotherapist is the only interpreting narrativist who conducts a living dispute with "authors" (termed "patients") concerning the meaning of their texts.

To clarify how a living dispute of text written by authors constitutes a psychotherapeutic dialogical bridge between the rational and irrational languages, I recount a personal experience:

One evening, in a public forum about the psychology emanating from the PaRDeS system, an historian and a novelist discussed this bridging theory. To dramatize my response to the challenging speakers, I claimed that it was difficult for me to argue with people, of which one speaks to the dead, and the other is a self-professed liar... To wipe off the naturally astonished, or rather startled, look from the audience's faces, I said defensively that, while everybody knows that historians usually interpret dead people's reported statements, the statement that authors are liars was made by a quite famous writer: Isaac Bashevis Singer purportedly said, "When I was a young boy, they called me a liar. Now that I'm all grown up, they call me a writer." The point I tried to make was that, in contrast to the contemporary novelist who, according to Paul Ricoeur, is "dead" from the moment that his story is published (like an historical figure who lived hundreds of years ago) because, as a rule, he does not discuss his novel with his readers, a psychotherapist's documented dispute of an author's experiential texts comprises a unique contribution to hermeneutic narrativism.

To buttress the claim that the psychological dialogue of texts contains a unique dimension, I recited a fabricated text from the thirteenth century that presumably explicates the psychological meaning of a cabalistic ecstatic experience (see pages 25-26 in the present book). By using concrete clinical case studies, it was possible to illustrate how psychopathological interpretations of extreme ecstatic conduct may entail crucial consequences for people's mental health.

As an example, on a psychotherapeutic level, the difference between talking to the dead and being dead when one is talked to is a living problem. Judy Carmel reports in her master's thesis how a bereaved father who experienced a mental breakdown twelve years after his son was killed in action was able to resume normal functioning due to her success in bridging this man's rational and mystic thinking. When the bereaved father was encouraged to "converse" and "interact" with his dead son without jeopardizing his membership in the community, he felt relieved.

There is a story about a Jew who sent his three daughters to a Jesuit college in order to express his atheistic-secular perception of life. Nonetheless, when these daughters returned home one by one with Chabad (that is, Lubavitch Hasidim, who typically perform outreach to secular Jews) boyfriends who searched for Jewish lost souls on the fringes of the campus, the father became so alarmed that he rushed to his former Reform rabbi to ask for his help—whereupon the "modern" rabbi surprisingly suggested to the father that he "check his *mezuzos*" (parchments containing text from the book of Deuteronomy rolled up in cases and attached to the doorposts of one's home, in accordance with Jewish law, and which are periodically checked to ensure their validity), a custom many Jews follow in times of misfortune.

It may thus be said that in fact we all "check our mezuzos" when we face irrational calamities. We all cross the bridge between our rational everyday life and our intuitive-prejudicial beliefs when we feel the need.

It is hoped that due to the widening of horizons since its initial publication, *Between Rationality and Irrationality* will strengthen and legitimize the proposed psychological bridge. Whether we will kiss our mezuzos goodbye when we leave home and no longer want them, or whether we shall accept them as part of our household and thus kiss them also when we come home, will depend entirely on our intellectual and emotional integrity.

Mordechai Rotenberg
February 2004

To the unforgettable memory
of my youngest son, BOAZ,
the child who prolonged my youth
and the man who taught me truth

Preface

As a phenomenologist who accepts people's subjective experiences as a canonical basis for his research method, I have no problem in joining those who believe that *every* book is largely shaped by the specific personal mood that imbued the author during the writing period that preceded the publication of his work. True, this book was written immediately after my beloved youngest son, Boaz, was killed in action in the Israeli army, as a result of which I felt more than ever a need to relate to the world of the transcendental unknown. I find it, accordingly, senseless to attempt the payment of dues to the scientific community to which I belong by endeavoring to play the role of the objective researcher because the clever reader will doubtless discover on his own my "Boazed" and biased subjectivism.

The Jewish pluralistic interpretation system known under the acronym *PaRDeS,* which will be introduced in this book, entails the potential therapeutic bridge between the rational-material and the irrational-mystic worlds that I have sought ever since I first immersed myself in studies about the Judeo-Christian impact on Western social sciences in the early 1970s. I have thus devoted this book to the study of psychotherapy as a dual, or a "dia-logic," discourse between the rational-cognitive and the mystic-schizophrenic languages. And I have done so only because this perspective incorporates my previous work on the impact of rational Protestantism (Rotenberg, 1978), Hasidic cabalism (Rotenberg, 1983), and the hermeneutic system of the Midrash (Rotenberg, 1987) on psychology. I also introduce the *PaRDeS* psychology because I believe that a psychotherapeutic theory should attempt to engulf all aspects of human behavior. Accordingly, although it is legitimate to concentrate on one cognitive-rational therapeutic method or on a narrative-storytelling salvation remedy, a comprehensive theory of psychotherapy must encompass treatment possibilities for rational and irrational behavior manifestations as they are apprehended in their specific cultural context.

Although, consequently, many psychological theories of therapy construct their treatment strategies on specific nomenclatures of personality types, the present point of departure is that behavior patterns are shaped by specific cultural reading codes. Hence, "problems of living" that may be read as a *text* must be interpreted in their specific religiocultural *context*.

It is with this comprehensive and culturally relativistic perspective in mind that we launched our dia-logo therapy project early in 1987. In this experimental treatment project an egalitarian norm of discourse was established according to which the therapist is committed to learn his patient's language rather than impose his own doctrinaire interpretation. Thus, a cognitive-rational interpretation that could be understood by a California existentialist would not be imposed on an oriental fatalist. Similarly, even subtle English humor would have to be interpreted by Americans and Israelis raised to appreciate largely slapstick as a different language. Likewise the wisdom of an engineer would have to be understood by the sophisticated humanists as a different thought system and not as "squareness."

Thus, parts of the psychotherapeutic texts discussed in this book are taken from the dia-logic treatment workshop I conducted during 1987 and 1988.

I am indebted to the Paul Baerwald School of Social Work at the Hebrew University for supporting this therapeutic project with a fund from the Warburg Foundation. I would like to express my thanks to Dr. Eli Frankel for his continuous support. I would like to acknowledge also with gratitude Michal Hakohen's and Graciella Spektor's contributions to this project in volunteering case material, critical advice, and general encouragement. To Abraham Werter, Chaim Cohen, and Naftali Fish, who worked on this project, go special thanks for their readiness to go along with my unconventional guidance in treating the cases described in this book. I am grateful to my colleagues Moshe Idel and Gershon Shaked for volunteering graciously vital information from their respective disciplines.

Finally, to my daughter, Michal, who read the manuscript critically, and to my wife, Naomi, who typed it in between her many more important obligations, I convey my respect, love, and appreciation.

Introduction

I am grateful to Allan Bloom (1987), who in his popular book has succeeded in demonstrating eloquently how the "American mind has been closed" because it has been dominated by German philosophy. Drawing on his compelling arguments, I find it worthwhile to begin my introduction with Bloom's claim, which raises the following rhetorical question:

> Who in 1920 would have believed Max Weber's technical sociological terminology would someday be the everyday language of the United States . . . ? The self-understanding of hippies, yippies, yuppies, panthers, prelates and presidents has unconsciously been formed by German thought of a half century earlier . . . and the new American life-style has become a Disneyland version of the Weimar Republic for the whole family. (p. 147)

If, accordingly, the permeating predominance of Weber's German "technical terminology" means, as I and others have repeatedly maintained (Rotenberg, 1978, 1983, 1987), that rationalism was accepted in the United States as the official, exclusive language of the country, "self-understanding" has been disseminated in its Waspy Darwinian expressive form, which Bellah and others (1985) termed the "first language of individualism."

It is the thesis of this book that if Weber and especially Michel Foucault (1967) are correct in their contention that since the rise of Protestantism in the sixteenth century, the "irrational language" of creative schizophrenia and mysticism has been banned in the West, then this monological language of "egoistic rationalism" has not only "closed the American mind" but also precipitated the crisis associated with terms such as *counterculture*, *psychedelic flights*, and *cultish plights*. This perpetual Western social crisis may be briefly reconstructed thus: Although the irrational language of mysticism may be banned, people's fears of the unpredictable, transcendental world of the unknown will always remain irrational.

It is consequently plausible to assume a connection between the Darwinian "Star Wars" competition during the twentieth century, which has resulted in increasing pressure being exerted on Western youth to excel in rational-technological achievements, and the growing popularity of Eastern mysticism among these same youngsters. In other words, the proposition here is that increasing demands to speak the language of technological rationalism have enhanced the need to learn the irrational language of mysticism. It seems, however, that neither the drastic switch to methods of Eastern mystic salvation nor the cultish flight to what can be termed the psychedelic drug world has succeeded in providing the vital bridging balance between the rational-material world and the irrational-mystic world to which young Westerners tried to relate.

If the search for pertinent salvation formulas to help people adjust to the unpredictable "imperfect world" in which we are doomed to live always begins in the religious domain, as Weber claimed, then the system for balancing the rational and the irrational worlds must indeed be sought in a religious text. I say "religious text" because it is through the doctrinaire texts by which religions exert paradigmatic impact on the secularized normative social order that disseminate from various religions. And if cultural therapeutic remedies, or actualization patterns, may be understood, as Weber posited, in terms of secularized salvation methods, then my effort to introduce the Jewish hermeneutic system known as *PaRDeS* might indeed contain the potential balancing bridge between the rational and the mystic worlds.

To be sure, whether it is the religious or the secular texts that entail therapeutic actualization remedies, our attention must focus on how to read and interpret these texts. Moreover, if indeed the religious texts produce the psychology of everyday life in respective cultures or, vice versa, if behind every psychology there is a theology, as I have often argued, then psychological conceptions of human behavior might function today as Platonic ideas. Consider merely how Freudianism, with its medically based authority, has been inculcated—via the media, literature, and so forth—as an unquestionable system for interpreting life throughout most of the Western and even within parts of the Eastern world. Indeed, Freudianism, as a Platonic idea preceding and shaping the real world, has been more widespread and effective than material Marxism, which seems nowadays to have collapsed in many communist countries.

Now, if religious and secular texts function as psychological Platonic ideas, which may shape behavior, then psychotherapeutic efforts to change behavior will require specific hermeneutic systems for reading and interpreting these texts.

The focus on reading and interpreting lives as texts obviously raises the problem of choosing a methodological authority in order to determine which reading code, or what I term metacode, may be used to establish the true meaning of the text. If only a univocal Aristotelian metacode is being used, then the art of deciphering the text may result in a fundamentalistic either/or interpretation of life. If, however, the Socratic dialogue is used as a reading metacode, then truth might ensue from an ongoing, ever-changing discourse between reader-therapists and their writer-patients.

It is in this dialogical sense that I introduce in this book the *PaRDeS* system as a pluralistic reading method for balancing the rational-material and the irrational-mystic languages. In order to present the Jewish *PaRDeS* as a therapeutic reading method, I have naturally incorporated ideas from theories of literary criticism, *deconstruction* and *reception.* Accordingly, this book is entitled *Dia-logo Therapy* not only to pay tribute to Martin Buber's I-thou philosophy and to Viktor Frankl's Logo Therapy, but mainly to advocate the idea that therapeutic truth may be established if the discourse between reader-therapist and writer-patient is based on the coexistence between two or more alternating (*dia*) systems of logos. Thus, a Jew who was raised with a *PaRDeS* metacode is trained to choose a *P(eshat)* (rational), a *R(emez)* (symbolic), a *D(erash)* (narrative), or even a *S(od)* (mystic) interpretation of life. By stressing that the *PaRDeS* encompasses a socialization system, I am in fact suggesting that it is the hermeneutic system that produces the psychology of everyday life because it is by absorbing the *PaRDeS* metacode (either by listening to sermons in the synagogue or by studying biblical commentaries) that the Jew learns how to choose between or to accept both the mystic and the rational reading of a text as a source of truth. Here, the *PaRDeS*, as a proposed system for balancing rational and mystic reading metacodes, impinges on the problem of the methodological authority mentioned above. The *PaRDeS* would require, accordingly, that the mystic language of *S(od)* and the rational language of *P(eshat)* employ equal positions as legitimate methods of interpretation. Thus, if a reader-therapist speaks the rational language of *P(eshat)* and the writer-patient speaks a schizophrenic language of *S(od),* then the discourse may not be dominated by one interpretive methodology. We may elucidate the "dia-logic" approach to the methodological authority as follows: Whereas students trained via the historical method know they have to establish truth by using primary sources, students trained to conceive truth from a phenomenological perspective know that secondary sources often exert greater impact on people's understanding of a text than do primary sources. Consequently, if historians find it necessary to preface their study by stating apologetically that they used only or mostly primary sources, our phenomenologist should state that he attempted to use mostly secondary sources for his study. Nonetheless, the *PaRDeS* system would require one, accordingly, to discard the dominance of one methodology by accepting various metacodes as a basis for the dia-logic discourse.

To explore possibilities for establishing dia-logic truth in therapeutic reading, the first part of this book attempts to draw on hermeneutic theories that focus on the relationship between the literary critic and the author of a text; the second part assesses possibilities of establishing an intrapersonal balance between mystic and rational readings of one's biography; while the third part concentrates on scrutinizing the interpersonal applications of "dia-logism." This book thus far might appear to the reader to be a study that attempts to apply the potential contribution of hermeneutics to psychotherapy. However, I would like to conclude this introduction by sharing also the hidden agenda that I hope will be manifested to the reader of this book. Put succinctly, since dialogues between literary critics and authors are, as a rule of thumb, not based on living discourses, whereas therapeutic dialogues contain disputes concerning the meaning of experiences described in the text, our study of the therapeutic discourse might enrich our understanding of the hermeneutic mystery of life. This tacit goal might be illuminated with a popular Hasidic anecdote:

A poor woman who was deserted by her husband went to her *Rebbe* [the leader of a Hasidic sect] and handed him a *quittle* [a piece of paper on which a Hasid spells out his or her request] asking him to do something so that her husband will return home. The Rebbe read the *quittle* and promised the woman that in due time her husband would return. On her way out, she was told bluntly by the Rebbe's *shames* [servant] that, in his opinion, her husband would never come back. A year passed, and the husband did not return. The bitter woman went to her Rebbe with a new *quittle* repeating the same request, and again the Rebbe promised that her husband would return, but the *shames* told her on the way out that her husband would never return. When the woman went a third time and the *shames* again contradicted the Rebbe's promise, the Rebbe reprimanded him vehemently by asking him to explain how he dared to contradict a Rebbe's promise? The *shames*, however, responded: "Rebbe, you looked at the *quittle* [a righteous Rebbe would not look at a woman] but I looked at the woman's face."

By telling this story I suggest that, whereas the literary critic is trained and committed to look only at the *quittle*—that is, the text—the psychotherapeutic reader-therapist is trained and committed to establishing truth by looking at both the text and the human face.

Part One

DIA-LOGIC TRUTH

1

Dia-logic and Dialectic Languages of Psychotherapy

This book endeavors to apply to psychotherapeutic interpretation the Jewish multilevel system of hermeneutics known under the acronym *PaRDeS*.[1] The *PaRDeS* system will be defined and introduced in Chapter 4 as a dialogic bridge between mystic-irrational[2] and cognitive-rational perceptions of life. The gist of this book's argument will be that an egalitarian dialogue is possible to the extent that two thought systems employ equal positions in the discourse that ensues from a literary or a psychotherapeutic exchange.

The study of the psycho-therapeutic discourse as a multi- or dia-logic system of interpretation impinges upon a central dilemma that perpetually rocks the discipline of psychology. What I have in mind is the ceaseless search for methodologies that are appropriate for establishing what is termed social scientific or psychological truth. It is well known, for instance, that even those who agree that people's lives may be interpreted as a literary or biographic text are divided between the objective, natural science oriented school of "explanation" and the subjective orientation associated with the Romantic-historicistic school of empathic "understanding."[3] According to the school of explanation, it should be possible for an authoritative interpreter to establish one authentic Aristotelian truth that would replace or eliminate all other attributed meanings to reality. In contrast, given the approach of the historicistic school of empathy, understanding experiences would imply that truth may be generated from a Socratic discourse between various interpretations of a described event or an author's intent.

In differentiating between structural explanation and Romantic understanding, Paul Ricoeur (1983) admits, however, that in both the objective kind of reading (explaining) a text as a closed, internal linguistic structure[4] and the empathic, subjective way of reading (understanding) a text in order to determine the author's intent, there is no living discourse[5] that may corroborate truth. That is to say, if by explaining a literary text according to philological rules patterned after the methods of the natural sciences, we may not speak about a living truth that generates discourse because the text is treated "as a worldless and authorless object" (p. 152), then philology that does not require a living discourse might be acceptable to Aristotelian believers in unipolar terms of truth. However, if understanding a text according to the Romantic-historicistic method of nostalgic empathy means likewise "to consider its author as already dead and the book as posthumous" (p. 147), then it is only the living kind of psychotherapeutic discourse that might now be propelled into becoming the true heir of Plato's dialogues. It is, after all, the psychotherapeutic text that preserves the living dialogue between a reader-therapist and an author-patient. Indeed, according to Ricoeur, "the text is a discourse fixed by writing" (p. 145), and since "writing as an institution is subsequent to speech" (p. 146),[6] it is thinking and the oral living dialogue that must be studied prior to focusing on reading or writing per se. Thus, dialogism in the context of psychotherapeutic text reading must be a major concept in our treatise, and will therefore be explored and defined in this chapter.

Moreover, dialogism, or rather dia-logism, becomes significant for literary and psychotherapeutic interpretation because it also explores the possibility of an egalitarian discourse between two people who use two or more alternating systems of logic. These two thought systems, to which I shall refer as dia-logism are the mystic-spiritual logos and the rational-material logos. It is, after all, the psychotherapeutic dialogue that forces a rational reader-therapist to converse with an author-patient who might speak the irrational-mystic language of schizophrenia.

Accordingly, another major goal of this chapter is to introduce dia-logism as an egalitarian model for psychotherapy, which obviates the otherwise inevitable manipulative superiority of the therapist. More specifically, it will be argued that it is the dia-logic balancing between the mystic and the rational thought systems that facilitates an egalitarian dialogue in psychotherapy.

To justify the need for psychotherapeutic dia-logism, the first part of this chapter will focus on demonstrating how efforts to formulate a humanistic, egalitarian I-thou conception of therapy have hitherto failed because they depend too much on an undifferentiated idea of dialecticism. In conventional dialectic psychotherapy, thesis must always be replaced by antithesis or synthesis and likewise the therapist's interpretation must always replace the patient's conception of his reality. Consequently, egalitarian dialogues in conventional dialectic psychotherapy are usually more ideal than real.

Let me therefore begin by reviewing critically the literature dealing with the concepts of dialogue and dialectic, and then introduce dia-logism.

DIALOGIC CONVERSATION VERSUS DIA-LOGIC INTERPRETATION

While the term *Dialecticism* is usually used to refer to historical processes or to a mode of thinking traceable to Hegelian philosophy, the term *dialogue*, which is associated with the names of Plato or Socrates and recently with Buber, call to mind a technique of conversation and a state of coexistence. The distinctions between a dialectic thought process and a dialogic I-thou technique of interaction or conversation should in theory clarify the difference between these two constructs.

It appears possible to speak about one dialectic philosophical thought process predicated on negating opposites in which the Platonic-Socratic dialogic conversation technique may or may not be used to facilitate or enhance the dynamics of dialecticism. Indeed, this has been Maurice Friedman's (1987: 7) observation that "the tendency of by far the largest and most dominant methodologies in most human sciences is to begin with dialectic and to examine dialogue as a part of that dialectic." One may notice, however, that (1) dialogicalism is treated on a philosophical level not only as a technique but as a representative of various schools of thought and that (2) on a social science level dialecticism is being used to refer to a multiplicity of processes.

Very briefly, in analyzing the nature of "the other," Michael Theunissen (1983) differentiates between ego-centered philosophers for whom "the other" constitutes the "alien I," or what is termed the "alter ego," and those for whom "the other" is a thou, that is, a second person who is to be addressed as a partner of the discourse in a dialogue. I shall return to argue that from an applied therapy perspective it appears useful to include both categories in a dia-logic system according to which the hyphen between *dia* and *logic* would stress that a genuine dialogue connotes the possibility of alternating between two modes of thought. Theunissen, however, labels only the second, interpersonal, I-thou category as the "philosophy of dialogue" or "dialogicalism"; whereas the first, intrapersonal, I-I category he terms "transcendental philosophy."

Tackling dialogism from a different angle, philosopher Hugo Bergman (1974) has used the term "dialogical philosophy" to designate a long line of thought systems that began with Kierkegaard and led to Buber. In differentiating between the Buberian dialogical principle and the Hegelian dialectic principle, Bergman says: "It is worthwhile to compare the dialogical principle and the dialectic principle of Hegel . . . [for] Hegel's synthesis swallows . . . the thesis and the antithesis into a more engulfing synthesis . . . [whereas] this is not so among those dialogic philosophers, according to whom the engulfment really preserves both" (p. 247-48). So the I remains I and the thou remains a thou.

Having demonstrated that in the philosophical domain, where the terms under consideration originated, dialogicalism is being used not merely as an encounter technique but as a philosophical system distinguishable from dialecticism and other processes, let us now see how these concepts are applied to the human sciences. To justify the need for a conceptual differentiation between dialectic and dialogic psychotherapies, I shall first examine the confounding and loose application of these constructs to the social sciences.

MULTIPLE OR CONFOUNDING DEFINITIONS OF DIALECTICISM

Two operations may assist us in showing how differential definitions of dialecticism affect praxis: (1) an assessment of the multiple use of dialectic conceptions in the social sciences and (2) a demonstration of how an undifferentiated application of a multiple definition of dialectic conceptions may exert a detrimental influence on a field as practical as psychotherapy.

In the 1970s several discourses about the contributions of dialectic to human developement made a noticeable appearance in the psychological literature. In his introductory chapter to one of these collected publications, which he entitled "The Multiple Meanings of 'Dialectic,'" Joseph Rychlak (1976) differentiates between Socratic-dialectical and Aristotelian-demonstrative reasoning strategies. Thus, according to dialectic reasoning, meaning is bipolar and truth may hence emerge only by contrasting opposites, as taught by Socrates, who would pose a question for his student and defend the opposing position because we may know right, for example, only by identifying what is left, and so we may recognize the positive by understanding the negative. Introducing Aristotelian unipolar and science-based reasoning, according to which there is only one truth, which must be reached through empirical, hard-nosed demonstrations, Rychlak speculates that if psychology wishes to adopt the scientific method, then dialectical theories are not amenable to psychology.

So far, Rychlak's differentiation between Aristotelian unipolar and Socratic bipolar truth concurs generally with Ricoeur's distinction between explanation and understanding. Contemplating the possibility of progress and human development entailed in the dialectic sequence of thesis, antithesis, and synthesis, Rychlak nonetheless gravitates in the direction of a positive vote for a dialectic psychology, but strangely enough only if it embraces a multiple definition of dialectic.

How is this inner contradiction between the singular or multiple definition of dialectic reconciled? In his effort to define the multiple meaning of dialectic (to be adopted by psychology), Rychlak seems to be forced to reject the dialectic formulation of historical progress that emanates from a Marxist dialectical materialism. By insisting that a confrontation of opposites must not necessarily lead to one final antithesis or synthesis, Rychlak accepts the Socratic assumption in regard to the bipolar nature of meaning. "Indeed, the dialectical process of discovery is never ending . . . [and] final answers are not always forthcoming. . . . The certainty which Marx assigned to the march of dialectic in material reality is thus not to be seen in the intellectual interpretation of dialectic proffered by Socrates" (p. 6).

Rychlak's endorsement of the Socratic multiple, open definition of dialectic because Marxian "class-struggle ideas are likely to call for a victory of one side over the other" (p. 14) in fact illustrates how formulations applying the dialectic idea are perpetually divided between the Darwinian-Marxian idea of replacement and the Socratic idea of open dialectic. For according to the Darwinian-Marxian notion, one new, "fitting" event, belief, idea, class, or son is to replace the no-longer "fitting" idea, class, or old father; and according to the Socratic dialectic, tension between two opposites may lead to higher levels of development by positing the possibility of diversity within unity, so that there is no need for one final synthesis negating its preceding thesis. Another similar example of the perpetual confounding oscillation between Marxian and Socratic definitions of dialectics, which to my mind permeates the literature in the social sciences, is Ina Rossi's (1983) attempt to differentiate between a Marxist replacement dialectic and a Socratic definition of dialectic in terms of open tension that does not require the elimination of thesis in favor of a new antithesis. Thus states Rossi:

> I understand social praxis as the acting out of the dialectic tension between the subjective and objective principles . . . which does not eliminate one of the two principles but reproduces their tension at a higher level. The performance of such dialectic tension is the key explanatory variable of social dynamics. (p. 320)

Like many other social scientists, Rossi used the term *dialectic* to refer to both the process of replacement and the dynamics of reciprocal complimentarity, which may reproduce the tension on ever-higher levels of development, although admittedly the latter "differs from the Marxist notion of the dialectic of opposites" (p. 35). Similarly, Rychlak insisted that "to freeze dialectic into a single, fixed definition would be to destroy it" (p. 2).

I could go on citing from another collection from the 1970s in order to demonstrate how the Marxian replacement conception of dialectic and the developmental notion of dialectic in terms of coexisting polarities are lumped under one heading and applied as a model for humanistic psychology (see Buss, 1976[7]) or as a paradigm for paradoxical psychotherapy (see Weeks, 1977[8]). I think, however, that unless we move on now to examine how a confounded conceptualization of dialectic affects a field as practical as psychotherapy, our theoretical differentiation between coexisting polarities and the replacement of opposites will remain a matter of sheer semantic meticulosity. I shall therefore begin by redefining the terms under consideration.

I propose now to reserve the term *dialectic* only for the Marxian replacement process and to use the term *dialogue* to describe reciprocal tension. Accordingly, "only the term dialogue differentiates between replacement situations in which there is no "dialogue," between the 'replacer' and the opponent who is to be 'replaced' or rather eliminated, and the dynamic situations in which a constant coexisting 'dialogue' between seeming opposites may prevail" (see Rotenberg, 1987: 28). Moreover, since from our discussion above it became evident how the definition of otherness appears crucial for philosophers of dialogue, let me also redefine "the other" in the proposed terms. Bergman, you recall, interpreted Buber's "other" in Socratic terms of tension in which the I and thou in dialogue may not eliminate or swallow each other into a new synthesis; whereas Theunissen focused on another definitional aspect of otherness when he reserved the title "dialogicalists" only for those who consider "the other" as a partner in a discourse but not for those who consider "the other" as the "alien I" or "alter-ego" of the self. I, however, would propose that the critical question for psychotherapy is, not whether "the other" is an internal alter-ego I or an external thou, but whether the psychotherapeutic relationship between any I and thou is defined in Marxian dialectic replacement terms or in Socratic terms of dia-logic tension, in which case polarities are not eliminated but propelled via mutual recognition to ever-higher levels of development.[9]

To defend dia-logism on the intrapersonal, I-I and the interpersonal, I-thou levels, I shall attempt to show how the detrimental impact of an undifferentiated definition of dialectic may be better understood when one examines its application to a practical field like psychotherapy.

DIALECTIC AND THE MISSIONARY THERAPIST

Let me begin by examining Gerald Weeks's assertion that "therapists with dialectical orientations would help the client develop as many alternatives as possible . . . [because] the therapist's role is not one of manipulation from a superior position" (1977: 283). Weeks's paradoxical tension therapy, which is to be fostered, for example, in the case of mates who avoid conflict and confrontation to protect their precarious mutual "love," is clearly not intended to eliminate one of the marriage partners but to strengthen the relationship between them. Nonetheless, how are we to understand Weeks's notion of manipulation, which dialectic therapists do not use? Does "manipulation from a superior position" imply an Aristotelian, unipolar conception of truth that is to replace all other interpretations of reality, or does it include the possibility of a Socratic multidefinition of truth generated through discourse?

Because it seems almost impossible to avoid a certain degree of manipulation even by a therapist who "develops as many alternatives as possible," I would like to introduce here the concept *missionary therapist*. The Aristotelian missionary therapist is a person who, because of his conviction that he represents "a superior position," like the religious missionary manipulates another person "to accept the one and only fundamentalistic 'true' interpretation of reality, religion or biography" (see Rotenberg, 1987: 30). In contrast, the Socratic open therapist is a practitioner who "develops as many alternatives as possible," but who would not coerce or manipulate a client to accept one interpretation against the other. It is, accordingly, the problem of the tyrannic replacer who is expected in the dialectic class struggle to eliminate "the other" (position or opponent)[10] that Buss (1976) or Weeks (1977) overlook when they apply Marxian dialectic to humanistic and psychotherapeutic psychology.[11] The clear distinction between the Socratic-Buberian dialogue and the Hegelian-Marxian dialectic is hence not merely a semantic problem or a matter of technique when these conceptions are applied to psychotherapy.[12] Two examples from the clinical literature will illuminate the problem under consideration. The first example illustrates merely how the use of dialogue as a technique to be employed in the dialectic process makes it difficult to distinguish between the Marxian I-*or*-thou therapist and the Buberian I-*and*-thou therapist. The second example elucidates this problem through the analysis of a clinical case.

In *The Psychoanalytic Dialogue* Stanley Leavy (1980: 13) makes the following statement in reference to the term *dialectics*, which he uses repeatedly: "I would like to use it rather loosely as a process of arriving at a conclusion . . . through the confrontation of different views." Although this loose definition essentially concurs with an applied Buberian I-*and*-thou formulation of therapy, in regard to dialogue Leavy says the following:

> In the dialogue with persons one is never in the position of putting nature to the question. . . . For as soon as we talk together we are not strange to one another; we acquire one another's words and accordingly live in one another's world. It is impossible for the astronomer to do that with a star, or the geologist with a rock, or even the physician with the patient's cardiovascular system. . . . The rock and even the patient enter the observer's world as objects for some kind of manipulation. To be sure the patient in psychoanalysis is also the object of manipulation, in that he seeks treatment from another competent to produce change . . . but the actions of the analyst . . . take place through an exchange. (p. 31)

I have quoted Leavy at some length because prima facie it appears that he defines the psychoanalytic dialogue as a dia-logic exchange ("we acquire one another's words and . . . live in one another's world'') that takes place between patient and doctor during the dialectic process in order ''to arrive at a conclusion . . . through the confrontation of different views'' (p. 13). Thus, again in his definition, dialogue is to be employed as a therapeutic technique in a dialectic process that presumably concurs with the Socratic-Buberian I *and* thou, who are to coexist and not replace each other. The problem in Leavy's formulation is, however, not the manipulation of the patient, which we said is inevitable in psychotherapy to a certain degree. It is, rather, the self-contradiction inherent in Leavy's attempt to introduce the psychotherapeutic dialogue as a dialectical treatment method that rests on ''the confrontation of different views'' (p. 13) while referring only to the one psychoanalytic doctrine of humankind, which by definition may not allow interpretations that differ from the psychoanalytic dogma. In other words, since psychoanalysis constitutes, not a neutral encountering method, but a fundamentalistic belief system about human nature and human change, the analysand's ''different view'' that his troubles were caused by a neighbor's magic curse, for example, or by God's punishment or even by his boss' conditioning-reinforcement system are a priori unacceptable interpretations that the analyst must strive to uproot by means of his rational ''missionarizing'' techniques. Consequently, the problem of differentiating between a Socratic-Buberian dialogue of productive I-*and*-thou tension and the Hegelian-Marxian dialectic of I-*not*-thou replacement is crucial in psychotherapy. Thus, using the term *dialectic* ''loosely as a process of arriving at a conclusion . . . through the confrontation of different views'' (p. 13) is even more misleading when the fundamentalistic metaimage of humankind is disguised under a ''neutral,'' yet self-contradicting title, *The Psychoanalytic Dialogue*, in which case ''missionarizing'' comprises a subtle confrontation which aims to inculcate one Aristotelian dogma of truth.

By presenting a case used in the clinical literature, I would like to demonstrate now how therapeutic applications may vary according to underlying metabeliefs even when the notion of dialectic is interpreted differentially somewhat along the lines proposed here.

DIA-LOGIC TRANSACTION AND DIALECTIC INTERACTION

In their comprehensive discourse of paradoxical psychotherapy Gerald Weeks and Luciano L'Abate (1982) introduce John Dewey and A. Bentley's (1949) philosophic distinctions among self-action, interaction, and transaction in a chapter entitled ''The Dialectics of Psychopathology.''[13] It would be unduly burdening to the psychologically oriented reader to reiterate here Dewey and Bentley's philosophical differentiations among these categories. What should be of interest from the present perspective, however, is how a psychotherapeutic school labeled transaction attempted to apply Dewey and Bentley's concepts. For example, John Spiegel (1971: 25) quotes Dewey and Bentley thus: "*Transaction* is inquiry of a type in which existing descriptions of events are accepted only as tentative and preliminary . . .[and] interaction views things as primarily static." Further, Spiegel (p. 26) maintains that Dewey and Bentley "view a transactional description as essentially circular proceeding from knowing to known and back . . . [and their] linear logical procedures are fitted to interactional observation."

Even more relevant for the present applied perspective is Roy Grinkers and others' (1961: 20) differentiation between the above categories:

> The interactional only tells us about an unidirectional effect, the influence of one person on another. . . . Transactional, on the other hand, implies a relationship of two or more individuals. . . . Neither is isolated. Each has an effect on the other which is specific to the situation in which they exist. . . . The process is reciprocal and cyclical . . . and ever changing.

Thus prima facie, contrary to its common use, *interaction* represents a Marxist dialectic, I-*not*-thou replacement approach to therapy (the linear, unilateral effect of therapist on patient) and *transaction* stands for a Buberian I-*and*-thou orientation toward therapy (the circular, bilateral approach in which "each has an effect on the other").

Using the transactional terminology, we may be puzzled, however, to find the following treatment of a case described by Spiegel (1971):

> A twenty-three-year old, highly intelligent girl came for treatment with the problem of feeling generally frustrated and "lost" in her adjustment to life and specifically unable to realize her ambition in her chosen career. . . . She had a Ph.D. in mathematics but was unable to do much with it. Perhaps, she speculated, she had chosen the wrong field. Maybe she was more suited to the arts; she always found herself interested in aesthetic problems. . . . She asked me if I had seen a recent performance of "Don Juan in Hell" from *Man and Superman*. . . . I did not answer the question. The patient paused for a moment, and then, perceiving that I would not answer the question, she continued. She had already learned from previous transactions that I would decline implicit roles into which I was being inducted through a question. . . . In continuing after the pause, the patient delivered a highly perceptive account of Shaw's intention in the Don Juan interlude, of the actors' interpretations, and of her reactions. The account was so long that I finally interrupted to ask if she knew why she wanted to tell all this. . . . To make this transaction explicit, I now told the patient that I thought she must be feeling disappointed because she had hoped to interest me in the quality of her grasp of aesthetics. . . . She immediately covered her face with her hands and declared herself to be horribly embarrassed. Her face felt hot and red, the whole room felt hot—so intense was her feeling of shame. She felt that I had reprimanded her, as if she were a child. . . . I waited some moments until she became calmer. Then I speculated aloud that her expectation that I would accept the role of appreciator—of

one who puts great emphasis on artistic achievements—must have been learned in some previous experience. In response she told me that her father was greatly interested in intellectual and artistic pursuits and could seldom make contact with anyone except at this level. When she was a child, dinner-table conversations used to consist of long orations by father on some intellectual topic—conversations which she was hardly ever allowed to enter, on the ground that she was not qualified. . . . She kept her face averted from me, and her whole attitude was one of shrinking away, as if she desired to be invisible. The shame of having revealed her intention to me and of having failed was reinforced by the memory of failures in the past. It was clear that some activity on my part was indicated in order to help her to master the overwhelming shame. But what role was to be chosen for this purpose? . . . I could have reassured her directly . . . by affirming my appreciation of her abilities in the area which she had just attempted. . . . This is a perfectly feasible transaction in a psychotherapeutic procedure. The objection to it was that under the circumstances it would have appeared artificial, as if applied only to ease her pain. Instead of this, I pointed out that by placing me in her father's position, she neglected to explore the possibility of my seeing any values in her personality other than intellectual achievement. (pp. 318-323)

Following this treatment case carefully, one is immediately struck by the explicit observation that the term *transaction,* which allegedly stands for a circular systemic process in which therapist and patient presumably affect each other, is being used to describe an "interactive" linear procedure. The cardinal question that now arises is whether Spiegel's therapist should be viewed as a tyrannic therapist who "missionarized" and manipulated his patient, who was thereby being punished for leading the dialogue? More poignantly, the question that now propels our thesis to its culminating epitome is whether egalitarianism is a feasible reality or an impossible ideal in psychotherapy. In other words, would a genuine transactional I-*and*-thou dialogue in which subsequent reassurance would indeed not have appeared artificial have been possible if the therapist would have allowed the patient to feel superior to him in the area of arts?

From the present vantage the answer seems to be that the only chance for an egalitarian psychotherapeutic discourse seems to be available in the proposed concept of dia-logism, which assigns equal status to different thought systems. If two logic systems—whether on the interpersonal, I-thou level or in the intrapersonal, I-I relationships—are viewed as two languages, then a reader has no need to feel superior or inferior if he or she learns to master "the other" language.

Thus, the time has come to introduce the dia-logic conception to refer to the possible coexistence of artistic and scientific, or mystical and rational, orientations through psychotherapy.

HEMISPHERIC ORIENTATIONS AND DIA-LOGIC THERAPY

The notion of a Socratic-Buberian tension between opposites needed to facilitate growth and work out differences, instead of avoiding conflict, is usually accepted without challenge until we raise the question of whose opinion is to predominate. Accordingly, such declarations as "the therapist's role is not one of manipulation from a superior position" (see Weeks, p. 283) may represent nothing more than lip-service to humanistic ideology unless we apply them to praxis. After all, even in Buber's (1974: 97) "inclusion dialogue," manipulation of patient by therapist is unavoidable, since "the analyst rules by means of his systematic and methodological superiority." True, for according to Buber (ibid.) "healing through meeting" is possible once doctor and patient leave the therapy room to step forth together "into the air of the world where self is exposed to self." But is it really the therapy room or the doctor's predominating control of a therapeutic language that makes manipulation from a superior position inevitable? Thus, humanistic nonmanipulative psychotherapy is a myth unless the dia-logic I-thou within and between people is formulated in terms of multiple or dual languages and modes of thought.

A dia-logic conceptualization of psychotherapy, in which the Marxian clinical class struggle must not end in the therapist's predominating superiority that results from the inevitable "victory of one side over the other" (see Rychlak, p. 14) is possible by drawing on knowledge available in studies on brain functioning. Researchers of cerebral lateralization have repeatedly claimed not only that there are two modes of thought—one associated with the left side of the brain and the other with the right—but that overactivity of one side may inhibit the functions of the other and cause depression or other pathologies (see Ten Houten, 1982). As is well known, the left hemisphere is presumed to be characterized by a temporal-propositional and analytic or rational mode of thought while the right-sided way of thinking is assumed to be spatial-compositional and intuitive or spontaneous and emotional. Now, what is significant to our present perspective is not so much the neuropsychological correlates of brain activities with behavior but the more general sociopsychological observation that "the interaction of the hemispheres is apparently required not only for extraordinary abilities . . . but also in the creativity of the everyday world—including the . . . dialectics of participating in human relations, in discourse, in productive work, and in effective physiological functioning" (p. 34). In other words, we know that only brain researchers can establish empirically the degree to which various functions are associated with cerebral lateralization. Yet our major concern here is with the age-old consensus that dialectual thinking means also that creativity and growth may be enhanced if two modes of thought interact in the mind of one person.

Thus, what has been identified as a coexisting dialectic tension that is psychotherapeutically desirable may now be reformulated, not as a clinical class struggle in which it is impossible to prevent the manipulating superiority of the therapist that is due to his methodological control over the psychotherapeutic language, but as dialogue between two modes of human intellect. The use of the term *dia-logism* to refer to the possibility of therapy in which two alternative modes of thought are being juggled in the I-thou encounter comes to stress that if only one linguistic structure predominates the dialogue, the therapist's authority will always be threatened if his interpretation is not accepted. After all, since Wilhelm Dilthey's and Friedrich Schleiermacher's attempts to delineate the possibility of understanding a text, students of hermeneutics have known that the "cognitive superiority of the interpreter over the author" (see Bauman, 1978: 31) cannot be a matter open to question. Thus, the possibility for a dia-logic therapy lies in the coexisting I-thou tension that is accordingly not doomed to end in a "replacing victory of the therapist's side over the other [patient]" because in this event the patient's right-hemispheric interpretation could be accepted as an alternative version (of his biography) deriving from a different mode of thought. It is in the dia-logic sense of conversing in two or more thought systems that the psychotherapeutic discourse might hence be viewed as the legitimate heir of the Platonic dialogue.

The prefix *dia* in the hyphenated term *dia-logic*, which implies a desirable interactive or alternating coexistence of two modes of thought (see Friedman, 1987: 7), would refer now to a therapeutic system that is to harmonize or balance matter and spirit, or the mystic-emotional and the material-rational human elements, on the intrapersonal and interpersonal levels. Accordingly, if S. R. Tulkin and M. J. Konner's (1973: 34-35) observation is correct that "the Western world's emphasis on the mastery of abstract conceptual skills has blinded us to the potential development of other capacities which might be even more helpful in . . . 'advancing' our civilization," then dia-logic therapy may indeed be instrumental on a social and psychological level. Thus, not only could John Spiegel have allowed his patient to feel superior in leading the discussion on arts because this right-oriented language would not threaten his rational left-oriented language of therapy, but he could actually have focused on balancing the patient's inner tension between her overactivated Ph.D. training in mathematics and her need for a spontaneous artistic experience.

Moreover, dia-logic therapy should not be conceived only as a Western method for balancing conventional propensities toward arts and sciences; it should also be seen as a treatment system for reincluding the mystic "unreasonable" form of thought as a creative power. Thus, if R. Hertz (1960: 113) is correct in suggesting that "the constraints of a mystical ideal have . . . been able to make man into an unilateral being," then Foucault (1967) is also correct in contending that in the West it is only since the sixteenth century that one may witness how the fruitful dialogue between the rational man of reason and the creative madman of "unreason" is being broken. If indeed the new "language of psychiatry, which is a monologue of reason about madness" (Foucault, 1967, p. x) is as an instrument of power inherent in "knowledge"[14] being used to control, label, and confine all those who speak the unreasonable language of mysticism, art, and "madness," then dia-logic therapy may attempt to reestablish the link between what we have called here the mystic right-sided orientation and the rational left-sided orientation.

The dia-logic link, or rather that vital balance between the mystic and the rational languages of life comprised in the Jewish *PaRDeS* system of hermeneutics, will be developed and illustrated here as alluded to above, with clinical case studies. It is worth ending this chapter, however, with a classical Jewish case study from the sixteenth century that elucidates how the dia-logic collaboration between the Jewish mystic and rational modes of thought contributed to the formulation of the basic volumes of the Jewish legal system. The illustrative case refers to none else but the famous Rabbi Joseph Karo (1488-1575), the author of the legal codes Beit Yoseph and the Schulchan Aruch, which are being used to this day as the major source and guide for Jewish legal decisions.

Very briefly, Karo, who was a member of the famous circle of mystics in Safed, from whence cabalism disseminated in the sixteenth century, believed he was a recipient of a heavenly mentor. These revelations and communications with the heavenly mentor, whom he called *maggid* (an angel, mentor), were quite common among the cabalists. Communication with the *maggid* "were in the form of automatic speech coming out of Karo's mouth" (see Jacobs, 1978: 98).[15] Testimonies about the impact of these heavenly voices coming out of Karo's mouth include the following description:

> We heard a voice speaking out of the mouth of the saint, may his light shine. It was a loud voice with letters clearly enunciated. All the companions heard the voice. . . . It was an exceedingly pleasant voice, becoming increasingly strong. We all fell upon our faces and none of us had any spirit left in him because of our great dread and awe. The voice began to address us. (Jacobs, 1978: 100)

The point in regard to the above is not that such ecstatic meditations are unknown to the West, but that if Karo were a contemporary law professor, such testimonies about his eccentric behavior would have labeled him a schizophrenic, got him fired, and then got him hospitalized for hearing or being guided by voices—and we would have lost the Jewish legal code. In fact, the case of Karo, in which the ecstatic expression of the mystical language probably energized the rational thought system, may be termed mystic or divine in religious circles and inspirational or intuitive among seculars, but both may facilitate growth through the dia-logic balancing of the two modes of thought.

The notion of dia-logic balancing may also be understood as a mechanism of "contraction". Human development through a dia-logic system would be possible through the cabalistic principle of contraction, according to which one side's expansion of any I is possible through the contraction of its counter thou (see Rotenberg, 1983). Consequently, dia-logic growth may be understood in the cabalistic sense of give and take, which posits that the desire to give via expansion is equal to the desire to receive, which is possible only through the contraction process of mutual opening up (see Ashlag, 1965). To be sure, the opening-up principle of contraction does not imply that a Buberian coexisting dialogue is impossible when only one mode of thought is used in the therapeutic encounter. It suggests only that contraction, in terms of a diminished need for a "missionarizing" control, is more likely to occur when "the other" language does not threaten the only predominating mode of thinking.

In conclusion, the formulation of a dia-logic system of therapy and human development in terms of two languages or modes of thought that coexist on the intrapersonal and interpersonal levels appears possible by adopting the dynamic paradigm of contraction. Accordingly, it is neither Aristotelian explanation nor Diltheyan understanding, but the dia-logic discourse that may reconstitute the Socratic living dialogue. A spiral growth of the total system may therefore accrue only when I and thou learn that no strength is lost by contracting one mode of thought in order to listen and learn the other's language, because neither partner would feel so threatened as to need to "missionarize" the other side.

Our focus on the living discourse as a key for ascertaining the possibility of a dia-logic truth compels us to examine the nature of the relationship prevailing between readers and writers or speakers and listeners at large. Having thus defended the need for dia-logic languages in psychotherapy, I will explore in the next chapter the possibility of establishing a dia-logic truth according to Jewish hermeneutics.

NOTES

1. The acronym *PaRDeS*, which will be defined and discussed in Chapter 4, generally designates a fourfold system of exegesis used mostly by cabalists. The capitalized letters *P R D* and *S* (in Hebrew the *a* and *e* vowels are not needed) stand for *peshat* (plain meaning); *remez* (hint) which refers often to allegorical meaning; *derash*, which means narrative, homiletic; and *sod*, which refers to mystic-secretive or symbolic interpretations.

2. Although more will be said later about the relationship between the irrational, the unconscious, and mysticism, here it seems pertinent to point out that the thinking of such a major Jewish authority as Rabbi Kook (see Ish-Shalom, 1990), like many other Jewish philosophers, seems to be guided by the idea that one must accept the tension between the mystic and the rational as a bridging key for apprehending Jewish hermeneutics.

3. On the dispute between the Romantic approach to hermeneutics, with its nostalgia for the past, and the school of Enlightenment (*Aufklarung*), with its

struggle against prejudices, see Chapter 2 and Ricoeur (1983: 63-100). Here it seems sufficient to state that the historical school appears to draw on the Romantic notion, according to which it should be possible to recapture the intent of earlier authors by means of empathic understanding.

4. Although Levi-Strauss's (1963) structural analysis complies with the rules of explanation because it studies societies by using the system of signs that constitute their language, in fact only the real, living form of speech responds to the concrete, surrounding world. To lift the suspense between the text, the surrounding world, and the inner experiential world of the subject, Ricoeur (1983: 158) introduces the concept of appropriation, referring to interpretation of a text that culminates in "self-interpretation." To my mind, however, it is still only the living discourse occurring in psychotherapy that might enhance real understanding of self and the other.

5. Bergman (1974: 16) indicates that beginning with Descartes's "I think, therefore I exist" (*Cogito ergo sum*), in German ego-centered philosophies the singular person lives in a Leibnitzian isolated monad as a result of which "there is no discourse in the world."

6. If writing is a corrupted (see Derrida, 1978) or a contracted (see Rotenberg, 1983) form of speech, then dia-logic reading expands meaning because it allocates equal space for contrasting interpretations.

7. At the outset of his analysis, Allan Buss (1976: 249) maintains on the one hand that "dialectic as a method involves the notion of *dialogue* where 'truth' is increasingly approximated through a clash of opinions, and conflict is resolved at higher levels of analysis." On the other hand, Buss (ibid.) asserts that "the purpose of the . . . article is to trace the development of the dialectic from Hegel to Marx with special reference to humanistic psychology." Besides the fact that the term *dialogue* is used by Buss to designate a technique in the dialectic method (which involves the notion of dialogue as a clash of opinions), we do not know whether a Hegelian-Marxian conceptualization of a humanistic psychology interpreted into terms of clinical self-actualization posits the possibility of development only by means of the elimination of the previous self (as would happen in the Marxian class struggle) or whether it would allow for a coexisting inner dialogue between two (clashing) sides or phases of the self.

8. While Weeks (1977: 281) asserts that the humanistic metabelief "is used . . .to guide the process of psychotherapy, . . . the therapist's . . . reactions to and expectations for his clients," he also states that a person "is always becoming that which he is not, and not that which he is" (ibid.). One must therefore wonder whether this hermeneutic metabelief still draws its ideology from a Marxian replacement version of dialectics if a person grows only by "becoming that which he is not."

9. Friedman (1987: 12) distinguished between dialogue and dialectic along somewhat similar lines: "*Dialogue* recognizes differences and never seeks for simple agreement or unanimity. *Dialectic,* in contrast, . . . excludes the reality of the 'between' and with it the recognition of real otherness as that which can be affirmed even in opposing it."

10. Indeed, this is what Marx and Engels (1978: 120) declared in their famous manifesto: "The Communists . . . openly declare that their ends can be attained only by the forcible overthrow of all existing social conditions."

11. From the above perspective, it is important to point out that after rejecting

Hegel's status-quo dialectic because according to Hegel's idea history and progress ended with the establishment of the secular Prussian state, Buss adopts unequivocally Marx's notion of dialectics. Thus, humanistic development and self-actualization are to be accomplished by "negating one's present state" (1976: 253); this means that in terms of a Marxian class struggle, in order to become humanistic one must eliminate or replace the old self or class-based society.

12. A general observation that strikes the reader is the way these dialectic psychologists from the 1970s are inconsistent in attributing to Hegel one of the major uses of dialectics. Whereas in his discussion of "dialectical movements across history" Rychlak (1976: 3) quotes Hegel as stating that "this development took the form of repeated *theses, antitheses and syntheses*," both Weeks (1977: 281) and Buss (1976: 251) declare that "Hegel was viciously opposed to . . . the dialectic involving the well-known sequence: thesis, antithesis, synthesis."

13. At present I shall not focus on Weeks and L'Abate's formulation because their notion of dialectics leans toward a Socratic-Buberian I-*and*-thou dia-logic formulation, but I shall concentrate on those who seem to subscribe to a psychodynamic metaimage of humans.

14. Here is the place to comment that Foucault's thesis about the controlling power inherent in the possessors of knowledge pertains mainly to a closed system of knowledge. Accordingly, the danger that people will be "missionarized" and manipulated by other people in the name of knowledge exists mainly in societies where knowledge is acquired secretively through specific initiations confined to a family, a clan, a class, or a professional group (see Funkenstein, 1989). However, in societies that have an open, Jewish-style system of knowledge, where at least in theory the rules for multiple interpretations of the text are transparent and available to everybody, the possibility of controlling knowledge, as such, should be less powerful.

15. Karo's dia-logic technique will be described later by quoting directly from his Hebrew text *Maggid Meysharim*. Here I used Jacobs's translated citations simply as a matter of convenience.

2

Contraction, Deconstruction, and True Interpretation

What can we learn about the psychological "true" meaning of human experiences by comparing literary and psychotherapeutic dialogues? For the sake of parsimony both the literary critic and the psychotherapist may be seen as readers of a text written by an author (of a novel) or a patient (of a life story), whom we shall call writer. Let us begin by examining a typical paragraph written by a literary critic in which a citation from the author's story entitled *Samuch Venire* is being used as a basis for his commentary. In order that the passage may be read as a dialogue, I have inserted in parenthesis the words *author* and *critic*.

> *(Critic:)* The self [the "I"] . . . torn and divided, reflected its state of disconnection, its desertion, its being left hanging between contrasting worlds. This is what happens at the end of the story *The Last Bus:*
>
> *(Author:)* How much I needed at this hour to be helped [defended?] against those who don't love me and one of them is my enemy. But the one who could have driven me was busy with his [own] affairs. (*Samuch Venire:* 113 . . .)
>
> *(Critic:)* Loneliness and desertion are a result of the egocentric trend, which knows only itself, due to the breaking of the wall of relationships which was erected by traditional Judaism." (Kurtzweil, 1970: 332)

The interpretations preceding and following the paragraph cited from *The Last Bus* by the world-known Nobel Prize winner S. Y. Agnon were written by Agnon's most famous literary critic, Baruch Kurtzweil. Although these critical psychosociological interpretations were published during Agnon's lifetime, Agnon did not respond to them, for most authors do not react or refute interpretive criticism concerning their work. Indeed, a well-known anecdote told that whenever Agnon was asked to explain a putative meaning in one of his stories, he was said to have replied, "Ask Kurtzweil!"

Did Kurtzweil destroy, control, misinterpret, or distort Agnon's truth, or did Agnon preempt, neutralize, or even "kill" or destroy Kurtzweil and/or his truth by not responding? (Part of Kurtzweil's eventual suicide was attributed to his presumed bitterness for not having been recognized as an independent creative author.)[1]

Before attempting to address the above queries, let me introduce an interpretation of a text written in a different context:

> I said: "I wonder if my vacation may have been stirring such thoughts of my waning interest in my profession." Mr. R. replied: "I'm not sure how to understand what you mean. . . . I think you responded defensively to the idea of a psychiatrist switching to photography." He looked away and his body seemed shrunken in its stance. (Schwaber, 1990: 230)

True, the above excerpt is obviously taken from a psychotherapeutic dialogue in which the author-patient's critical-verbal (misunderstanding and blaming of therapist) and physical-semiotic (shrunken stance) responses to the reader-therapist's interpretation are reported. Consequently, the possibility of preserving the author's truth appears more plausible in this therapeutic text as compared to an author's truth qua truth in literary texts. For the therapeutic living dialogue between a therapist's interpretations and a patient's responses differs from the writer-reader or author-criticizer relationship, in which "the writer does not respond to the reader," as Ricoeur (1983: 146) claimed, and in which case one may consider the author "as already dead and the book as posthumous" (ibid.: 147).

But are there any other efficient methods or necessary conditions for avoiding textual destructions or "killing" of authors in literary interpretation? Humanistically oriented psychotherapists, educators, and criminologists influenced by Nietzsche or by Foucault have repeatedly claimed that knowledge used for socialization or interpretation (e.g., psychiatric knowledge) usually generates a controlling effect over the person socialized or over the interpreted text (see Cohen, 1985). The discourse in the following chapter will focus on demonstrating how dialogic interpretation not only may be imperative for minimizing the controlling effect in psychotherapy but may contribute to a better understanding of deconstructive interpretation possibilities in literary criticism.

In *Re-biographing and Deviance* (Rotenberg, 1987) I have demonstrated how the Jewish midrashic (commentary) system rehabilitates biblical role models by contracting the sins attributed to them in the Bible, that is, by minimizing them through reinterpretation. Citing a clinical case of a woman for whom Milton Erickson (see Haley, 1973) invented a new happy past under hypnosis, I have claimed that the midrashic model, which *re-*

biographs the old past instead of inventing a new past, seems preferable (to other dialectic death-rebirth models) as a therapeutic reframing[2] model because it allows the re-biographed person to maintain a consistent total identity, instead of erasing or ignoring his failing past. Within the present context the question that presents itself is, however, not whether my re-biographing or Erickson's reframing is essentially more effective, but which of the two—inventing a new past or reinterpreting the old past—complies more with criteria or truth. Put in more succinct and poignant terms, what is the possibility of truth in psychotherapy?

One should ponder further and ask why it is permissible to invent or reinterpret biographic data for midrashic-homiletic or educational purposes and, indeed, is even required, as Theodore Sarbin (1981) has argued, in dramatic stories or in biographic novels, whereas most psychotherapeutic "denominations" usually reject biographic distortions as defensive projections. Prima facie, however, it appears that difficulty in preserving biographic truth characterizes psychotherapeutic texts more than literary texts and biographic novels. On the one hand, therapeutic interpretations are expected to be not only truthful but also useful (i.e., therapeutic); on the other hand, patients as authors of biographic texts tend usually to misrepresent their failing past by using so-called defense mechanisms.

As alluded to, I intend to demonstrate that paradoxically in psychotherapeutic texts truth may be preserved precisely because the author's resistance, rationalization, projection, surrender, or general response to the suggested and presumably helpful interpretation is usually reported, in contrast to the literary deconstructed text, where the author's response to interpretation is usually lacking. In the first part of this chapter the differences and similarities between literary and psychotherapeutic interpretations will be examined by encountering dia-logic contraction with dialectic destruction of texts. Second, the psychiatric concept of self-deception will be used to demonstrate how the dia-logic struggle with deception paradoxically contributes to the preservation of truth in psychotherapeutic texts. Finally, the midrashic method of *al-tikrei* will be introduced to demonstrate how the dia-logic system of interpretation may be used as a model, or metacode, for reframing therapy and for literary deconstruction.

TRUTHFULNESS AND USEFULNESS IN PSYCHOTHERAPY

How is the problem of true interpretation being treated in psychotherapy? Existential psychotherapists who have abandoned the need and requirement to establish the historical truth of biographic events adopted a phenomenological definition of narrative truth by declaring that a persons's present experiences represent his or her subjective truth. Although this arbitrary definition of truth may become true in its consequential imprint on a person's behavior, it may obviously be grounded in false expressions or in forced reflections. That is to say, existential phenomenologists have not provided means to determine when and whether people will for various reasons misrepresent themselves or purposely distort their experiential accounts. As suggested, a person who seeks psychotherapeutic help might have good reasons to lie about his past failing identity or conduct or he might be tempted to misrepresent autobiographic data according to what he believes would please the therapist, whose help he seeks.

The problem of manipulating the therapist in order to comply with his version of truth, as Donald Spence (1982) described, or of being manipulated by the therapist to accept his one and only "truthful" and presumably "useful" interpretation, as Roy Schafer (1983) prescribed, raises another question: Whose truth is to predominate, the therapist's or the client's? Here our discourse may be divided between the unipolar Aristotelians, who believe there is only one truth that must replace or reject all other previous truisms as false, and the Socratic bipolar definition, according to which truth, which is never final, emerges by contrasting opposites.

Viewed from the biographic perspective, our dispute might also be understood (as discussed in Chapter 1) in terms of the differences emanating from accepting the historicistic philosophy of Romanticism (i.e., the school of understanding) or the one associated with the school of Enlightenment (*Aufklarung*) (the explanation discipline). Although these differences are beyond the scope and interest of the present work,[3] it is worth noting that the Romantic approach with its nostalgia for the past (see Ricoeur, 1983) would engender an enslavement to a historical truth, whereas critical *Aufklarung* would promulgate the replacement of anachronistic prejudices with new, useful, narrative truisms.

At any rate, the question in psychotherapy is, now, whether definitions of what is truthful and useful are guided by a dialectic or a dia-logic metacode (key or belief) for interpreting life and behavior. As specified in my previous works (Rotenberg, 1983, 1987), the term *dialectic metacode* refers in psychotherapy to a tacit belief that will guide one side (usually the therapist) to "missionarize," that is to manipulate the other side (usually the client) to accept one fundamentalistic interpretation of life, which is to eliminate or replace in a Marxist sense all previous understandings of growth possibilities. By contrast, a dia-logic metacode refers in psychotherapy to a belief according to which growth and therapy are possible through the coexistence of a multiplicity of interpretations of life from which one is free to select the narrative that appears useful for correcting one's biography.

I have maintained, further, that whereas the dialectic metacode is traceable to the Hegelian notion that antithesis or synthesis must always replace thesis, the dia-logic metacode is grounded in the cabalic notion of contraction, according to which divergent interpretations are, not replaced or erased, but contracted to evacuate space for other alternative and alternating viewpoints. Here is the place to stress that the Jewish midrashic system of biblical hermeneutics concurs with the contraction metacode because the multiplicity of biblical commentaries, accessible to everybody via studying or listening to oral sermons, comprises a socialization system that offers a free choice between various interpretations of texts and lives that are alternately contracted to make space for each other. The concrete question of how to ascertain a therapeutic dialogue in which a therapist does not "missionarize" the patient to accept a specific true interpretation of his or her life story remains open however.

The question here is, to what extent is the therapist as a text reader entitled to control the reinterpretation of the living text "written" by the patient, who is its sole and authentic author? This last problem of dia-logic versus dialectic relationships between a writer-author and the reader-interpreter has been dealt with extensively within deconstructionist circles.

It is common knowledge that many philosophers, literary critics, and social scientists who have set out to explore the possibilities of interpreting, reading, or criticizing texts are now associated with the popular term *deconstruction.* While some deconstructionists adhere to a dialectic orientation, others subscribe to what I would describe as a dia-logic point of view. According to the former orientation, contemporary readers always destroy (replace) the text written by a "dead" author (see Ricoeur, 1983), whose authentic frame of mind they cannot grasp because he or she has either not responded or because he or she indeed died a long time ago. In contrast, adherents of the latter approach believe it possible to capture the main thrust of an author's spirit or frame of mind by empathizing and "understanding" the author's language.[4] Jacques Derrida has been said (see Norris, 1982: 31) to define deconstruction as "an activity of reading which remains closely tied to the text it interrogates, and which can never set up independently as a self-enclosed system of operative concepts." Thus, Derrida, one of the leading figures of deconstructionism, is from our perspective a dia-logist because for him critical reading that becomes writing is a dynamic activity that must maintain a continuous dialogue with the original text and because for him "there is nothing outside the text" and thus it cannot turn into an independent methodology: "The deconstructive leverage supplied by a term like *writing* depends on its resistance to any kind of settled or definitive meaning" (ibid.).

Moreover, although the critical reader-writer is to remain "closely tied to the text," deconstruction according to Derrida is an activity that is creative and dynamic, and not structurally static (in Levi-Strauss's terms). Deconstruction may thus be understood as an infinite living dialogue between the signifier (the person who attributes meaning) and the signified (the assigned thing or object). This dynamic circular process in which the reader becomes a deconstructive writer who is to be eventually deconstructed by new readers-writers is elucidated by Derrida's (1978) concepts *difference* and *aporia.* By *difference* (or *differance*), which entails the two French verbs "to differ" and "to defer," Derrida seems to designate writing as an endless process of unstable interpretative writing that differs and deviates from the previous text and hence its meaning should always be deferred. Conceived in the present dia-logical terms one may say, then, that although the notion of differing may comprise a process that takes place in the interpersonal arena of space, the idea of deferring the attribution of meaning may also constitute an intrapersonal dialogue in time. The term *aporia* refers similarly to the paradoxical, unsettled nature of writing, which conveys suspicion, unease, skepticism, and the doubtfulness with which one should accept the meaning of writing.

Thus, Derrida's deconstructive writing deviation as an infinite process of dialogue between a signifying reader and a signified text is somewhat akin to the Jewish concept of oral law, which remains open to infinite new interpretations. But how are we to know whether in spite of his alleged good intention to "remain closely tied to the text," the deviating signifier does not destroy the "autistic" signified text? In other words, unless we let the author respond to the signifier's deconstructive writing, how are we to determine whether the interpreter is not manipulating or dialectically replacing the meaning of the defenseless text? In fact, sometimes living authors complain that theatrical interpretations of their novels either vulgarize or destroy their intended creations. But what is the meaning and reliability of, say, the cabalic "dead" mysticist's report wherein are described his ecstatic experiences of hundreds of years ago (see Idel, 1988b) as compared to the contemporary psychotherapeutic text that records disputes between patients and therapists discussing ecstatic behavior experienced by the former? Indeed, if one follows Howard Kurtzman's (1987) attempt to apply deconstructionist ideas to cognitive psychology, according to which "the mind . . . is a 'scene of writing' . . . in which texts are constantly created and altered" (p. 62), then the alleged goal of interpretation is to replace all previous meanings of the text, since "the mind-machine overpowers or distorts the stimuli according to a particular interpretive schema" (p. 63). Thus, maintains Kurtzman, to establish "what the signifier 'means' is ultimately determined only by the signifier's criteria" (p. 64). The signifier's schema or criteria would, accordingly, constitute a philological or historical methodology that presumably ascertains the utmost objective reconstruction of the author's authentic truth. But this does not mean that other methodological criteria examining the same experiences would capture the same authentic truth of the author. In any event, Kurtzman's schema or criteria guiding the direction and nature of interpretation, which concurs with our conception of metacode, could then be examined in the context of the therapeutic dialogue.

Earlier I suggested that interpretation in the context of the therapeutic dialogue is by definition committed not only to decipher the true meaning of the living text but also to guide or correct it according to the presumed needs of the person whose identity is affected by a reading of his lifestory text in one way or another.[5] Further, I have claimed that though this commitment to a corrective interpretation might lead the therapist to distort the patient's biographic text, the patient's proclivity either toward excessive blaming of self or of others for his past failures might tempt him to misinterpret his biography in a direction that differs from the therapist's version. Thus, Derrida's *differance* between text and context is prima facie magnified in the therapeutic dialogue because of the contradictory distorting needs and interests of patient (writer) and therapist (reader). It is hence the therapeutic dialogue that exposes the problematic relationship between interpretation and truth. It is, however, also precisely by examining the living therapeutic arena that one might demonstrate how the patient's biographic text is either dialectically destroyed or dia-logically preserved. The key for understanding the text is obviously the criteria, schema, or interpretive metacode used by the reader-therapist and writer-patient.

If the therapist's interpretation is guided by a dialectic metacode, then one may discover how the patient's old understanding of his biographic text is slowly destroyed and replaced by one new, fundamentalistic, Aristotelian true interpretation of the biography. If, however, interpretation is guided by a dia-logic metacode, then by following the textual and contextual interchange between patient and therapist one may discover how the Socratic-Platonian dialogue has brought about a selection of one interpretation without destroying or replacing the alternative version. Although in both cases we may witness a deconstructive process of interpretation, the contribution of the therapeutic interpretation is that in both the dialectic and the dia-logic interpretation exchange the writer's or reader's resistance, consent, or surrender *is reported* if it was indeed accurately recorded.

Therefore, it should be possible to determine the degree to which a signifying interpreter controls or destroys or is being contolled or destroyed by the signified author.[6] In other words, it is by examining the interpretive debate in psychotherapeutic texts that one might learn to determine whether the signifier's or the signified's Aristotelian truth predominates or whether truth is extracted and selected from the Socratic discourse between them. Before we indulge in discussing the difference between dia-logic and dialectic interpretations of psychotherapeutic texts, let me elucidate the difference between the psychotherapeutic and literary text at large by considering the following case.

In an esoteric cabalistic manuscript from the year 1290 the following discourse was reported:

Cabalist (mentor): I went over your notes and I was pleased to learn that yesterday you used the meditative technique of combining holy letters. I think, however, that you got the computations all wrong.

Novice: I followed the instructions as taught by you in the name of our master, Rabbi Abulalfia.

Cabalist: What happened as a result of your meditation?

Novice: I felt numb and all of a sudden I saw a light which became increasingly stronger. I looked for the source of that light but couldn't find it but then I felt that the light radiated from my own body.

Cabalist: How did it feel?

Novice: Well, I was overwhelmed with joy and a feeling of sweetness permeated my entire being.

Cabalist: How come that after that elating experience, I heard that you fought again with your wife?

Novice: Because she forgot to irrigate the garden and now all vegetables are rotten and worthless.

Cabalist: A real cabalist would attribute spiritual meanings to such material events in order to elevate his experiences.

Novice: (Breaks down in tears) Actually, I felt so frustrated in the evening because I couldn't get the letter combination in the right order.

Cabalist: But you stated a minute ago that you saw a vision of shining light which filled you with joy!

Novice: I was afraid that you'd expel me from the group if I wrote that I felt nothing.

Obviously, a manuscript describing such an encounter, which presumably took place in the thirteenth century, was never found, for even nondisputed reports of personal mystic experiences from that era are quite rare. If, however, in the year 2490 two manuscripts will be discovered in which a specific meditative-ecstatic experience is described, one would probably comprise a poetic, literary description of the experience and the other would probably include a psychotherapeutic dispute concerning the self-deceptive phases and the interpersonal obstacles to be overcome in order to reach the prescribed and desired state. Naturally, the psychotherapeutic text would be more useful than the literary manuscript for deducing the true meaning of the mystic experience under consideration.

By keeping these two writing styles in mind, we may turn to examine now the contribution of psychotherapeutic encounters to the problem of true interpretations. An example of a dialectic therapeutic exchange is the Freudian concept of self-deception. The dia-logic interchange might be illuminated by demonstrating how the midrashic interpretive system of *al-tikrei* is used practically in reframing therapy. I intend to argue, accordingly, that although in dialectic interpretations one Aristotelian truth is to replace all other "false" readings, paradoxically, examination of self-deception in action demonstrates that there is more than one version of truth.

SELF-DECEPTION AND DIALECTIC INTERPRETATION

Self-deception has been defined and described as an act of interpretation in which a person writes or narrates his biographic life story. For example,

Herbert Fingarette (1971), whose work is often cited as a pioneering point of departure, states that the self-deceiver who "is forced to fabricate stories in order to keep his explicit account of things and the way things really are in some kind of harmony . . . does not spell out that he is doing this" (p. 62). Sarbin (1981) similarly defines self-deception as autobiographic narrative plots, and he provides several examples of narrated self-deception. The one that, according to him, may be found in typical psychiatric studies describes a 19-year-old girl who is brought to a mental health center because she refused to believe that her brother was killed in a car accident, probably because "the accident had occured a half-hour after she and her brother had engaged in a . . . bitter quarrel," as a result of which she shouted, "I hope you get smashed up in your car" (p. 222). Another case cited by Sarbin involved the refusal of newspaper-reader responders to believe what they saw in photographs from the Mai Lai massacre. Sarbin concludes that "to 'believe,' say, a photograph of the finish of a horse race, and 'not to believe' a photograph of the Mai Lai incident in the same newspaper would influence a critical observer to consider self-deception as a proper description" (p. 224).

Schafer (1987) defines self-deception as a problem of multiple selves. He suggests that people use various defense mechanisms to narrate or tell stories concerning events that happened in their lives. As a psychotherapist, Schafer is aware of the possibility that self-deception grounded in such defense mechanisms as projection, repression, denial, or resistance may constitute an arena of contrasting interpretations offered by patients and therapists. Thus, a patient's description of altruistic dependency may be interpreted by the therapist as a defense against greed and envy; hostility may be interpreted as a defense against clinging dependency, or vice versa, clinging dependency may be interpreted as a defense against hostility. To elucidate this struggle between the patient's and the therapist's interpretations, Schafer uses the example of a woman about whom he states, "Although the subject defensively believes consciously that she is engaged in reading purely for scholarly purposes, the analyst is able to interpret that she is reading also and perhaps mainly in order to bring herself into a sexually excited state" (p. 326). In another example of self-narrated deception Schafer describes a teacher who derives pleasure from treating his students cruelly by maintaining that he is a dedicated teacher. Schafer argues that this teacher could be said to deceive himself if "a psychoanalytic examination of his life history, fantasies, dreams, conduct in love, etc., strongly supports 'sadistic' as the description that best fits his personality" (p. 341).

From the present perspective it is unnecessary to agree or disagree with Fingarette's or with Sarbin's definition of self-deception or to agree with either the patient's or the therapist's interpretation in Schafer's cases. It is also not imperative within the present context to tackle the very intriguing question why Sarbin's Mai Lai case or the case of disbelief in the brother's death in a car accident or Schafer's teacher fits the category of self-deception rather than deception of others. What does seem central to our discourse, however, is that Sarbin, Schafer, and others provide ample evidence that the therapists as signifying text readers and patients as authors of signified texts have good reasons to distort truth. For defensive reasons the patient will tend to misrepresent his failing past, and the therapist might distort the patient's past presumably in order to correct his or her life. Nonetheless, the point is that it is paradoxically *because* of the inevitable distortions that one may best examine the problem of true interpretations by studying psychotherapeutic texts. Both the patient-writer and the therapist-reader use cultural-ideological metacodes in writing their interpretations so that the resulting text will sound plausible. The question is only whether the metacode used is focused on one dialectic, Aristotelian interpretation that is to replace all other interpretations or on a dia-logic Platonian or Buberian truth that emerges from the coexistence of multiple exchanges between patient and therapist.

A definition of self-deception as a psychotherapeutic reading that clings to an orthodox psychoanalytic metacode not only is dialectic (see Rotenberg, 1987) but allows the acceptance of only one fundamentalistic, negative interpretation. Indeed, Schafer states:

> Repression that appears to have enabled the subject to endure terrible events of childhood, one wants to say . . . had been an essential means of adaptation. . . . *In a clinical context,* later on, when this victim's suitability for psychoanalytic treatment is being assessed, the analyst wants to emphasize the . . . pathological rigidity and scope of defensive repression." (p. 330)

The case of self-deception as presented by Schafer and others demonstrates unequivocally that there is more than one version of truth. To explore this paradox I will next introduce a dia-logic metacode, in which truth emerges from an encounter between two contrasting interpretations according to which pessimistic and optimistic interpretations coexist. Thus, before exploring the more complex phenomenon of the *PaRDeS,* which offers a simultaneous mystic and rational reading of the text, let us establish first the possibility of a dia-logic truth that may emerge between any two opposing interpretations of reality.

AL-TIKREI: THE DIA-LOGIC RECOMPOSING METHOD

I have suggested that in literary criticism it is difficult to determine the extent to which the signifying deconstructor is in fact destroying the authentic truth of the signified test, although allegedly he "remains closely tied to the text" (see Norris, 1982: 31). Although my argument rests on the assumption that in contrast to psychotherapeutic interpretations the literary author rarely responds to critical interpretations, this does not mean that it is always the signifier who destroys the signified text. The implication was also made that it *could have been* Agnon's (the author of the signified text) refrainment from responding that "killed" Kurtzweil. What could then be the dia-logic principle that would ascertain the possibility of therapy and creative literary progress in which neither the author nor the reader must destroy each other's truth?

The midrashic Hebrew concept *al-tikrei* means literally "don't read," which is an abbreviation of the sentence "don't read (the text) like this, but through a switching or changing of the letters in the biblical text read the verse or word in a different way with a different intent." There are about 180 *al-tikreis* in the talmudic and midrashic literature (see Zipor, 1987), some of which remarkably affected socialization throughout the ages because they were either used in prayers and/or turned into popular slogans.

The *al-tikrei* play-on-words method, which laid the foundations for a very flexible norm-changing system derived either from changing and switching letters in the text or from breaking words into several words, includes the following famous examples: The biblical statement that in the two Tablets that were given to Moses, God's words are *"charut al haluchot"* (Exodus 32:16) are reread as *"cherut al haluchot"* (Fathers 6:3) because in Hebrew *charut* means "engraved" and *cherut* means "freedom." The normative implication is that one who studies the Torah (the *Luchot,* i.e., the Tablets), is a free person. However, this normative impact of *al-tikrei* was further expanded and developed by reading into it also freedom to interpret the Torah, freedom from kingdoms, freedom from the angel of death, and freedom from sufferings (see Zipor, 1987). Thus, the more one studies the Torah, the more freedom he or she acquires to interpret the Torah. Consequently, one becomes free from tyrants and tyrannies of all kinds. An example in which one word is broken into two words, which facilitates a therapeutic-repentative rereading of a biblical verse, is the following talmudic *al-tikrei*: "Rabbi Yochanan said, anyone who observes properly one Sabbath, even if he is an idol worshipper as Enoch, is being pardoned [presumably concerning all sins], as it is written: '*Kol shomer Shabbat* [anyone who observes the Sabbath] *mechalelo* [keeps from violating it] [Isaiah 50:7], *al-tikrei* [don't read] *mechalelo* [keeps from violating it] *ela* [but] *machul lo* [he is being pardoned]'" (Pesachim 117:b).

One of the most famous *al-tikreis*, which every person recites daily in his morning prayers, refers to the verse *"verav shlom banayich"* (Isaiah: 54:13) in regard to which the Talmud says, *"al-tikrei banayich ela* [but] *bonayich"* (see Berachot 64:a). Although there are many more *al-tikreis* in the Talmud and in the midrashic literature, it is the above *banayich-bonayich al-tikrei* that might be most useful in illuminating the dia-logical principle that emanates from this interpretive system. The above-cited verse in Isaiah, *verav shlom*, states that peace will be brought upon your (the Israelites') children (*banayich*), but the talmudic deconstructionist rereads it as *bonayich*, which means "your builders." The question which might be asked, then, is whether this *al-tikrei* comes to replace and erase the previous textual reading of *banayich* or rather adds to it another alternative reading possibility that might stand in a dia-logic relationship with the old reading.

Rabbi Judah David Eisenstein, the editor of the *Otzar Yisrael* encyclopedia, states that both Maimonides and Nachmanides stressed that the *al-tikrei* method comes only to add another possible alternative interpretation of the bibilical text—and this, indeed, comprises what I have termed a dia-logic, or alternating, hermeneutic system. Thus, the rereading of *bonayich* (your builders) is not to replace dialectically the *banayich* (your children) but to facilitate the dia-logic possibility of accumulative progress according to which "your children" (*banayich*) become "your progressing developers" (*bonayich*). Indeed, to prove this point Eisenstein cites many midrashic sources that demonstrate how the *al-tikrei* may be understood only in dia-logic-progressive terms, and he draws on the following compelling example: The Bible states "*Ushmartem et hamatzot* [thou shalt observe the unleavened bread]" (Exodus 12:17) "*al-tikrei matzot* [the unleavened bread] *ela* [but] *mitzvot* [commandments]" (Mechilta). Put in simple terms, this *al-tikrei* means that one should observe not only Passover but all commandments, that is, since everyone knows that on Passover one must observe the *matzot* (eat unleavened bread), the *al-tikrei* of observing all *mitzvot* (commandments) comes only to add and expand the norm.

The *al-tikrei* method must, then, be understood as a dia-logic theosophic metacode underlying the possibility of a recomposing or reframing therapy in which the selection of a suitable optimistic rereading of one's biography emerges out of the exchange between patient and therapist. Selecting the old interpretation of a text is, accordingly, not a regression but a circular spiral, a progressive regression—as would happen if the fashion in Paris "progresses" (i.e., changes back) to the Renaissance style of clothing. A reemphasis on the reading of *banayich* (your sons), which aims to reconnect the *bonayich* (the progressors) to the loose roots of their parental heritage, is therefore not a regression but a spiral "ascent via descent" progression. Indeed, here the Hasidic process known as "ascent via descent" constitutes not only an intrapersonal creative-optimistic understanding of manic-depression (see Rotenberg, 1983) but an interpersonel concepualization of progress.

Moreover, interpersonal or intrapersonal truth must now be understood, not as an Aristotelian I-*or*-thou dichotomy in which one true antithesis or synthesis replaces a false hypothesis, but as a Buberian I-*and*-thou possibility in which the new reading of the text constitutes a new composition that includes both contrasting possibilities through the contraction process. Thus, if a "patient" was raised to read his or her biography by using a pessimistic (e.g., original sin) metacode, the reinterpretation of this biography with an optimistic (e.g., Hasidic) metacode does not erase or replace the earlier reading but only adds a new dimension.

This process has been termed reframing (see Watzlawick, 1978), but since the literature of reframing somewhat disregards both the framework that provides the cultural metacode and the possibility of progress, I prefer the term *recomposing*. Recomposing not only refers to a settling reconciliation of contrasting entities through a rearranging or a reframing process. It also connotes the creative process of listening to the reading of an old text with a new melody or with a different intonation so that a broader progressive composition is created. Recomposing differs from re-biographing (see Rotenberg, 1987) only in that it refers mainly to singular events in one's biography. Let me illustrate recomposing by using some examples.

Sarbin (1981: 224) was correct in stating that "the sentence 'I am deceiving myself' is self-contradictory like the sentences 'I am lying,' 'I am sleeping' and 'I am hallucinating.'" From this perspective if a patient tells his therapist that he had a very constructive childhood when "in fact" he had lived through "terrible events" (see Schafer, 1987), he is presumably deceiving himself or others only if he was trained or tamed by his parents, educators, or therapist to read his biography with a metacode that interprets "terrible events" as traumatic and pathological. If, however, the patient was trained to use an optimistic metacode in which "terrible events" may be understood as being possibly constructive for adaptation, the therapist, especially the psychoanalytic therapist, might say that the patient is deceiving himself because for him there is only one dialectic truth; but in fact the patient is not deceiving himself.

In contrast to the dialectic therapist, for whom there is only one Aristotelian truth (usually that terrible events are pathological), for the dialogic therapist both possibilities—that of "terrible events" as indeed terrible and that of turning such events into constructive adaptations—are true possibilities. Thus, an *al-tikrei* (a "don't read" message) of "terrible events" as constructive rather than as destructive does not come to erase their destructive element but to add the constructive potential. Accordingly, neither the destructive nor the constructive components of "terrible events" are to predominate as the only true interpretive possibilities, but they are to be mutually contracted in order to be recomposed as an expanded possibility of growth.

Hence recomposing constitutes a creative possibility in which there is no self-deception because one learns to reread events and experiences by adding new interpretation metacodes. Hasidic tales that recompose poverty, sinning, or misfortune, by providing an optimistic metacode for re-biographing, do not eliminate the sad-negative aspect inherent in poverty and sinning. Their intent is only to recompose these situations into growing possibilities of "ascent via descent." Howard Polsky and Yaella Wozner

(1989) have classified such tales under the heading of reframing, but they may be better understood in *al-tikrei* recomposing terms because by reading-listening to one's life episodes with the added tunes of optimism, one hears an entirely new melody.

Here are two examples that deal with sinning and two that deal with poverty:

1. The Merry Sinner

In Lublin lived a great sinner. Whenever he wanted to talk to the rabbi, the latter readily consented and conversed with him as if with a man of integrity and one who was a close friend. Many of the Hasidim were annoyed at this, and one said to the other: "Is it possible that our rabbi—who has only to look once into a man's face to know his life from first to last, to know the very origin of his soul—does not see this fellow as a sinner? And if he does see it, that he considers him worthy to speak to and associate with?"

Finally, they summoned up courage to go to the rabbi himself with their questions. He answered them: "I know all about him as well as you. But you know how I love gaiety and hate dejection. And this man is so great a sinner! Others repent the moment they have sinned, are sorry for a moment, and then return to their folly. But he knows no regrets and no doldrums, and lives in his happiness as in a tower. And it is the radiance of his happiness that overwhelms my heart." (Buber, 1978: 315-316)

2. The Gamblers

A Hasid complained to Rabbi Wolf that certain persons were turning night into day, playing cards. "That is good," said the *tzaddik* [righteous man]. "Like all people, they want to serve God and don't know how. But now they are learning to stay awake and persist in doing something. When they have become perfect in this, all they need do is turn to God—and what excellent servants they will make for him then!" (Buber, 1978: 161)

In both of these tales it must be obvious to the reader that the pious Hasidic rabbis did not approve of sinning. The tale comes only to add the optimistic dimension of gaiety and persistence, which are positive qualities to be either emulated by others or used eventually and hopefully for repentance by the sinners themselves. Whereas recomposing progress in the two tales about sinning depends on behavioral changes, in the two following tales about poverty, growth is strictly a matter of *al-tikrei* (don't read) only pessimism; that is, also read optimism in the "terrible event" of poverty you encounter.

1. Why the Pious Are Poor

The Besht was asked why the pious are poorer than the impious. In reply he narrated the following parable:

"A king desired to please his loyal courtiers and announced that each would be granted his particular wish. Some asked for honors; others asked for wealth. But one of them said: 'My wish is to speak to the king three times a day.'"

"We, the pious, prefer communion with the Lord thrice daily above all honors and riches, and God grants us our wish." (Newman, 1975: 323)

2. The Choice of Poverty

Said Rabbi Nahum Tzernobiler: "Between poverty and wealth, I always choose poverty. It is the best shield against egotism and against every evil of the spirit. It is the least costly, the most easily attainable; it need not struggle against jealousy and competition; it need answer no questions or suspicions; it is understood without comments and without explanations. I beg of you, my good friends, not to deprive me of this great treasure." (Newman, 1975: 324)

When Tevyeh, Sholom Aleichem's hero in "Tevyeh the Milkman" (dramatized as the musical *Fiddler on the Roof*), turns to God, he is aware of the Jewish-Hasidic norm that there is no shame in poverty; but, alas, in his plea to God he cries, "It is also no big honor!" Since in both tales the bitterness of poverty is not denied because it bestows "no big honor," there is no self-deception if one learns to see also the optimistic, constructive side inherent in this "terrible event," for there is also "no shame in poverty."

Midrashic re-biographings are, hence, not to be understood as distortions nor as corroborations of biblical texts, but as *al-tikrei* systems that contain dia-logic metacodes according to which truth constitutes a composition of contrasting positions. It is thus the genuine dia-logic contraction and expansion of expressed and recorded emotional optimism and rational pessimism comprising the psychotherapeutic text that might be most relevant for examining deconstructive possibilities in literary criticism and of growth potentialities in socializing systems. Accordingly, if novels, for example, are permeated with popular psychoanalytic interpretations, one must realize that such insights encompass by definition only a one-sided, fundamentalistic understanding of reality (see Felman, 1982, and Rimmon-Kenan, 1987). By contrast, dia-logic options offering alternating psychological interpretations of the human situation could enrich the writer's and the critic's vistas considerably.

So far I have demonstrated how contrasting interpretations of poverty as bitterness and poverty as happiness may be recomposed into an I-*and*-thou conglomeration of truth that entails the possibility of progress by using the dia-logic *al-tikrei* metacode. My final task is now to illustrate how the psychotherapeutic text may further enhance the possibility of recomposing truth by examining how interpretative disputes are used in a dia-logic sense.

Although in the Hasidic tale the dia-logic *al-tikrei* metacode is available for emulation, we still do not know whether the Ḥasid indeed chooses the optimistic understanding of poverty unless we examine his response to the suggested interpretation. When Viktor Frankl (1970) describes how he reframes or recomposes suffering into a meaningful ontology, it is only the reported response to Frankl's interpretation that convinces us that his patient's text becomes true. In one case Frankl describes an elderly doctor who became severely depressed after his wife's death. To Frankl's question what would have happened if he had died before his wife, the doctor answered, "This would have been a terrible blow for her" (p. 136). Frankl then developed his interpretation by adding the following: "You see doctor, . . . you are the one that saved her from this suffering [your death]" (ibid.). In the case of a mother of an only crippled son who was about to commit suicide, Frankl reports the woman's response to his interpretation of her life as being meaningful because of her devotion to her son: "I myself may reflect calmly on my life because I can say: my life was full of meaning and I tried my best to actualize this meaning. I did for my son the best according to my ability. My life was not a failure" (p. 141). Thus, it is not only that it is possible to compose the dia-logic truth by adding the emotional-ideal dimension of meaning to the unerased rational-real dimension of suffering but also that the truth becomes authentic because a patient who is the author of his own biographic text reported it.

However, since Frankl did not record his patients' disagreements to his suggested interpretations, we still do not know whether he "missionarized," that is, whether like a charismatic therapist he manipulated them to replace dialectically their own version of truth. For that matter, the cabalic text describing an ecstatic experience of mystical self-annihilation (see Idel, 1989b) or a Christian text describing mystic mood swings referred to as "the dark night of the soul" (see Underhill, 1974), might very well account for culturally ideal rather than real states because no corroborating disputes over the authenticity of these experiences are reported in the text. Thus, optimal dia-logic truth available in psychotherapeutic texts emanates from the reported reader-writer disputes over interpretations of reality and experiences, and apparent progress may become true progress to the extent that we know how candid and effective was the dialogue between the world-mending *bonayich* (the building therapists) and the *banayich* (the sons and heirs of their parental legacy).[7] This also means that one may progress while *hanging on* to parental tradition or that one might regress because parental *hang ups* condition one.

To illuminate this dia-logic possibility let us return to one of Evelyne Schwaber's (1990: 237) cases:

> Mr. J. told of how after his wife had hit him when he was joking with her, he'd hit her back, harder (though he felt clearly in control). . . . I talked with him about what was evoked in him that had led him to hit her. He spoke of knowing his tendency to hurt those weaker, just as he had been the little brother whom the bigger boys would hit. As he went on, he seemed to be engaging in a useful piece of clinical work—except for one problem. His affect remained heavy, even more weighted down as he pondered these things. I noted this to myself, thinking that it was a clue to something not yet understood, or perhaps to a way in which he felt not understood. When I reflected on what may have been taking place this hour, I

observed something which I at first resisted recognizing in myself. I felt on the side of his wife. I didn't want him to hit her and I was engaged in trying to help him "analyze" what had led him to do that. That is, I had an agenda, well-intended as it may have been, to help him, by analysis, stop this behavior. I rationalized my interpretive endeavors as analytically appropriate, and indeed, he seemed to work seriously with them. Only his affect remained a clue to something not yet recognized.

The next day he returned complaining that he hadn't liked the session, he didn't like what I was saying; it seemed to him I was conveying that it was his problem. "Rather than?" I wondered . . . "that she's a bastard. . . . " Then I learned more of what had bothered him about his wife's response; he'd thought things were warm and loving between them and was taken aback, startled by her gesture. It evoked an old history of his relationship to women—of surprise hurts when they were least expected.

I did not then need to say, or even to think, she's a bastard, nor did I need inwardly to feel myself an advocate of his hitting his wife, to still recognize and respect his wish for me to see his point of view and his feeling.

The text cited above contains a tale about a man who hit his wife. The reader-therapist first interprets this text in realistic-rational terms of the weak victim being attacked by the strong, wicked aggressor (reportedly a husky man over six feet tall). However, because of the author's refutation of this interpretation, another, more emotional interpretation emerges that portrays the aggressor as a rejected, love-seeking victim. What is true and what is a lie? Is the man a "bastard" or is the woman a "bastard"? By now the reader would agree that in this story as in many other tales, there are no lies but that the truth that emerges is to be understood in the recomposing terms of the dia-logic coexistence between the real-rational truth of wife beating and the emotional-ideal truth of love seeking.

After our explorative excursion into the general possibility of establishing dia-logic truth, in the next part of this book I shall study possibilities for balancing people's irrational and rational worlds as they experience them on the intrapersonal level.

NOTES

1. A concrete case that attributes the suicide of a literary critic to a humiliating incident during which he was mocked publicly by a powerful author whom he dared to criticize is the following. In the introduction to M. M. Feitelsohn's *Selected Works* (1970), a description is provided how the powerful, conceited author known under the pseudonym Mendele the Book Seller, humiliated Feitelsohn (1870-1912) in public. A. B. Yoffe, who wrote this introduction, states that this incident testifies once again how some complacent writers are intolerant to creative interpretations and that since "shortly after this incident . . . Feitelsohn . . . committed suicide, it was commonly agreeable to see in the mentioned incident one of the main causes for his desperate act" (p. 6).

2. The cultural bias and the semantic problem associated with the term *reframing*

will be discussed later in this chapter when the preferable term *recomposing* will be introduced.

3. Since the problem of psychology as a "pendulum" discipline perpetually oscillating between association with the natural and humanistic sciences was mentioned in the beginning of Chapter 1, any elaboration on this issue would be superfluous and redundant.

4. Here it is of interest to point out that Ezra Zion Melamed (1978), who is undoubtedly one of the contemporary leading authorities on biblical and talmudic hermeneutics, has differentiated between the concepts *derash* and *peshat* in a way that is highly relevant to our present discourse. The two categories of biblical interpretation *peshat* (simple, straightforward) and *derash* (searching, narrating), about which more will be said later, were understood by Melamed in a way that is akin to the dispute between the Romantic and critical modes of interpretation discussed here. Melamed states:

> The way of *peshat* thus constitutes an attempt to approach and reach the understanding of the text and its meaning in the way it was said at the time. The *darshan* [the interpreter using *derash*] on the other hand, introjects into the text, which he interprets, part of his own intentions and thoughts of his heart, sometimes advertently and sometimes inadvertently. In other words, the *darshan* is subjective in his interpretation and the *pashtan* [the user of *peshat*] endeavors to be objective. (p. 6)

5. Here is the place to stress that although in his efforts to formulate a rational theory of truth Jurgen Habermas (1980) opts for what he terms a "monological language," he would have probably admitted that in the present context the dialogical language does not occupy a subordinate position because it fulfills a vital social function. Habermas thus regards Derrida and Foucault as antirational Nietzscheans who disguise the will to power as a will to truth because they breed anarchistic theories of meaning, yet he overlooks the potential truth emanating from the psychotherapeutic dialogue. Monological languages in which meaning is univocal because arguments are propositional and hence capable of embodying unequivocal deductive inferences may, according to Habermas, produce a true social consensus. On the other hand, a dialogical language that constitutes the everyday discourse and that proceeds in hermeneutic circles derived through mutual interpretations and negotiations of meaning is consequently incapable of providing rigorous inferences for the establishment of truth.

Although Habermas nonetheless concedes that for the purpose of social protest or for emancipation from a dominant power, the dia-logical negotiation of meaning is often more efficient than the static-rigid monological language, he seems oblivious to the possibility that it is precisely such negotiations that are often the major guardians of truth. It is in this sense, then, that the psychotherapeutic dialogue concerning self-deception should be understood as a contributor to methods endeavoring to recover truth.

6. Foucault's thesis about the controlling power inherent in knowledge is indeed compelling (see Sheridan, 1982) but we might overlook the danger of a reversed situation. Although psychiatric and criminological knowledge might usually encompass controlling power over the "mads" and the "bads", the manipulative "conning" power that many criminals exert over naive practitioners in the helping professions seems to constitute part of the everyday reality in correctional and psychiatric institutions.

7. Philosopher Franz Rosenzweig (1977:92) uses this *al-tikrei* in discussing the possibility of an anti-Hegelian dia-logic progress. Challenging Hegelians like Toynbee, who evisioned the possibility of progress via the exclusive emphasis on *bonayich* because presumably the state of *banayich* perpetuates the fossilizing regression to archaism, Rosenzweig calls for a renewal of the state of *banayich*:

> This turning backward while life's trend is forward, is for the nations of the world a difficult task . . . while for us this determines the essential feeling of our lives . . . the feeling that we are sons to our fathers and fathers to our offsprings . . . since by being "banim" [sons] we are "bonim" [builders].

Part Two

INTRAPERSONAL DIA-LOGISM

3

Unconsciousness: The Underground for Irrational Mysticism

If what is termed the unconscious[1] is indeed structured like a language, as Freudians and neo-Freudians like Jacques Lacan maintain, then a simple question must be raised: Where, when, and how may someone learn this language? Indeed, states Lacan (1970: 103), "What the psychoanalytic experience discovers in the unconscious is the whole structure of language." Thus, a language, we are told and taught, is governed by specific rules of syntax and symbols that constitute the communicable associations between a signified thing and the person who signifies it. Any language as a thought system providing the cultural metacodes that guide the signifying process must therefore be learned, either through natural socialization or in any Berlitz type of school for acquiring new languages.

Due to the intricate process of interpreting the dubious nature of symbols, we would then usually say that X masters a language if what he said was understood by Y or Z, who speak the same language. Accordingly, if symptoms of mental illness are to be understood as an unconscious language that "fixes in a system the signification inaccessible to the conscious subject," as Lacan (1966: 22) postulated, then this subject speaks a language he does not master because the linguistic "system of signification" he himself uses "is inaccessible" to him. Moreover, if indeed "the 'unconscious psychic processes' [are] 'the appropriate and justified expression for an established fact,'" as Freud (1938: 542) insisted, and "the unconscious is the larger circle which includes the smaller circle of the conscious" (ibid.), then the unconscious language masters its speaker.

Now, if the analyst as a reader is presumed to understand a text written by a patient-author who does not master the language in which he or she expresses himself, then we have an absurd situation according to which a Frenchman may be persuaded to believe he recited by heart an ancient poem in one of the Indian esoteric languages about which he never heard before. The situation in which the patient-author is mastered by his or her own unconscious language is often attributed to the reality that the language under consideration "applies to the . . . unconscious in which logic does not exist" (see Lemaire, 1977: 201); consequently, it is impossible to learn this irrational language because it encompasses no logical rules. But then again, if "elect" analysts are capable of learning to master the language of irrationality, which is hazardous for people's mental health, then certainly chances to prevent or to minimize mental breakdown might be increased if everyone could learn to master the mystic-irrational thought system we call the unconscious language. By inserting here the idea that learning to master the irrational language of the mystic unconscious may prevent mental distress, I am *ipso facto* reiterating what George Albee (1983) and other "preventionists" have claimed all along. I thus agree that whereas the field of general medicine focuses on preventing plagues that have beset humankind *before* they infect the population, mental health services are mostly concerned with treating people only *after* they have been inflicted with problems of mental disorder. My point of departure comes to stress only that in addition to teaching Westerners the Darwinian rational language of survival by means of enhancing their self-esteem, competence, and competitive "coping skills" (ibid.), preventionists have to reckon with the reality of the "unreal" and teach its mystic-irrational language.

Indeed, it is the thesis of this chapter that while the unconscious may control people's conscious thinking and precipitate mental breakdown because irrational-mystic thinking was banned in the West by being excluded from the "text," prevention of psychosis may be enhanced by grafting, including, and teaching the irrational-mystic language as part of the text people ought to learn as part of their respective socialization in the society that reared them. The Jewish multiple hermeneutic system known as *PaRDeS* demonstrates how the narrative system of *derash* constitutes the socialization components for teaching people how to re-biograph their failing identities by legitimizing the bridging between reading their frightening or puzzling experiences through the rational (*peshat*) and/or the irrational (*sod*) thought systems. I shall introduce the *pardesian* hermeneutic system later, in Chapter 4, but first, here, I will (1) establish the association between irrationality and the unconscious and (2) explore the differential meaning attributed to irrational mysticism in the pre- and post-Protestant eras.

THE MYSTIC LANGUAGE OF UNCONSCIOUS IRRATIONALISM

In Walter Kaufmann's (1961: 237) vivid, fictitious dialogue between Satan and a theologian, we find the following:

Theologian: You seem to feel that the Old Testament was enough.

Satan: After all, it invented me.

Theologian: The Jews took you over from the Persians; so by the same token you could stop with Zoroastrianism. . . .

Satan: But the Old Testament gave me my name. And the Zoroastrian Ahriman had to fight all the time against the god of light. . . . I am much more civilized, I don't like to fight. I like to talk.

Referring to the Book of Job, which "invented Satan," Kaufmann in essence says that you may control irrational fears of mystic satanism by including him in your text so that you may not have to fight in the dark with the Satanic eternal forces of darkness but maintain a civilized dialogue with Satan, who now has a name and who "likes to talk."

In psychological terms this would mean that if a frightened person rushes to a psychotherapist because he or she heard the voice of Satan or was persecuted by Him, the therapist could say, "Relax! You will not be excommunicated as a schizophrenic because we have a book about it!" (that is, the language of Satanism comprises a legitimate part of the text). This therapist might then proceed to help our frightened "patient" to "re-biograph" himself by using Job's dialogue with God, which ended in justifying and compensating Job, or by using cabalic or midrashic paradigms for normalizing the hearing of voices[2] or the transmigration of a dear deceased's soul.

In discussing the mental problems of Western people who hear voices or see visions and hence perceive themselves as mentally ill because they do not have a "therapeutic book about it," Carl Jung (1978: 31) describes the panic that seized a rational theologian who encountered such inexplicable mystic experiences:

What psychologists call psychic identity, or "mystical participation," has been stripped off our world of things. But it is exactly this halo of unconscious associations that gives a colorful and fantastic aspect to the primitive's world. We have lost it to such a degree that we do not recognize it when we meet it again. With us such things are kept below the threshold; when they occasionally reappear, we even insist that something is wrong.

I have more than once been consulted by well-educated and intelligent people who have had peculiar dreams, fantasies, or even visions, which have shocked them deeply. They have assumed that no one who is in a sound state of mind could suffer from such things, and that anyone who actually sees a vision must be pathologically disturbed. A theologian once told me that Ezekiel's visions were nothing more than morbid symptoms, and that, when Moses and other prophets heard "voices" speaking to them they were suffering from hallucinations. You can imagine the panic he felt when something of this kind "spontaneously" happened to him. We are so accustomed to the apparently rational nature of our world that we can scarcely imagine anything happening that cannot be explained by common sense. The primitive man confronted by a shock of this kind would not doubt his sanity; he would think of fetishes, spirits, or gods.

In contrast to the panic-stricken fear of voices and visions that could paradoxically seize many Western theologians (Christian or Jewish) who presumably "have the books" about mystic "irrational fears" but most probably do not believe in them because of their rational upbringing, I find it pertinent to describe here briefly a therapeutic approach developed in an outpatient psychiatric clinic that treats ultraorthodox Jews in Jerusalem.

Although according to the present thesis a fear of the irrational world of the transcendental unknown is universal, I think that such fears might be magnified under the following intertwined circumstances: (1) if the people encountering such fears reside in a country at war and (2) if consequently or independently the person who experienced such a frightful encounter is newly orthodox.

Among the many cases treated in the clinic under consideration, the case of Ezra (see Witztum, Buchbinder, and Van Der Hart, 1990) who was a newly orthodox (repenter) young man, and the case of Avraham (see Bilu, Witztum, and Van Der Hart, 1989), who was traumatized, though not hurt physically, after having experienced an incident during which several hand grenades exploded next to him, are of particular interest to the present perspective. Both Ezra and Avraham were haunted and persecuted by angels (demons?) with whom they maintained audiovisual contacts. In both cases symptoms of hallucinations, paranoic depression, physical self-neglect, and an encounter with a deceased father were part of the experience, so that prima facie they could be considered as typical schizophrenic patients.

It is, however, the fact that medications and conventional hypnotic or cathartic treatment methods were admittedly ineffective in both cases until a dialogue with the angel-agent of the "unknown world" was attempted that makes these cases relevent to our present point of departure. Thus in the case of Ezra tremendous improvement was noticed immediately following an ecstatic exorcistic ritual performed according to a formula read from the mystic *Book of the Angel Raziel* (see Dan, 1972). Similarly, in the case of Avraham the combination of recruiting a deceased Jewish *zaddik* (righteous man) who helped to exorcise the angel-agent and the reading from the book of Psalms resulted in Avraham's ability to return to an imaginary Paradise that was paralled by the concrete regaining of the family paradise he was able to live in and enjoy once again.

The details of these dia-logic treatment sequences are insignificant here; what is significant is that the irrational universal fear of the transcendental world, which was accelerated in these two cases, was not subdued by rational manipulations but by using the specific "cultural books" that provided the proper language of conversing with it. The therapeutic possibility of "having a book about it," which means practically that rational and irrational thinking are part of the living text, obviously requires a system for teaching multiple linguistic structures so that a person may master his emotions and thoughts and not be mastered by them.

Now, if Max Weber (1970) is correct that since the rise of Protestantism, which began in the sixteenth century, we are witnessing in the West the gradual predominance of rational, calculated thinking as a sole criteria and evidence for salvation and divine election, then it is plausible that socialization would aim to inculcate only the language of rationality. Likewise, if Foucault (1967: X) is correct that until the Renaissance "madness and non-madness, reason and non-reason are inextricably involved: inseparable" while "the end of 18th century, affords the evidence of a broken dialogue . . . in which the exchange between madness and reason was made [because] the language of psychiatry, which is a monologue of reason about madness, has been established only on the basis of such a silence," then indeed Protestantism has banned the irrational thought system. Consequently, if Western Protestantism has excluded the mystic-irrational language from its text, one may wonder what happens to people's eternal irrational fears of the transcendental unknown, and the unexpected unrationalizable predicaments that will forever haunt people in our "imperfect world," as Weber (1967) posited?[3]

To be sure, the presumed Western condemnation of irrationality since the Protestant era was not confined to the domain of people's fears of the metaphysical world of the unknown. The undemocratic banning of people's subjective feelings and belief systems by social scientists who took the positivistic oath of allegiance has precipitated an unbalanced study of human behavior. Alan Sica (1988: 6) put it most eloquently when he stated that

> this "growth of reason in the West," considered a moral good, has taken on an axiomatic quality as if post-feudal history can be well represented as a deliberate escape from bondage to irrational (and unrationalized) beliefs and acts. This encourages ignoring social behavior that does not observably subscribe to rationality, conceptually defined (or to aspects of its formal expression, logical positivism).

Accordingly, I would like to suggest now that the term *unconsciousness* was conceivably adopted by psychopathologists as an underground category to host and deal with the irrational-mystic thought system precisely because the Western no-exit situation that tabooed "un-reason" did not succeed to free people from their irrational fears. It is thus claimed here, not that the unconscious is a *myth*, but that the unconscious is *mystic* in the sense that it provides a rational *license* to redeem the irrational from its *silence* (a cabalist could attribute mystic meanings to the above letter-reversal exercise). By using an underground, or rather "under the counter,"[4] category that exists outside the text, analytically oriented therapists might then handle people's irrational thoughts without legitimizing them by claiming to master the language of the unconscious, which they would allegedly convert to rational consciousness.[5]

Indeed, although many psychodynamic psychologists eschew a direct association between irrationality and the unconscious, a typical writer on psychopathology like Arnold Buss (1966: 126) recapitulates Freud's formulation of the unconscious as follows:

> Freud brought to fruition the notions of unconscious that had been developing since Descartes,[6] and, more than those before him, brought conscious and unconscious into sharp opposition. The unconscious is essentially irrational, dominated by primary process (hallucinatory fantasy) wish fulfillment and the pleasure principle. It has no sense of time and contains ideas and motivations that may be mutually incompatible but that nevertheless are not in conflict. . . . The conscious is essentially rational dominated by secondary process (imagination in the service of planning) and the reality principle.

Following such definitional descriptions of the unconscious, it is, in fact, not surprising that even psychoanalysts like Donald Spence (1987) admitted that it would be impossible to establish the very existence of the unconscious in a particular patient. Spence hence indicates that since

> Freud made it clear in his definitional monograph that . . . the processes of the system Ucs. have the following features: "Exemption from mutual contradiction, primary process, . . . timelessness and replacement of external by physical reality." . . . Some of these characteristics make it almost impossible to verify our assumptions about a particular patient's unconscious [*because*] this principle would seem to imply that a complete account of a particular unconscious would not necessarily show any logical sequence or hierarchy of ideas. (p. 31)

True, the struggle between the rational realists and irrational idealists is as old as history. It is, however, this Cartesian-Freudian dichotomization between the rational conscious and the irrational unconscious that broke the vital dialogue between the creative world of ecstatic unreason (the pleasure principle) and the confining world of reason (the reality principle) by declaring that thoughts or knowledge derived through mystic-ecstatic experiences are not only false but mentally dangerous. It is with this Cartesian division in mind that we will turn now to examine the role irrational ecstatic folly played in the production of knowledge and truth in pre-Protestant thinking.

PHILONIC FOLLY AS A SOURCE OF LIFE AND KNOWLEDGE

I have maintained so far that the unconscious is an underground or "under cover" category that was a clever invention to handle people's unshakeable irrational-mystic thoughts, which were tabooed with the beginning of the age of reason ever since Protestant rationalism successfully permeated the Western world. I have suggested, further, that by excluding the irrational-mystic language from the curricula, an absurd, dangerous situation[7] was created whereby the unconscious language of folly supposedly dictates and controls the language of consciousness and personal responsibility as portrayed, for example, in Freud's (1955) famous writing-pad analogy. Indeed, Otto Rank (1978: 26) one of Freud's outstanding ex-students, who did not accept the theory of the dictatorship of the unconscious, states that "the 'psychology of the unconscious' unveils itself as one of the numerous attempts of mankind to deny the will in order to evade the conscious responsibility following of necessity therefrom." Rank's theory of the cure inherent in people's conscious-rational "will" does not teach them how to control their irrational fears from the transcendental "imperfect world" of unpredictable calamities. However, there is no "will" that can cancel one's fears in the midst of experiencing, for instance, the horrors of a flood or an earthquake. So Rank's "will" does not bequeath people with a therapeutic *tool* to help them remain *cool* in facing an erupting volcano.

In the following I shall demonstrate that in pre-Protestant formulations, irrational-mystic thinking was included in the text because it was accepted as a legitimate source of knowledge and that the teaching of the language of mysticism and of irrational ecstasy was effective in many ways. I shall do so by showing how irrational mysticism functioned as a paradigmatic "book" that helped one to understand and accept unexpected atrocities. More importantly, I shall claim that it was useful as a preventative immunizing measure against mental breakdown because the function of folly was understood as a source of life and progress, and not of death and decadence. It is well known that such pre-Protestant writers as Erasmus, the author of the influential *Praise of Folly,* and Brand, in his classic *Ship of Fools* (*Narrenschiff*), lamented the condemnation of folly and its resultant excommunication of fools from the bosom of European societies.

According to Michael Screech (1988: XVII), Erasmus's folly refers to "a form of a religious ecstasy which is indistinguishable from a bout of temporary madness." Screech's (p. XXI) erudite study shows how one may understand Erasmus's eulogy of folly if one realizes how Erasmus was influenced by the neo-Platonic pseudo-Dionysus "he came across in Italy," and especially if one notices "how powerful a contribution Plato had made to the doctrines of ecstasy with his teachings in the *Phaedrus* about the divine forms of madness which produce prophets, poets and lovers."

Now, my reference to the Erasmian praise of folly will not add much to Foucault's thesis about the "broken dialogue" between the "straight" world of reason and the "creative" man of unreason unless I demonstrate (a) how irrational ecstatic folly was considered as a legitimate source of truth because of its capability of producing the highest kind of knowledge and (b) unless I show how in the pre-Protestant era learning the language of madness functioned as an immunization device that helped minimize mental breakdown. It is of interest here that in regard to the first point, Screech (1988), for example, emphasizes that Christian notions of ecstasy owe their understanding not only to Platonic thought but also to Jewish thinking mainly as formulated by the first-century Jewish philosopher Philo. To see how mystic folly was a widely accepted source of knowledge in the early Judeo-Christian era, let us turn now to consider briefly Harry Wolfson's (1947) important study of Philo's philosophy in which he compares systematically Plato's and Philo's notions of ecstasy.

Recalling the mutual energizing system operating between the sensual-emotive and the rational-cognitive approach to life, it is worthwhile to notice at the outset that Wolfson (1947: 4) finds it important to begin his discussion by stating that Philo "was merely reechoing the view common to Plato, Aristotle and the Stoics. All of them, in different ways, believed in the existence of a reciprocal relation between sensation and reason." Reading on in Wolfson's Philo, one receives the definite impression that in fact Philo's holistic approach is far more dynamic than that of his contemporaries when he describes how the union of the faculties, "intertwined and clinging to each other, . . . move in rythmic concord mutually receiving and repaying benefits" (1947: 20).

Nevertheless, in regard to the source of knowledge, both Plato and Philo seem to agree on two basic notions that are either blurred or disregarded in contemporary psychological theories: Namely, (1) there is a difference between knowledge of the mind, consisting of rational knowledge based on what we would term today the science of empirical testing, and knowledge of the senses, consisting of sensation and opinion; and (2) the highest form of knowledge, which includes ideas and the ability to tell future things, does not rest on sensation but is acquired through what Plato called philosophic frenzy or, in Philo's terms, through ecstatic prophecy.[8] These two important points are made here not only to demonstrate that these ancient philosophers believed that the highest form of creative knowledge mastered by poets, prophets, and lawgivers may be produced only through mystic ecstasy and frenzic folly; they are made also to stress that these philosophers differentiated between knowledge derived through the senses and knowledge acquired without their assistance. I emphasize this distinction to remind the reader that both contemporary neuropsychologists interested in the study of hemispheric lateralization[9] and psychologists focusing on cognitive and emotive aspects of behavior tend to lump together sensual and mystic expressions either as a right-hemispheric activity or as a personality predisposition (see Rotenberg, 1987).

Moreover, since pleasure is "connected by Philo with sensation" (Wolfson, 1947: 10), one may wonder further why interpretations of Freudian psychology classify the pleasure principle as part of the irrational unconscious (see my earlier quotation from Arnold Buss)? It is hence not only that early philosophers like Philo shunned such confusing, simplified associations between the reality principle and rationalism (although crib-deaths, earthquakes, and floods are realistic, they are certainly not rational), to which I shall return later. It is, rather, their understanding of the bridging relationship between ecstatic pleasure of the senses (which might be very rational) and the achievement of mystic-irrational knowledge, which may explain also their functional conception of folly.

In other words, the question to which we should address ourselves now is the classic one: "If it is so good, why is it so bad?" That is, if ecstatic folly is a source of creativity that may produce poetry, prophecy, and even love and law, why was it excluded by the Protestants from the text and context of life, as Foucault insisted, or as a living reading or writing method, as Derrida (1978) would have it? Now, for the skeptic, eyebrow-lifting readers who at this point would say, "What has creativity to do with the problem of the unconscious?" let me remind them that since Freud's time Frederick Myers's (1903) theory about the unconscious as the source of intuition and creativity never ceased to exert its impact on "creative" thinkers (see, for example, Harman and Rheingold, 1984).

The answer, which relates to my second and major proposition, posits that since the inception of the Protestant age of reason, irrational mysticism was not tabooed only because it did not comply with the rational, calculated, and positive criteria for salvation and the establishment of Aristotelian truths. More importantly, I postulate that the language of irrational folly was excluded from the text mainly because it was identified with death and damnation.

I shall show below that whereas the pre-Protestant thinker saw ecstatic folly as a functional activity that infuses people with the energy of life because it operated as an immunizing method for overcoming the fear of death, for the Protestant-Calvinist, irrational folly was synonymous with Thanatos (death wish) because it carried the signs and symptom of incurable damnation. I shall therefore introduce now a major point of departure by positing that by equating mystic folly with death and damnation, the post-Protestant West is governed by the unconscious fear of death (the death-wish hypothesis), whereas the pre-Protestants and the Easterners use mystic folly as an immunization device to control their fear of death.[10]

THE BOOK OF FRENZY AGAINST THE FEAR OF DEATH

It should be well known that it was John Calvin (1939: 129) who, in his famous Institute of the Christian Religion, first associated the symptoms of damnation as representing and deserving death when he stated, for instance, that "it is a notion commonly entertained, that God . . . adopts as his children such as he foreknows will be deserving of his grace, and devotes to the damnation of death others whose dispositions he sees will be inclined to wickedness and impiety." It is also well known that the practice of witch hunting and execution of those who in our day would be defined as fools or as mentally ill began with the rise and spread of Protestantism in the sixteenth century. It is therefore unnecessary to reestablish the empirical connection between damnation and the mental illness metaphor (see Rotenberg, 1978).

One should agree, however, that if since the age of reason "folly . . . would be one and the same with death itself," as Foucault (quoted by Sheridan, 1982: 20) rightly indicated, then the exclusion of the irrational-mystic language[11] of folly from the book of life does not automatically eliminate people's irrational fears of the "reality principle" of unexpected death and disasters.

Of course, it is true that in the face of only one legitimate language of rational socialization in which material success is its only sign of salvation, the invention of the unconscious as an underground category to deal with people's irrational fears seems to be an inevitable solution, as noted, because people were not socialized to speak the language of ecstatic folly. However, if the unconscious language of irrationality masters people's conscious behavior, a language and a book are needed in order to restore the normal situation that allows people to master their own language, especially if it connotes death and damnation. Philo had such a book, used for teaching the language of ecstasy, which produces the highest kind of prophetic knowledge[12] and which I claim instills the energy of life because it functions as an immunization against the fear of death, as I hope to demonstrate next.

Philo's book is the Bible, and his role models are Abraham, Moses, Ezekiel, and other prophets, so that the possibility of a mutual energizing process between ecstatic unreason and the reasonable activity of lawmaking may be learned from Moses. But what comprises this dynamic ecstatic folly that I claim functions as an immunizing system triggered by the fear of death? What marks the difference between the deterministic hypothesis of the death wish and the free-will postulate of immunizing folly against the fear of death?

Let us read carefully Philo's descriptions of, or rather prescription for, reaching the state of ecstatic frenzy. In discussing the rhetorical question "Who could be the heir of divine and incorporeal things?" Philo (1949:

4:317) uses Abraham's dispute with God and interprets the verse "He who shall come out of thee shall be thy heir" (Genesis: 15:4) as follows:

> Therefore, my soul, if thou feelest any yearning to inherit the good things of God, leave not only thy land, that is the body, thy kinsfolk, that is the senses, thy father's house [Gen.XII,1], that is speech, but be fugitive from thyself also and issue forth from thyself. Like persons possessed and corybants, be filled with inspired frenzy, even as the prophets are inspired. . . . Such is the mind, which has this inheritance.

Whereas the above description refers strictly to a religious experience, which today could be entitled "do-it-yourself steps for attaining prophecy," the actual prescribed procedure contains what most writers on mysticism would consider as efforts of the soul to leave the body. Even more pertinent is Philo's prescription for attaining the higher mystic knowledge by means of the same process when he interprets how God "led Abraham outside":

> He led him outside and said "Look up into heaven" [Genesis 15:5]. . . . [He led him] outside of the prison-houses of the body, of the lairs where the senses lurk, of the sophistries of the deceitful word and thought; above all He led him out of himself, out of the belief that he thought and apprehended through intelligence which acknowledged no other authority and owed no allegiance to any other than itself. (pp. 321-325)

Now, it is striking to observe that according to most pre-Protestant writers the procedure to reach the state of folly known as *unio-mystica* (uniting with God) and the state of creative inspiration actually follows the process of dying, during which the soul leaves the body. According to Screech (1988: 49), "For centuries before Erasmus, ecstasy had come to mean the state of a Christian who had been raptured outside himself, his soul 'leaving his body' in the process." Hence, maintains Screech (p. 57), "Erasmus finds strong Christian authority for interpreting ecstasy as a divinely induced insanity . . . induced by the soul's striving to leave the body." Patterned after the popular notion of living in Christ, Screech (p. 56) explains how by following the idea of "ecstatic rapture" one may understand how "lovers live not in themselves but in the one whom they love, their souls departing from their bodies and entering that of the beloved, in a mutual exchange."

The creative joy and prophetic-knowledge usually attributed to children, fools, and the Renaissance court jester might, then, be explained as follows: If a person was able to penetrate the heavenly domain of the transcendental unknown that everybody fears, if a person "has been there" because he was temporarily dead when through his ecstatic-psychotic behavior his soul left his body, then (1) he has certainly a good reason to be happy because he became immunized against the state of death and (2) he has probably acquired part of God's wisdom and protection. In a series of experiments comparing the mystical experience of *unio mystica* with meditation, hypnosis, and the LSD trance, Alfred Lord Tennyson observed that the common feeling in these states was of a loss of consciousness and of joy due to the impossibility of death (see Merkur, 1989: 128-129).[13]

To be sure, by "ecstatic prophecy" I obviously do not have in mind those quietistic forms of frenzy, individual or collective, that bring about a total breakdown of personalities. These trance states of uncontrollable possession, which were described by Benjamin Uffenheimer (1987) and others are incapable of triggering any prophetic visions or creativity. Hence, the kind of frenzy presumed to enhance prophetic vision and creativity must be understood as an ecstasy that crystallizes one's personality (see Uffenheimer, 1987). This creative folly in which one does not obliterate one's self concurs, in fact, with my cabalic formulation of the contraction paradigm (see Rotenberg, 1983). Accordingly, temporary death is a process that refers only to a desire of the soul to leave the body via the body's efforts to contract its normal controlling activities and thereby make room for the souls, which may now expand their ecstatic elevating aspirations.

Returning to the medieval theory of folly, it is of interest to note that Walter Kaiser's (1963: 8) indication that "the feeble-minded were considered by the Middle Ages to be under the special protection of God" because "Christ himself had . . . given the example by favoring fools, and idiots and children" is generally tantamount to the famous Jewish saying "The Lord protects the fools" (Psalms 116:6) and the talmudic slogan declaring, "From the day the Temple was destroyed, prophecy was taken from the prophets and given to fools and babes" (*Baba Batra* 12:b).

Moreover, the belief that the child's and the fool's "soulless" natural state is "devoid of reason" because it is uncontaminated by society's twisted and biased norms in fact provided the rationale and license for the "fools" to criticize the accepted order with their prophetic wisdom. However, the Renaissance cult of the "wise fool," during which the professional fools imitated the "natural fool" either in the king's courts or as heroic characters in Rabelais's, Shakespeare's, and Cervantes's classic literary contributions, seems to have vanished after the Protestant dogmatic language of reason was successfully disseminated in the European countries. Thus, in the pre-Protestant era the highest kind of knowledge—creative inspirations, achievements of the genius,[14] prophetic muses, and ecstatic love and joy—is paradoxically attainable by approximating or simulating the dying process, that is, by separating the soul from its body.

How should we extricate this paradoxical paradigm? In my study of the psychosocial dynamics of cabalistic Hasidism (see Rotenberg, 1983), I have interpreted the famous Hasidic notion of descent for the sake of ascent as a desensitizing immunization device. I suggested, accordingly, that one may understand Hasidic normative prescriptions as instructions for overcoming depression or the feeling of failure. Thus, the Besht (1975: 30) who was the founder of eighteenth-century Hasidism, states, for example, that the verse "'There is no righteous man on earth who will do good without sinning' [means] that when a person does only good the evil impulse seduces him, whereas when the evil impulse realizes that he has in him a part of the evil inclination, he will leave him alone." The prescription against the disease of temptation described in the Besht's book is thus portrayed as a straightforward immunization manual that may be read as follows: "Consume or introject a small dose of germs (e.g., anti-evil impulse germs) that cause the disease that threatens to contaminate you, and your organism will develop natural antibodies against the illness under consideration."

I would like now to expand this immunization model by suggesting that normative prescriptions for attaining ecstatic folly, in which one's soul strives to leave the body, may also be conceived as immunization procedures against the fear of death because by means of this process of temporary death, one enters the domain of the mystic-transcendental unknown in order to learn to master what one constantly fears. Put differently, I suggest that by consuming small doses of death, so to speak, one learns to control the fear of death.

Thus, acquiring the irrational language of mystic folly may be instrumental in preventing permanent psychotic detachments from reality provided that indeed "there is a book about it." It would accordingly be conceivable that if individuals encounter stress, disaster, or manic joy, they need not be overly alarmed if they will be allowed to understand their resultant experiences (delusions or hearing voices) either in the rational language of reason or in the mystic language of unreason, which they learned to master in the course of their socialization.

As alluded to in the beginning of this chapter, a Cartesian linguistic model will be of little help to the modern person unless a linking dimension is available to enable the bridging between such rational and irrational thought systems. This linking dimension may be found in the Jewish multifaceted interpretation system known as *PaRDeS*, which will be the focus of the next chapter. *PaRDeS* contains a narrative language of *derash*, which may be viewed as a comprehensive therapeutic system for re-biographing because it links the rational language of cognitive *peshat* with the irrational language of mystic *sod.* By introducing *derash* as a comprehensive therapeutic system of re-biographing that may bridge between cognitive *peshat* and mystic *sod*, I will demonstrate how re-biographing as the pivot of *PaRDeS* meets the basic requirements of a comprehensive psychotherapy because of two reasons: First, it does so because unlike many fragmented therapeutic procedures it strives to encompass the remedy not only for what is usually termed neurotic behavior but also for so-called psychotic conduct. And second, it does so because it attempts to relate not only to people's situational here-and-now problems but to their total biographic identity which includes their past failures and their future aspirations. In other words, *pardesian* re-biographing aspires to bridge between the rational and the irrational forces people encounter in their interpersonal space and between parts of their past and future identities operating in their intrapersonal time perspective.

NOTES

1. I should caution the reader at the outset that a discussion of the unconscious as a linguistic structure designating pathological processes must be distinguished from the loose use made of this term in popular literature to refer to spontaneity, thoughtlessness, or unawareness. Sidney Rosen (1982: 59, 60) describes, for example, how Milton Erickson established a rapport with a farmer in order to sell him some books:

> Here, Erickson is recounting how he had unconsciously acted . . . to achieve his purpose . . . to sell books. . . . He had "thoughtlessly" picked up some shingles and had scratched the hog's back as he was talking to the farmer. The farmer unconsciously responded to a man whom he felt to be a kindred soul.

Donald Spence (1987) has used the term "substantive unconscious" to refer to its usage as a system with clear rules, while its popular usage, in which it means unavailable to awareness, he has termed "descriptive unconscious."

2. A good example of how the midrashic "book" may be instrumental in normalizing such schizophrenic manifestations as hearing voices is the talmudic concept of *bat kol.* Max Kadushin (1972) explains how rabbinic philosophy established a state he termed "normal mysticism," according to which pople are urged to experience God in mundane things such as their daily sustenance, the very experience of daylight, or loving kindness. Thus, the term *bat* (daughter) *kol* (voice) means only a derivative voice from heaven "something like an echo" (p. 262). After the death of the last prophets, this voice "lacks authority" and is hence "not associated with any experience of God" (ibid.). On the interesting connection between the *bat kol* and the use of children's innocent statements at the temple or school, see Saul Liberman (1984).

Psychotherapeutically, then, for modern people seeking existential and transcendental answers to their irrational fears and experiences (e.g., hearing voices), this would mean that there is a "book about it." This therapeutic book of "normal mysticism," which contains such concepts as the "miracle" (*nes*), the "revelation of God" (*gilluy shechina*), and so on, does not dictate people's behavior as does a Freudian unconscious, but it may be used as a paradigm that legitimizes and normalizes some mystical experiences. With it our rational-modern "seeker" who heard voices could feel less threatened by psychiatric excommunication, accepting "normal mysticism" as a possibility that presumably some people experience.

3. It should be pointed out here that although Weber's thesis about the "universal need for salvation" emanating from the reality of an "imperfect world" urges concentration on studying people's irrational fears, his own evasive ambivalence about the place of irrationality in human behavior permeates most of his writings. Thus, states Alan Sica (1988: 5) succinctly:

Wishing or theoretically demanding submission to rational consistency from social actors will not make it so. It will not lessen the empirical prevalence of irrationality in meaning-seeking activity. This, Pareto's major thesis, was boldly brushed aside by Weber and tends, accordingly, to be ignored or denied by today's researchers.

4. In *Damnation and Deviance* (1978) I have described psychopathy as a clinical "wastebasket" category that clinicians continue to use "under the counter" to refer to "cureless evil people," although the term *psychopathy* was eliminated from the 1968 edition of the American Psychiatric Association's *Diagnostic and Statistical Manual* (DSM). While I accept that physicians, for example, need such a wastebasket category as "allergy" in order to host temporarily those illnesses that do not yet have a clear scientific etiology with its compatible prognosis, here my reference to the unconscious as an underground category is different. It is accordingly claimed, not that the unconscious-irrational thought system does not exist, but that it was banned by the Protestant augment of rational salvation.

5. In his erudite analysis of Freud's psychoanalysis, Philip Rieff (1961: 35-36) makes two points that are of great relevance to the present discourse. The first is about the nonrational, godlike, mystic nature of the unconscious: "The unconscious functions for Freud as a 'god-term' . . . because it is both fundamental to and inaccessible to experience. . . . The unconscious is fertile 'nature,' the womb of darkness." In his second point Rieff (p. 103) enlightens us that as a committed rationalist Freud maintains that psychoanalysis constitutes a dialectic process in which rational consciousness replaces the irrational unconscious: "Though he insisted on the pre-rational core of human nature, Freud remained a rationalist. . . . Little Hans was correctly cured—by rational enlightenment. When he was enlightened as to his real motives, his emotions were checked." Quoting from Freud's *Introductory Lectures,* Rieff (p. 104) then emphasizes that "the task of the psychoanalytic treatment can be summed up in this formula: everything pathogenic in the unconscious must be transferred into consciousness."

6. According to Henri Ellenberger's (1970: 312) comprehensive study of the unconscious, "It was Leibnitz, who proposed the first theory of the unconscious mind supported by purely psychological arguments."

7. This absurd postulate according to which the language of the unconscious, which one did not learn to master, controls and dictates the speaking conscious language and behavior is further complicated by considering the psychodynamic self-contradictory concept of unconscious motivation. While the term *unconscious* connotes determinism the word *motivation* implies a belief in free will, and therefore the term *unconscious motivation* appears as another clever invention to circumvent the Protestant taboo in order to defend wickedness, which should have otherwise been labeled as a sign of damnation (see Rotenberg, 1978). Indeed, such naive philosophers as John Hospers (1966: 26), who accepted blindly this psychoanalytic category, stated that the criminals

should not be held responsible [because] the deed may be planned, it may be carried out in cold calculation. It may spring from the agent's character and be continuous with the rest of his behavior, and it may be perfectly true that he could have done differently *if* he had wanted to; nonethless his behavior was brought about by unconscious conflicts developed in infancy, over which he had no control and of which . . . he does not even have knowledge.

8. It seems that a major thesis in Wolfson's study evolves around the difference

between Plato's and Philo's conceptualizations of prophecy. Thus, states Wolfson (1947: 10), "Philo identifies his third and highest kind of knowledge, the knowledge of the ideas, with prophecy thus substituting the term prophecy for the Platonic term recollection." It is of interest to note here, that when Gershom Scholem (1972) differentiated between the "restorative" and the "utopian" patterns of messianism, he never associated the restorative kind with Plato's "recollection" and the utopian type with Philo's notion of prophecy. After all, Philo's insistence that prophetic knowledge does not constitute a recollection of preexisting ideas seems to deserve the credit of an original departure from Plato's deeply entrenched philosophy of primordial ideas. Although Scholem's concern was with messianic forces, I think that his utopian category, which entails forces of inspiration that "are nourished by a vision of the future" (1972: 3), seems to comprise a "restoration" of Philo's notion of prophecy.

9. Here it is of interest to notice that Eugene d'Aquili (1983) proposed that the process of myth formation occurs on the dominant (left) side of the brain as part of an analytic, cognitive, problem-solving activity. However, a ritual act such as the meditative *unio mystica*, which unites such opposites as God-man, according to d'Aquili marks a cognitive shift from the dominant (left) to the nondominant (right) hemisphere. Whereas d'Aquili views the ritual performance as a mythic activity that reconciles opposites like good and bad, the present perspective considers the narrative process of imaginative re-biographing as a more appropriate bridge between the rational and the irrational languages the modern person uses when he is caught between the natural and the supernatural worlds. In other words, I contend that midrashic narration, which allows the use of the imagination, parable, metaphor, or tale to re-biograph one's lifestory, constitutes a more functional bridge between one's corporeal reality and one's need for a more ideal, incorporeal relationship with it.

10. Observation of Western people's everyday behavior might provide ample evidence that they are motivated by the fear of death rather than by their desire to experience it (i.e., the death wish). Here, however, it might be appropriate to indicate that the suicidal trends observed among Shiites and other Moslem fighters in Iran, Lebanon, and Israel most probably reflects an extreme form of immunization against the fear of death. Thus, mystic and fatalistic conceptions of incarnation and of the paradisiacal world that awaits man (especially martyrs) after death might infuse people with a feeling of courage and indifference in the facing of their own or of one of their closest kin's death.

11. In a modern philosophical novel that uses ecstatic cabala as its background, Umberto Eco (1989) echoes these dangers of mystic irrational thoughts. If we agree, however, that by warning against the dangers emanating from mystic-irrational thinking one does not eliminate people's fears of the supernatural, then learning the cabalic language might still teach people how to overcome these fears, whereas a demonic language of determinism might reinforce such fears.

12. Unlike most contemporary academic writers on mysticism Philo accounted "of his own personal experience of prophetic inspirations" (see Wolfson, 1947: 54).

13. Here, it should be stressed that our emphasis is on establishing the connection between ecstatic folly and the unconscious, yet many writers consider this mystic experience or even madness per se as a higher state of consciousness. Thus, Lillian Feder (1980: 280) states in her study, for example, that

what primarily distinguishes the modern approach to the mind through the nonrational primary process from earlier ones is not only the cultural adaptations of psychoanalytic discoveries, but beginning with Nietzsche, the growing belief that, since God is dead, the individual consciousness supersedes all authority. This consciousness, restricted for millennia by its rational masks and lies, can be freed, it is assumed, only by a return to its eternal roots in the primordial processes manifested in madness.

14. According to Evelyn Underhill (1974: 65) the "higher mysterious powers of the genius "lie very near the normal threshold of consciousness" and according to Willis Harman and Howard Rheingold (1984: 7) the older term *genie*, which implies that "talented individuals must possess the aid of a genie," reflects the idea that even today the genius possesses unconscious insights that may be liberated.

4

PaRDeS: The Narrative Link between Cognitive and Mystic Therapy

According to Gershom Scholem (1977: 60), the thirteenth-century cabalist Rabbi Moshe De Leon claimed to have coined the term *pardes* when he stated in his book *Hanefesh Hachachama* (*The Wise Soul*) (1290) that "I called its name P.a.R.D.e.S. [and presumably the last part of the book was named *Sefer Ha-Pardes*] on the account of a famous matter which I formulated in the secret of four ways: . . . *peshat, remez, derash, sod*." For the present discussion the etymological history of the concept *P(a)RD(e)S* (in Hebrew the *a* and *e* vowels are not needed) is insignificant, but it is important to know that the *P(a)RD(e)S* idea means, generally, that the Torah and other sacred texts may be interpreted on four levels or, rather, according to four different thought systems.[1] Thus, *P(eshat)* (simple) stands for the simple, straightforward, literal, and rational meaning of a verse, which could be understood as going by the written letter. *R(emez)* (implication) refers to the philosophical truth inherent in an allegoric or symbolic meaning of a word derived either by reading a word or several words as an abbreviation of other words or by breaking a word by recombining the letters of a word into a new word in order to derive a new meaning from the text. *D(erash)* (search, interpret) refers to the narrative and ethical interpretation of a word or paragraph by using an analogic story and parable or by using any other method that activates the imagination to expand, broaden, or change the meaning of the text according to traditional Midrashim. *S(od)* (secret) refers to specific texts that include mystic-irrational interpretations of the scripture according to prestructured paradigms as outlined, for instance, in cabalic books. Scholem (1974: 172) cites sources indicating that the four exegetic categories that came to be known under the acronym *PaRDeS* "served only as a general framework for a multiplicity of individual readings . . . which . . . was expressed in the widespread belief . . . that each single Jew approached the Torah by a path that he alone could follow."

To minimize misguiding generalizations, I should insert at the outset two precautionary comments: (1) The earlier use of the term *pardes* referred only to mystic *sod* or other esoteric (hidden) interpretations of such events as Genesis. (2) The Rabbinic rules determining the circumstance allowing the deviation from *peshat* in favor of a more creative interpretation of *derash* or *sod* was a highly disputed matter.[2] From the present dia-logic perspective one might point out, however, that although Maimonides (*Talmud Torah* Chap. 1:37), the famous twelfth-century rationalist, used *pardes* in its earlier sense,[3] he repeatedly accentuated the idea of studying the scripture on different hermeneutic levels. For instance, Maimonides specified in one place (ibid.) how people are to divide their daily studies into three parts that include one-third of mystic (*pardesian*) or *derashic* interpretations, and elsewhere Maimonides (1965: 12) teaches how to differentiate between the inner (esoteric) and the external (exoteric) meaning of various passages.

Likewise, if discrepancies between the literal *peshat* meaning of a verse like the biblical (Exodus:21:24) eye-for-an-eye principle of retribution and its *derashic* interpretation as monetary compensation reflected severe exegetic tensions, in essence the present notion of *PaRDeS* "has become a household word in Jewish exegetical terminology" as van der Heide (1983: 153) maintained. Thus while the question of interpretative authority was not undermined (see Weiss-Halivni, 1990), the dia-logic notion of multiple meanings that coexist was persistently maintained. To be sure, by emphasizing the dia-logic nature of *PaRDeS* one should not overlook the various hermeneutic hierarchies inherent in this multiple interpretive system. In fact, these four hermeneutic levels[4] were so ranked that once *peshat* (rationality) and once *sod* (mysticism) were considered most important in the hierarchy (see Sandler, 1955).

Accordingly, the open, noncanonical nature of *PaRDeS* contains, on the one hand, a most important psychological guide for interpreting the living text while, on the other hand, it entails obstacles inviting an oversimplified anthropomorphic misconstrual of text and context. This double-edged sword embedded in the *PaRDeS* system may be understood by following a dispute that evolved around the connotation of the Hebrew word *be'ur* (interpretation or translation). In a sixteenth-century text attributed to Joseph ibn Gikatilla (see van der Heide, 1983) the point is made that, since the word *be'ur* comprises both the Hebrew word *bor* (meaning pit) and *be'er* (meaning well or spring), *pardesian* interpretations of the Torah should be utilized in the second sense to uncover the deeper mysteries that flow from the spring of divine wisdom. One may, however, understand *be'ur* as an open system which follows the biblical popular slogan stating that "the ways of the Lord are right, and the just shall walk in them; but the transgressors shall fall therein" (Hosea, 14:8). From our psychological perspective this would mean then that such a *be'ur* conceptualization of the *PaRDeS* encompasses a component that would constitute a safeguard against fundamentalistic trends. One might hence view, for example, the fact that the famous eighteenth-century Jewish philosopher Moses Mendelsohn termed his translation of the Bible *Be'ur* as no sheer coincidence, because his famous *Be'ur* was conceived by many in Hosea's terms.

In any event, whether, by following the notion of *be'ur,* the *PaRDeS* scheme contains more *pit*falls than *spring*boards (or vice versa) for interpreting the written text in its living context, as a psychological system it constitutes a model for choosing between multiple interpretations of life because the idea that *PaRDeS* connotes a coexistence between the natural and the supernatural was systematically preserved. Indeed, Scholem (1974: 233) stresses that Nachmanides, the thirteenth-century cabalist, "knows the danger of spiritualization and he is not worried about it in the realm of *sod*, because the unknown is inherently intertwined in the known and in the action which without it the mystic symbol has no existence at all."

The dia-logic interconnection between mystic and rational interpretations of the text may also be understood in the open, noncanonical status of various mystic categories. On the one hand, in postexilic times permission was given to disregard such supernatural revelations as a *bat kol* (a voice from heaven)[5] or dreams (Sanhedrin 30:a); on the other hand, it was well known that some sages even settled *Halachic* (legal) matters according to responses communicated to them from Heaven via a dream or other mystic revelation (see Margaliyot, 1989). This dia-logic, open status of semimystic categories seems to contain a most significant psychological device for bridging between people's natural and supernatural reality. Accordingly, one is free to perceive a *bat kol* (the lowest rank in prophecy) as a mystic experience; but if, say, due to a rational upbringing, one interprets the hearing of voices in schizophrenic terms, one is allowed to understand this experience as an inner voice that functions as a reflective echo or as a synonym with wisdom that only borders on prophecy. Indeed, Reuven Margaliyot (ibid.: 34-35) states that according to talmudic sources

> some say that no voice would be heard from heaven but from one voice another voice comes forth as often happens when one hits forcefully (e.g., an iron) and hears another voice . . . generated from it from far away. . . . This voice exists by itself in the blowing wind and Rabbi Saadya interpreted that he hollers within the mountains and the voice responds to him from within the broken mountains and caves of the rocks, and the expression *bat* (daughter) indicates that one does not hear the real voice . . . that it appears as if it responds to the person who hollers towards it.

From the present socializing, psychotherapeutic perspective this would mean that if no interpretation is erased but introduced via teaching and preaching, then the process by which the ordinary Jew, who studies or listens to *derashot* (sermons), will selectively apply a particular biblical interpretation to his personal needs will follow automatically. It means also, however, that he might prefer to resort first to the kind of interpretation which will be termed here the "metacode" (mystic or rational) that was accentuated during his socialization.

In fact, one should emphasize here that there is a belief that the heavenly Torah was handed down to man in letters that were not divided into words, so that people will be forever forced (see Heineman, 1974) to rearrange its letters into new words to corroborate the imperative possibility of "seventy faces to the Torah" (which implies the idea of multiple interpretations). Here one should stress further that the *PaRDeS*, as a multiple scheme for interpreting life, comprises a challenging paradox to the methodological dilemma that has confronted the discipline of psychology (see Chapter 1) since its inception. It is commonly accepted that usually only religious doctrines breed fundamentalistic dogmas, whereas secular ideologies or theories adhere to the formulation of alternative disprovable sets of hypotheses. Paradoxically, it seems, however, that while in religious systems of exegesis such as the *PaRDeS* alternative interpretations must function as tentative sets of hypotheses, secular ideological theories such as Freudianism and Marxism have disseminated fundamentalist dogmas, which in the case of the latter have even instigated the harassment of individuals and wars between nations. At any rate, returning to *PaRDeS* in the present context, since interpretations must follow specific midrashic and cabalistic books that comprise the basic narrative and mystic paradigms for role modeling, for our therapeutic purposes *PaRDeS* may be conceived as a threefold scheme. Accordingly, one may incorporate *remez* (see ibid.) under the general heading of *derash* because, on the one hand, it means literally "hint or allusion," which pertains to mystic *sod*, and, on the other hand, it practically comprises specific narrative and hermeneutic techniques.[6]

Using the broader *derash* category, which is the epitomizing pivot of therapeutic re-biographing constituting the potential bridge between the rational and irrational interpretations of one's experiences, we may turn now to compare the *PaRDeS* system to modern trends in psychotherapy.

COGNITIVE THERAPY (RATIONAL *PESHAT*)

In the preface to Rian McMullin's (1986: XIII) comprehensive *Handbook of Cognitive Therapy Techniques,* which appears to constitute a representative demonstration of how-to apply cognitive psychology to therapy, we find the following personal account:

Cognitive restructuring therapy (CRT) is one of the newest approaches to counseling being used by psychologists, psychiatric social workers, psychiatrists and other

> mental health professionals today. . . . Periodically, I would meet with other therapists . . . in order to exchange ideas and discuss common problems. It was during these deliberations that we became aware of a particular type of client that we were encountering in increasing numbers. . . . The typical profile for this client was that he or she was from an upper-middle-class background, well educated and a very high achiever. Nevertheless, the client suffered from what we then referred to as "free-floating anxiety." . . . They would become visibly agitated, perspire excessively and become inarticulate and nervous to the extreme, as though their very lives had suddenly been put in jeopardy by some unseen threat.

In defining the essential practical steps that follow his approach, McMullin (p. V) stresses that the process by which "the therapist helps clients to change their irrational beliefs . . . from those that are unrealistic and harmful to those that are more rational and useful . . . is the main emphasis of this particular handbook."

What comes through very clearly from this preface is that even presumed rational, upper-middle-class, well-educated high achievers do not succeed to shake their irrational fear of death, reflected in their "free-floating anxiety" (as though their very lives had been jeapordized). Also obvious is that the cognitive therapist is committed to eliminate irrational beliefs (possibly by accepting the Protestant taboo that equates irrational folly with death and damnation), although paradoxically, according to our immunization formula, irrational-ecstatic rapture might be a very useful device against the fears of death.

Thus far we might conclude that cognitive therapy teaches only the language of rationality as taught by Aristotle's "book of logos," according to which truth might be established only by "what is verifiably real" (McMullin, 1986: 157). As such, it complies in essence with the criteria of logical *peshat*, with one important difference: that it neither accepts the language of unconscious irrationality even as an underground category dictating conscious activities nor conceives the unconscious as a language that creates life by overcoming the fear of death. Indeed, states McMullin, "the process is not based, in our view, on getting in touch with hidden elements inside one's subconscious" (p. 149). Even more succinct is Aaron Beck (1979: 316) when he compares psychoanalysis with cognitive therapy:

> In contrast to psychoanalysis, cognitive therapy deals with what is immediately derivable from conscious experiences. The cognitive therapist does not look for hidden meanings in the patient's thoughts, whereas the psychoanalyst deals with them as symbolic transformations of unconscious fantasies.

What consequently follows is that as a predominant language of rationality, cognitive therapy might indeed be helpful only as a counseling technique suitable for selective-elective upper-middle-class, well-educated achievers who have not encountered serious stressful predicaments.

Accordingly, if fear of death persists in spite of the rational *peshat* interpretation, cognitive therapy is unsuitable in this case. However, the rational language of *peshat*, learned only as one possibility in the multichoice *PaRDeS*, functions so that if one's reality is "irrationally" too stressful, he or she might choose the book of mystic *sod* in order to re-biograph his or her lifestory according to its proposed paradigm.

To understand how midrashic re-biographing might help modern people to bridge between the irrational and rational hermeneutic thought systems, let us consider briefly the differences between *sod* as a part of the multilinguistic structure of *PaRDeS* and Eastern mysticism as a singular predominant thought system.

MYSTIC THERAPY (IRRATIONAL *SOD*)

By defining mysticism as an experience in which "the larger share of the work is done subconsciously," as Underhill (1974: 63) contended, we are speaking in fact of an irrational language of intuition (p. 82) that one learns according to specific books offered in various cultures. Accordingly, the object of the "mystic's adventure" would constitute in therapeutic terms "the apprehension of a direct communion with that transcendental reality" discussed by Underhill (p. 68).

Although some Western Christian traditions have used mystic models to preach and teach salvation, the practice of mysticism in the broadest psychotherapeutic sense is usually associated with various Eastern methods. Whether defined as a healing ceremony in which the healer acts as a mediator between the patient, his group, and the supernatural world, in Jerome Frank's (1961: 62) words, or whether called enlightenment, as D. T. Suzuki (1964) described the Zen Buddhist experience of *satori*, Eastern mystic experiences refer by and large to a process of human efforts to penetrate the frightening realm of the transcendental-supernatural unknown.

I find, therefore, Alan Watts's (1975: 47) all-encompassing concept of liberation still most appropriate to refer to most Eastern mystic practices. For in his classic *Psychotherapy East and West* he states, "It is almost invariably assumed that *nirvana* or *moksha* means release from the physical organism and the physical universe, an accomplishment involving powers of mind over matter that would give their possessor the omnipotence of a god." The nature of such "acquired" occult powers is not as important to the discussion here as is the assumption that omnipotent, godly powers might be acquired via the process of entering (uniting with) God's domain via the process that I have termed "temporary death" (liberating the soul from its physical organism)—which fits our proposed immunization paradigm.

But here again only by reading carefully Jung's forward to Suzuki's

(1964) *Introduction to Zen Buddhism* might one realize how Eastern mystic therapy is proposed, not as a complementary method to other approaches to therapy, but as an all-engulfing philosophy of life that Western people are not really capable of understanding. Unlike Rudolf Otto (1976: 14), who believed that "in mysticism there are indeed strong primal impulses . . . which . . . are completely unaffected by differences of climate, of geographical position or of race," already on the first page of his extensive introduction Jung (see Suzuki, 1964: 9-10) expresses a basic ambivalence about the suitability of Eastern ineffable mysticism for Westerners: "It should not be too difficult for the Western mind to grasp what a mystic understands by enlightenment . . . *Satori,* however, depicts an art of enlightenment which is practically impossible for the European to appreciate."

Indeed, such statements positing that "a direct transmission of Zen to Western conditions is neither commendable nor even possible" (Suzuki, 1964: 26) appear repeatedly in Jung's introduction. However, since Zen demands a total emptying of the ego, it seems that this quietistic language abolishing I-ness is diametrically opposed to the language of rationality. Thus states Jung (ibid.: 27): "If the psychotherapist finds time from his helpful activities for a little reflection . . . it may dawn upon him . . . how contrary to life are all rationalistic reductions." This is not to suggest that in the East the rational language needed for everyday terrestrial living is not taught at all; what is suggested here is that as a psychotherapeutic system of salvation, the Eastern Zenlike book of life focuses primarily on teaching the irrational-mystic egoless language of *satori.* However, the Jewish mystic language of cabalic *sod* is offered as but one alternative in the *PaRDeS* system.

Since we are interested here in the psychotherapeutic possibility of choice between the rational-cognitive and the irrational-mystic interpretations of one's failing biography, let us turn now to discuss briefly the narrative language of *derash* (and *remez*), which I claim functions as a dia-logic bridge between rationality and irrationality.

NARRATIVE RE-BIOGRAPHING (IMAGINATIVE *DERASH*)

Consider the following reminiscence of a woman's family life cited by Daniel Goleman (1985: 16):

> I am very close to my family. They were always very demonstrative and loving. When I disagreed with my mother she threw whatever was nearest at hand at me. Once it happened to be a knife and I needed ten stitches in my leg. A few years later my father tried to choke me when I began dating a boy he didn't like. They really are very concerned about me.

Although abhorred by this recollection, I believe that if a cynical interpretation of the above statement is ruled out, then sophisticated readers must accept this woman's assertion as an honest declaration possibly nourished by a cultural metacode that associates physical expressions (including punishments) with caring even if they believe that it constitutes a defensive, self-deceptive act of rationalization. Now, imagine that in regard to a similar chain of events a woman recalls that her folks would always say, "Honey, do whatever is best for you!" even when she was desperately expecting their disapproval because in her view she was going wild or dating the wrong boy. Suppose that this woman, who has apparently internalized a cultural metacode that differs from that of the first woman, would eventually interpret her parent's attitude toward her as neglect and disconcern. Which of the two opposing interpretations should be stamped as true and which as false?

Obviously, there is no unequivocal way to establish an Aristotelian true-false dichotomy if one accepts the idea of cultural metacodes. But beyond the impact of cultural metacodes on interpreting personal experiences, the contradictory accounts described above demonstrate that people have a basic need to tell their lifestory in a coherent manner or as a complete plot (see Sarbin, 1989). A noncoherent autobiographic account in schizophrenic terms is hence phenomenologically as true as a "falsified" (self-deceptive) self-narrated lifestory because both accounts were influenced by a certain belief that functioned as a metacode. The former might be influenced by a belief in the very existence of schizophrenia, and the second by a belief that the very self narrated act of retelling of one's miseries as a coherent story eliminates or destroys the foundations of the previous miserable self-perception.

Thus, it is phenomenology that applied the method of collective *history* to the biographic method of one's telling *his story*. Consequently, phenomenology uncovered an interesting paradox; in individual psychology the concept of truth is by definition false if it disregards personal experiences. Indeed, re-biographing as a therapeutic perspective is indebted to the phenomenonological methodology, which, by using such case studies as cited above, was able to prove the necessity to accept the truth inherent in people's subjective experiential accounts because it is impossible to apply a true-false dichotomy to autobiographic interpretations.

In *Re-biographing and Deviance* (1987) I have demonstrated at length how the midrashic thought system provides a cultural metacode for re-biographing people's failing pasts. It is therefore unnecessary here to over-burden the reader with tedious midrashic examples. However, if we accept that people need cultural metacodes for retelling their distressing lifestories, in a coherent (though not necessarily pleasant or favorable) way, then we need a variety of mystical, mythological, narratological, and logical texts or books that supply these metacodes. I may thus agree with R. D. Laing's (1967: 31) lamentation of contemporary conceptions of imagination when he stated that "fantasy as encountered in many people today is split off from what the person regards as his mature, sane, rational adult experience." I may also go along with his assertion that "fantasy is . . . sometimes the essential part of the meaning or sense . . . implicit in action" (ibid.). My only argument with Laing is that imagination and fantasy as a serious basis for personal re-biographing will be functional for the "mature, sane, rational adult" who experiences "irrational" fears to the extent that fantasy will be guided by specific culturally approved texts.

The *derash-remez* as a dia-logic pivot in the "*PaRDeS*" multihermeneutic system uses, as noted earlier, textual parables, anecdotes, and letter-rearrangement exercises, which are not detached from one's rational reality, but which allow the use of the imagination to expand and reorganize it in order to pattern one's re-biographed lifestory in order to make it bearable. True, students of Milton Erickson (see especially Rosen, 1982, and Gordon, 1978,[7] and even McMullin, 1986[8]) have used stories, fables, and fairy tales in guiding the process of reframing. However, since these reframers[9] usually use the "existential bible" as a guide for a situational here-and-now reinterpretation, they do not have a "book" that provides a metacode for learning the irrational language of mystic folly as an immunization device for overcoming the fear of death. The cabalistic book of mystic *sod* as part of the *PaRDeS* metacode provides the choice of a normative ecstatic technique like *devekut* (temporary death) practiced in communion[10] or *unio mystica* that may function as an immunizing process. Accordingly, if a person comes to a *pardesian* therapist after experiencing an atrocious calamity and/or after a "psychotic experience" (e.g., hearing voices), this *pardesian* therapist might first attempt to use the "cognitive" *peshat* approach. Only after realizing that the person's struggle with the transcendental unknown is not yet resolved might the therapist resort to the *sod* interpretation. Put in Derrida's (1978) terms of *differance,* in *pardesian* therapy meaning is always *deferred* so that a *different*, personally more suitable interpretation might be inserted. Emphasis on differential interpretation allows less dependency on differential personality theories.

The re-biographic dialogue between the rational and irrational as mutual energizers would thus largely concur with Bruno Bettleheim's psychotherapeutic use of fairy tales.[11] Bettleheim's (1977: 7) model for teaching fables, myths, and fairy tales may be understood as a method for teaching the language of the unconscious in order to control irrational fears: "When unconscious material *is* to some degree permitted to come to awareness and worked through in imagination, its potential for causing harm—to ourselves or others—is much reduced; some of its forces can then be made to serve positive purposes."

To grasp the plight of the Western person, who seems to be haunted forever by his irrational fears of the unpredictable transcendental world because he or she did not learn the language of mysticism in order to control the unknown, one needs only to follow the periodic popularity of Zen, Hare Krishna, Cabala, and the cultish psychedelic practices in Western countries.[12] It is therefore worthwhile to refer to some examples demonstrating how the mastering of the *pardesian* dialogue between the irrational and rational interpretation of texts has been used since early times to alleviate personal distress.

PARDESIAN RE-BIOGRAPHING IN ACTION

The Historical Case of Rabbi Karo

Earlier, in discussing how Rabbi Joseph Karo, the sixteenth-century author of the monumental Jewish legal code books, interacted with a mystic angel (see Karo, 1960), I maintained (see Chapter 1) that Karo's mystical-irrational experiences most probably energized his intellectual-rational activities.[13] By using Karo's classical case, it is thus possible to demonstrate how familiarity with a *pardesian* multithought system may function as an energizing mechanism between the mystic and the intellectual, whereas in today's West, speaking the language of mystics, that is, conversing with angels, would most probably result in one's being diagnosed and incarcerated as a schizophrenic.

Following the midrashic paradigm of re-biographing (see Rotenberg, 1987), it is possible to show now not only how the mastering of the *pardesian* languages might be instrumental as an energizing mechanism but how it might be used therapeutically to alleviate concrete personal predicaments via re-biographing. For example, by using the perspective of "re-biographing," Moshe Idel (1989a) was able to demonstrate how one of Rabbi Karo's *pardesian* biblical exegetic exercises seems to be associated with alleviating personal suffering. Very briefly, in his mystic-cabalic commentary on the Torah, Karo (p. 48) accounts that one Saturday the mystic figure (angel) to whom Karo referred as the *maggid* (the preacher) informed him that he will "tell him the secret of his own incarnation and the secret of his wives." Implying that the sudden death of Karo's two sons and their mothers is associated with a certain punishment for which Karo repented, the *maggid* stressed that he will derive great pleasure from the sons that his third wife will bear (p. 30).

The point is that a week later Karo developed a complicated cabalistic interpretation concerning the geneology of David's Messianic Kingdom on the basis of the story of Judah and Tamar (Genesis: 38). As is well known, Judah's oldest son, Er, was killed by God, although allegedly he did not sin, whereas his second son, Onan, was killed by God because he masturbated.

Karo (p. 36) goes on to point out that the fact that Er was killed although he did not sin is due to the mystic reality, that "it is known that a first born is incomplete," so that he disqualifies for a task of being the original conceiver "out of whom the kingdom of the house of David will disseminate." Karo thus stresses that it was "Peretz, who was the third"[14] and who was the forefather of David, and who "is preferable for being the one out of whom the kingdom of David will be constructed" (ibid.).

Now, for the psychologically oriented reader it would be too intricate to recapitulate Karo's cabalistic explication of how the intratransplantation of feminine and masculine holy sparks made his third wife's pregnancy possible,[15] and it is not necessary to reiterate here Karo's cabalistic—*sefirotic*[16] calculations about the third son's messianic destiny; but one point seems highly revealing from our re-biographic perspective: Idel indicates that since in the Lurianic cabala and in the book of Zohar, Er and Onan are described as evil-natured, Karo's tendency to play down the evilness of Judah's two older sons suggests a strong re-biographic trend in Karo's commentary.

It is not only that Karo claimed overtly that his third wife's soul constitutes an incarnation of Ruth, from whom King David descended that makes it relevant here; it is also the fact that the *maggid*'s point about the messianic quality of the third son comprises "high secrets that cannot be found in any book" (p. 36) that reinforces the therapeutic element in Karo's re-biographing.

We have, then, a classic case of how it is possible to alleviate severe personal distress (here, the sudden death of two sons and their mothers) by using *pardesian* therapy, which in this case allowed Karo to use the *derashic* technique of re-biographing in order to choose an irrational-mystic interpretation for his otherwise unrationalizable reality, because "he had the cabalistic book about it."[17] Put differently, by mastering the prestructured mystic language of *sod*, Karo could switch from his everyday, legalistic, language of *peshat* in order to re-biograph his personal tragedy into a therapeutic messianic ascent-via-descent lifestory. In this way, for those who have internalized the dia-logic metacode of *PaRDeS*, re-biographing may work as a preventative method against psychosis.

One could go on to demonstrate how a Hasidic leading figure like Rabbi Nachman of Bratzlav used the *pardesian* therapy to re-biograph his periodic depressions via the mystic notion of cabalistic *tikun* (correction of souls) (see Green, 1979). One could also show how the Hasidim converted cabalic mysticism into a narrative story-telling method, as well as present some contemporary case studies in which cabalistic ideas were used as therapeutic interpretations of severely disturbing experiences. But since such neotherapies usually advocate cabalic applications, not as one out of three or four chooseable possibilities in the *pardesian* hermeneutic system, but as a singular possibility that is to replace all other options, one would wonder how this dialectic kind of cabalism differs from other Eastern mystic practices that seem ineffable for Westerners.

Since I claimed that the application of *PaRDeS* to therapy must begin with learning, I would like to conclude this presentation by describing briefly, not a therapeutic success story (even partial failures are rarely reported in the clinical literature), but how the language of mysticism could be understood and taught as a method for preventing and/or mitigating psychopathology.

The "Berlitz" School for *Pardesian* Mysticism

Throughout my presentation I have stressed time and again, that if the unconscious is to be understood as a language dictating deviant conduct, a comprehensive psychotherapeutic theory must comply with the following criteria:

1. It has to address itself not only to "neurotic achievers," who speak the language of rationality, but also to "irrational psychotics."
2. It has to offer a preventative system by teaching people to master the language of the irrational unconscious.

To back my argument I have used the Jewish *pardesian* language as a case study in order to show how people can be socialized to read reality and re-biograph their lifestory in either irrational-mystical or rational-intellectual terms. I have thus stressed that this preventative therapeutic-socializing system of "having a book and a language about it" is possible because the ordinary Jew who listens weekly to *derushot* (sermons about the Torah) in his respective synagogue is trained to choose either a cabalistic-*sod* or an intellectual-*peshat* interpretation of the biblical text because he is familiar with both languages. I have maintained, further, that by using the imaginative language of *derash* people might re-biograph their lifestories between *peshat* and *sod*.

Since, obviously, the hypothesized relationship between the *pardesian* socialization model and the prevention or the combating of psychopathology must await more empirical and clinical verification, a preliminary question for the modern person is whether a *pardesian* multithought system might be acquired by adults in whom the *pardesian* hermeneutic system was not inculcated during their childhood.

I would like to suggest now that seminars and institutes conducted by contemporary popular movements for repenters (*baaley teshuva*) provide good case laboratories for assessing this possibility. Thus, unlike the switching from a rational to an irrational orientation to life described under the title *Snapping* (see Conway and Siegelman, 1978), in the seminar described by Michal Fachler (1988) the *PaRDeS* system was used to explain Judaism in the logical language of *peshat* and in the mystic language of *sod*.

A good example is how, side by side with attempts to provide logical and even "scientific" proofs concerning the truth inherent in the Torah by using techniques that might be classified as *derash* or *remez*, the cabalistic method for understanding the mystic meaning of letter combination was introduced. Thus, first the mystic meaning of the alphabetic letters were explained, and subsequently the composition of special words was analyzed so that a practical methodological guide for deriving personal meaning by dissecting Hebrew words was provided. For example, if the Hebrew word *gilgul* (rolling or incarnation) contains parts of the words *galut* (diaspora, rejection) and *geula* (redemption and attraction), that means that cabalism provides a cyclistic ascent-via-descent model for understanding life. I have used the case of the "*pardesian* Berlitz School" mainly in order to demonstrate how secular adults seem capable of absorbing a new mystic metacode to the extent that it is derived from "a book about it."

This minor linguistic exercise, if adopted for re-biographing in the case of personal suffering, is obviously more effective the more one internalizes the religious belief system that goes with it.[18] Thus, Dr. Philip Berg (1986) demonstrated, for example, how by means of cabalistic calculations the belief in incarnation helped a family to believe that their dead son's soul (or spirit) transmigrated into a newborn nephew: "The spirit of the deceased Aryeh and of baby Aryeh strengthened the moral consciousness of the family, changed their lives and brought family members closer to each other" (p. 62). One may assume, however, that in relation to irrational fears and queries regarding the transcendental world of the unknown, so-called secular people will usually seek rational (*peshat*) answers and so-called religious people will accept mystic (*sod*) interpretations provided they "have a suitable book" and a language to apprehend and master their own experiences accordingly.

Nonetheless, in our dia-logo treatment project we noticed to our surprise that among our religious geriatric cases some were at first quite reluctant to re-biograph their past miseries according to circular mystic-cabalistic terms I had presumed to be most suitable for old age (Rotenberg, 1987).[19] Mr. J., for example, who was in his mid-seventies, suffered from an obsessive-compulsive need to wash his hands, which he eventually admitted was related to his experiences during the Holocaust, which caused his unshakeable guilt feelings. Mr. J., who is now a religious person who allegedly succeeded in raising a "nice" family, seemed first to be guided by an original-sin metacode when he spoke about his impenitent sins such as eating nonkosher food even when he had a chance to eat kosher food. This observation, which first puzzled us, was soon disentangled when we learned that during his youth Mr. J. was not immersed in learning Jewish texts as were observant Jews. Thus, it was only after months of intensive work with Mr. J. during which we indeed blamed him for using a non Jewish self-blaming belief system (metacode) while we simultaneously persistently urged him to think about the cabalic paradigm of *tikun* (correction), with which he was generally familiar, that he began the process of re-biographing.

I conclude this chapter with this brief account of Mr. J., who finally began literally to write his re-biographed lifestory by using mystic ascent-via-descent interpretations, to demonstrate that *pardesian* re-biographing is not necessarily a domain of those who were all along so-called religious Jews but that it may be learned if "there is a book about it."

The possibility of mastering one's own language of the irrational unconscious seems, hence, to depend on the availability of cultural paradigms providing mystic orientations to life, paradigms all would be free to adopt when their "imperfect world" becomes inexplicable to them. The preventative possibility inherent in "having a mystic book and a language" could thus help Westerners mitigate their fear of death instead of accepting it as a predestined death wish emanating from their unshakeable state of damnation.

In the next chapter I intend to demonstrate how Hasidic-cabalistic techniques of mystic *sod* may be understood as an inner immunization mechanism that balances between the bipolar states of descent and ascent.

NOTES

1. The four letters *P, R, D,* and *S* that comprise the Hebrew word *pardes*, meaning literally "orchard," symbolize also immersion in dangerous theosophic speculations. According to Scholem (1977: 62) these four levels of Torah interpretation are tantamount to several Christian conceptions popular in the Middle Ages. Moreover, in his study of Christian biblical exegesis, T. Todorov (1982) also discussed four hermeneutic levels that might be traceable to the Jewish *PaRDeS* doctrine. Nevertheless, I have already indicated elsewhere (Rotenberg, 1987) that Todorov persistently indicated that "the Christian tradition of biblical exegesis . . . consists in restricting the proliferation of meaning, in seeking one meaning that is preferable to the others" (Todorov, 1982: 126). Accordingly, I have stressed (ibid.) that if indeed biblical hermeneutics exert paradigmatic influences on therapeutic possibilities, then unlike the *PaRDeS* system the Christian doctrines might contain a fundamentalistic trend that might be uncovered in certain therapeutic dicta.

2. Here I must concede that my (1987: 142) earlier understanding of Rabbi Saadia Gaon's (the *Rasag*'s) authoritative four-points position stipulating when an interpretation of a biblical verse may deviate from *peshat* was somewhat simplistic. During my 1989 membership in the Jerusalem Institute for Advanced Studies, I learned, for example, from Moshe Greenberg that *Rasag*'s interpretation rules may be so understood that if it is impossible to accept a literal *peshat* interpretation of a verse, then the *derash* acquires its sole, new committing meaning. However, in the same institute I also learned from Isadore Twersky that even the authoritative Maimonides (1960: 51) asserts that when in regard to an issue "two opinions are possible," one should not "accept his rabbi's proposition (*sevara*) by rejecting his

own proposition.'' In Twersky's view this statement reflects that Maimonides favored the coexistence of multiple opinions (if they could be backed by equally sound documented arguments) even if the disputers involve a teacher and his students.

3. Here is the place to stress that although Maimonides's (*Yesodey Hatora,* Chap. 4:13) use of the term *PaRDeS* comprises also the secretive act of genesis and the complicated act of *Merkavah* (the work of the chariot), which usually refers to a body of Jewish mystic literature, his interpretations of *PaRDeS* are by and large philosophical in nature.

4. Rabbi Meklenburg in *Haketav Vehakabala* (1924: Det. 9: 9) interprets the fact that the plural word *stones* was used in the scriptures to refer to the tablets Moses received at Mt. Sinai in order to stress the pluralistic hierarchy inherent in *PaRDeS.* He states that ''because there are four kinds of stones which alternate among themselves in strength and hardness . . . so the four facet principles which the *PaRDeS* doctrine contains alternate (are distinguishable) from each other in difficulty, contents and depth of inner intention.'' Thus, by using the plural word *stones* (instead of one stone) to imply that there are stones that are weak and hence dissolve easily whereas strong stones require great strength to penetrate their inner parts, the author equates *sod* with the diamond because it implies inner strength and beauty ''unknown to the masses and to the bulk of scientists'' (ibid.).

5. According to Margaliyot (1989: 34) the *bat kol* phenomenon may be further demystified by interpreting it as an unclear voice one hears from behind one's back.

6. Although the technique of letter combination (*zerufe otiot*) and the numerical technique of *gematria* are usually classified under the mystic-*sod* category, the practice of *notriquon* (the breaking of words) is usually listed under *remez* but used largely by cabalists (see Idel, 1988b). Considering *remez* as an instrumental *derashic* technique that helps people to bridge between their needs to interpret their life in logical-rational and mystic-irrational terms, it is of interest to mention here one of Freud's (1938: 152-53) uses of a mystic-numerical *notriquon* technique for auto-re-biographing. Very briefly, Freud recounts that in a letter to a friend he stated that after getting tired of proofreading *The Interpretation of Dreams*, he ''did not intend to make any further changes in it, 'even if it entailed 2,467 mistakes.''' Pondering subsequently about the unconscious (mystic) meaning of the number 2,467, Freud offered the following interpretation. Freud recalled that when just prior to writing this letter he told his wife he read in the paper that a certain inspector general with whom he was acquainted retired, she remarked, ''Then you too should be retired.'' Freud then recounted that when he first met this inspector Freud had just celebrated his twenty-fourth birthday. This, he explained, accounted for the 24 in the total number 2,467. Freud then added the number 43 (which was his age when he wrote the letter) to 24 and got the number 67, which comprised the second part of the number 2,467. Freud then concluded ''that not even the unintentionally thrown-out number 2,467 lacks its determination for the unconscious.'' Freud was thus an underground mysticist.

7. Unfortunately in some American how-to books that offer a commercial style of writing, the books' ideas are manifested not in the level of analysis but only in their attractive titles. Although the book under consideration carries the ambitious title *Therapeutic Metaphors,* the author does not take the trouble to differentiate between analogy, anecdote, metaphor, and story.

8. Although I agree with McMullin (1986: 139) that the selected "story must . . . bridge the Client's old, damaging belief and a new, perfected belief," I find McMullin's clever, how-to, commercial book another example of sloppy conceptual inconsistency. For instance, in discussing the use of stories and fables, he admits that the selection process might be retracted as follows: "Stories we heard . . . and the moral conveyed by them, whether true or false . . . found their way into our value system" (ibid.). Yet elsewhere (p. 115) he insists that "the philosophical underpinnings of cognitive restructuring are analytic philosophy . . . and their parent logical positivism. It is not phenomenology. . . . In the world of this philosophy truth and falseness can be ascertained." Although McMullin attempts to differentiate between truth with a small and a big *t*, I think that throughout the whole book he does not realize that by allowing the client to select out of many statements one that appears true for him, he subscribes to a strict dia-logical-phenomenological definition of subjective truth. It is certainly impossible that all optional statements (which are offered by the therapist as a consistent technique) may entail an Aristotelian truth.

9. The charismatic power of psychotherapeutic salesmanship in the United States never ceases to arouse my admiration. The concept of reframing became in a short time a most popular psychotherapeutic term in Western countries, and the double-bound, compartmentalized connotation of the term seems to cause no problems of cognitive dissonance or misconceptions. After all, since the term *framing* stands for a negative act of incriminative trapping, the expression *reframing* could be conceived as an attempt to "frame" someone for a second time. I am thus inclined to believe that an effective marketing campaign of a new messianic psychotherapy could succeed in promoting even "rechauvinism" as a desirable healing process.

10. The dispute between those who define the Hasidic-cabalistic state of *devekut* as communion or as *unio mystica* seems unsettled, but I think that the present formulation of ecstasy as an immunizing device against the fear of death might throw new light on this debatable issue. Ecstatic *devekut* might reflect a desire (for *unio mystica*) that in actuality paves the way for communion. Psychologically, this would mean that the desire of the soul to leave the body (the temporary death experience) immunizes the person against the fear of death, which in turn makes joyful communion possible.

11. I would like to stress that Bettleheim's (1977: 121) insistence that Freudian energy must be understood as a process in which "the id can provide the ego with the energy necessary to mold unconscious tendencies and use them constructively" concurs with the present dia-logical perspective. Thus, unlike Freudian dialectic conceptions that view the ego as a replacement for the id, in the *pardesian* dialogue irrational *sod* and rational *peshat* may not only coexist but energize each other.

12. It is with this yearning for the vital mystic reading of life in mind that one should perceive the recent popularity of Scholem's and mainly Moshe Idel's expositions of Jewish cabalistic texts. Thus, it seems that after extended tantalizing oscillations between uncontrollable psychedelic experimentations and the Eastern ineffable experiences, Westerners finally discovered that there is a book "about it" (cabalistic mysticism) that is more cogent to Westerners because it maintains a coexisting dialogue with their rational language instead of replacing it.

13. Underhill (1977: 66) would most probably interpret Karo's intellectual writings not in the present dia-logic terms, but as the automatic-writing phenomenon, the

kind she attributed to St. Theresa, "who declared that in writing her books she was powerless to set down anything but that which the Master put into her mind."

14. It is unclear why Karo labels Peretz as the third son of Judah, although according to the Scripture (Genesis: 38:5) Shela was the third and Peretz the fourth.

15. Karo's conceptualization of the feminine-masculine intratransplantation of sparks is similar to Jung's model of the anima-animus components, which according to him may be found in males and females alike.

16. Very briefly, *sefirot* are the ten basic cabalistic elements by which the functioning of the world is explained.

17. Indeed, it was because I knew "we have a cabalistic book about it" that I could understand how our suffering could be alleviated after my youngest son, Boaz, was killed in action in the Israeli army during spring 1988.

18. An excellent example of how the internalization of a mystic-*sod* language by a repentant scientist does not eliminate the rational-*peshat* mode of thinking is Professor Baranover's (1984) auto-re-biographed account published about 12 years after his emigration from the Soviet Union to Israel. Baranover, a prominent Soviet scientist who repented and became a devout Chabad Hasid, reports in his autobiography how every day he shifts orientations between his mystic (irrational) and his strictly scientific (rational) thought systems. Thus in the morning he functions as head of an important laboratory in one of the Israeli universities and in the evening he lectures about the Hasidic transcendental world of miracles, esctasy, and holiness.

19. Although elsewhere (Rotenberg, 1987) I advocated cabalistic studies for the elderly because its study was essentially forbidden for those under the age of 40, the reader is reminded that cabalistic texts by Nachmanides and others are traditionally taught and studied without any age limitations.

5

Depressed Mania and Spiritual Ecstasy

Would the use of a specific metaphor or metacode for categorizing and describing certain behavior patterns as deviant, erratic, or ecstatic determine also the kind of treatment to be prescribed for it? Would the epidemic state of mental health change in a Western state if it decides, for instance, to relabel "manic-depressive illness" as desirable creative ecstasy? Although conservative psychopathologists would most probably dismiss the second question by claiming that name tags do not change the incidence and prevalence of a mental phenomenon, they would have to agree that if a behavioral problem is defined in religious terms, they would not try to cure it with injections against infectious germs. Moreover, these "medical psychopathologists" would have to agree also that if the spread of a certain organic or social "illness" is caused by a deficiency of specific antibodies, then its preventative remedy must consist of early immunization or specific nourishment that counteracts this anticipated deficiency. In this chapter I will thus strive to demonstrate that after discarding the medical metaphor to define and treat so-called mania, the time is ripe to inculcate manic ectasy as a preventative remedy against schizophrenia.

Now, before my medically brainwashed reader classifies my enigmatic statement as "psychotic" (irrationally non-Western), let me explain my paradoxical intention. Following the assumption that ecstatic mysticism, which I claim functions as an immunizing device against man's fears of the irrational world of the transcendental unknown, was indeed banned in the West since the sixteenth century (see Foucault, 1967), thus causing the "deficiency," I propose here that as a bipolar disorder depressive mania may be understood as a desirable, dynamic model for balancing between people's depressing rational reality and their manic irrational ideality. In other words, I shall maintain that if the schizophrenic as representing the creative man who speaks the language of unreason was indeed excommunicated by the Western Protestant world of reason, then controlled socialization for switching between the manic and the depressive (or supressive) languages might "shrink" the deficiency in people's ecstatic antibodies against their irrational fears.

To establish the thesis that by learning the balanced language of manic-depressive switching between rationality and irrationality people may control their fears from the supernatural, let us first consider the impact of metaphorical changes on treatment strategies.

METAPHORS OF DEVIANCE AS METACODES FOR TREATMENT

In my study (Rotenberg, 1978) about Protestant Calvinism's impact on deviance and its treatability, I have shown how since ancient times the changing metaphors used to define deviance have in various ways dictated the means used for handling it. If, thus, in ancient times a favorable religious metaphor was used to define deviance so that deviant people were described as those possessed by a divine spirit, the concomitant social attitude toward them was that of reverence; and therefore no treatment was prescribed because they were considered "too sacred and good or too powerful for anyone to venture to reduce them to the unblessed state of normalcy" (Zilboorg, 1941: 23).[1] If in the early Middle Ages a subtle change was inserted into the "possession" model, so that instead of being possessed by the divine spirit, the deviant was said to be possessed by a demon, this "demonological" metaphor invented exorcism as a suitable treatment device. If in the late Middle Ages the "devilish" metaphor was introduced so that the deviant was viewed as the devil's victim, incarceration (excommunication) was its matching remedy. Similarly, if during the Renaissance the "Satanic" metaphor (which was now intertwined with free will[2]) was used to blame people for making a pact with the devil or for personifying Satan, the concurrent treatment was burning with or without trial by the notorious sadists of the inquisition.

In my search and effort to unravel and expound the cruel attitude toward the deviant which the "enlightened" post-Renaissance witnessed in Europe, I have introduced Calvin's "damnation" metaphor, according to which deviants were the born wickeds who deserve hell's treatment. I have stressed, further, that whereas the earlier, subtle metaphoric changes reflected the gradual degradation of deviants, the possession models still connoted the intrusion of an external entity (be it a spirit or a demon) that could in theory leave (on its own or via exorcism) the deviant, so that deviance was not yet viewed as being inherent in the person possessed by it. I have thus argued that if Protestant damnation is the first metaphor that stands for an innate, unchangeable state, then the presumed impact of Protestantism on modern society (see Weber, 1970) might imply that the contemporary medical metaphor of deviance connotes an incurable disposition, as many antipsychiatric or antilabeling theorists posit (e.g., Becker, 1963, and Laing, 1967).[3]

Accordingly, the question is now whether Ervin Goffman's (1956) and Thomas Szasz's (1961) call for discarding the medical metaphor of deviance, which was first so vehemently rejected, did after all open the arena for new, competing metaphors and metacodes for defining and treating deviance. It is with this metaphoric scheme in mind that I would like to examine now the status of the so-called manic-depressive phenomenon with its vicissitudes.

FROM EPIDEMIC TO EPISODIC MANIA

From the early 1950s through the 1970s typical writers on manic depression bluntly entitled their books under the general heading of psychosis. Thus, for example, Leopold Bellak (1952) entitled his book *Manic-Depressive Psychosis.* Elton McNeil (1970) who entitled his book *The Psychoses*, which according to him refers by definition to "a massive disintegration of the human personality in which the victim is no longer capable of dealing effectively with himself or his surroundings" (p. 12), includes manic depression as one of its major subcategories.

However, the American Psychiatric Association's *Diagnostic and Statistical Manual* (DSM), which is *the* definitory bible for the medically oriented mental health professions, came out in its 1968 (DSM-II) edition with their first evasive, stuttering definition in regard to this disorder. While according to the DSM-II "some psychotic phenomena may occur in manic-depressives, it allows only that these be secondary to the dominant mood disorder" (see Shopsin, 1979: 78). It seemed, hence, that the main embarrassing problem of diagnosis was associated with the fact that more and more it was found that those labeled manic-depressive simply failed to display an unequivocal detachment from reality, which is allegedly the major component constituting and justifying the classification of psychosis. Indeed, the authoritative Silvano Arieti (1974) stated in his study of schizophrenia that "severe thought disorders, like illogical remarks, incongruous statements, bizarre delusions or ideas of reference, are rare in manic-depressive patients" (ibid.: 79). Likewise, after reviewing six major textbooks Baron Shopsin (ibid.: 78) stated that "all [textbooks] implied that 'schizophrenic' symptoms—psychotic symptoms . . . were absent or rare in manic-depressive illness." According to Shopsin (ibid.), who in 1979 edited a book under the more neutral title *Manic Illness,* one may conclude that the term "schizoaffectiveness" seemed to function as a useful face-saver for the medically committed diagnosticians because now if some delusions or hallucinations occur, "in addition to affective symptoms, so-called 'schizoaffectives' are classed by DSM-II as having a subtype schizophrenia."

Nonetheless, here we come to our major point: The DSM-III published first in 1980, which was to state unequivocally (according to preliminary reports) that "a diagnosis of manic-depressive disorder would not be allowed when certain schizophrenic symptoms are present" (ibid.: 79), excluded this behavioral disorder altogether from the schizophrenic-psychotic category. The new category "affective disorders," which now includes all major affective disorders, is from now on defined as a "bipolar disorder," which even in the case of major depression "is distinguished by whether or not there has ever been a manic episode" (see DSM-III, 1980: 205). In cases of affective disorder there is no more talk about psychotic *epidemics* but about bipolar *episodes* of mood swings that may be controlled by lithium, much the same as a thyroid irregularity might be controlled by other medications. Interestingly, although for some peculiar (evasive?) reasons the DSM-III failed to provide diagnostic criteria for the subtype schizoaffectiveness, it states openly that this diagnosis "can be made whenever the clinician is unable to make a differential diagnosis between a major depressive episode and schizophrenia" (p. 213). Thus the divorce between psychosis and the bipolar episodes seems final because of or in spite of the availability of the schizoaffective clinical-wastebasket category.[4]

Is this subtle metaphoric change only semantic, or does it signify the beginning of a new *era* imbued with a new *aura* that brings under its wings the announcement of a new message of openness, which will help people to better *fight* their emotional predicaments and their *plight*? Put differently, does this quiet retreat from the medical metaphor reflect a silent admission that the manic-depressive behavior pattern is essentially not an illness but a cultural, relativistic mental mechanism that might be sometimes disordered and often very much in order? The question of whether manic-depressives are made to feel *at ease* or as being infected by a *disease* depends hence on the socialization metacode used variously in specific cultural groups. The metaphoric change may hence not be considered as a naive euphemism but rather as a new understanding of mysticism.

DEPRESSED MANIA OR MANIC DEPRESSION?

Elsewhere (Rotenberg, 1983: 146) I have stressed that although "the ancient Greeks and Romans observed that extreme states of excitement or elation and extreme depression or melancholy are cut from the same cloth, it was Kraepelin who is usually credited with first using the term 'manic-depressive insanity' in the late 19th century." I have accentuated further, that it was Rado who asserted in the 1920s that "the manic condition succeeds the phase of self-punishment [depressions] with the same regularity with which . . . the bliss of satiety succeeded to hunger" (ibid.). Pursuing the query about succession implicit in Rado's declaration, I have then indicated that it is not the question of whether the struggle between Eros and Thanatos, life and death, or melancholic *mourning* (depression) and exciting "*mornings* (mania) actually operates in an interrelated, cyclic regularity, which should be under scrutiny" (ibid.). Rather, my concern has been focused on two intertwined questions: (1) whether depression and mania are considered to be functionally or dysfunctionally related, and consequently (2) whether mania or depression is conceived as the predominant and/or the desirable state in life. Put in our present terms of cultural metacodes, the problem at stake here is whether the cultural metacode's stress is on manic depression or on depressive mania? Although in both cases depression and mania seem to be functionally related, in the first case the manic depression metacode would be conceived as a natural, temporary "rest" state from the ideal striving toward joyful-ecstatic living. However, the second metacode of depressive mania would typically be used by societies that fail or refuse to provide their people with institutionalized means for expressing their manic needs, in order to stress that mania is merely a temporary "escape" from the real (desirable?) predominant state of depression. Cross-cultural observations would probably reveal that the first category is more common in Eastern countries whereas the second is characteristically Western.

Indeed, in conventional Western psychiatric textbooks we find systematic and repetitive statements interpreting manic elation as a defense and a facade for covering the underlying predominant state of depression. In one psychopathology textbook the manic person is described as "humourous, optimistic and carefree. He describes himself as being on top of the world and full of pep. He radiates exuberance and vitality . . . [but] he vaguely realizes that his gaiety is a *facade,* a kind of desperate whistling in the dark" (Page, 1971: 235; italics added).

In another typical textbook, which relies on one of the most widely cited studies on manic-depressive disorders done by a team referred to as the Washington Group, Melvin Zax and Emory Cowen (1972: 200-201) conclude that "the Washington Group regarded manic behavior as a defense utilized to keep underlying depression from awareness. When it followed depression it was seen as a straightforward escape mechanism. Where mania was followed by depression the mania was simply thought to have failed as a defense." A most dramatic emphasis on the predominance of the depression metacode that prevailed in the 1970s may be found in McNeil's (1970: 114-15) survey of the psychoses: "The rapidly mounting spiral of frenetic activity of the manic reflects an attempt on his part to deny that he senses the massive depression that is about to engulf him. The manic runs away from depression by plunging into activity so all-consuming that it drowns out the 'quiet voice' of depression."

It follows from the above that psychiatry during the 1970s, which was ruled and dictated by the DSM-II, portrayed mania as a facade, defense, or escape from the culturally prescribed norm of flat, controlled, and inhibited or rather depressed mental state. Thus, depression functioned as a self-contradictory, double-bind metacode that on the one hand connoted a psychotic state of mental illness while on the other hand it reflected the predominance of the Western controlled and antiecstatic (manic) socialization ideal.

Thus, manic depression encompassed a dangerous double-bind metacode[5] that propagated the norm of depressed-inhibited behavior as a socialization ideal for which one may eventually be stigmatized as being mentally ill if one internalized it too seriously. This "you are damned if you do and you are damned if you don't" metacode is obviously not to suggest that people did not or do not suffer from depression or from dangerous, extreme mania. The present immunizing perspective comes merely to point out that the antimanic metacode might have driven some people into an absurd "no-exit" trap. Indeed, Albert Camus (1968) dwells brilliantly on this Western no-exit, double-bind metacode of depressive self-control. If his "stranger" or "outsider" would have fallen gravely ill or attempted suicide at the sight of his mother's death, society would have considered him a warm albeit weak human being who might require hospitalization as a mentally ill person with severe depression. He is, however, being condemned as a criminal psychopath, not because he killed a person, but because he displayed the very extreme norm of inhibited self-control so subtly fostered by Western society.

The question now is whether the newly discerned nonmedical[6] metaphor of bipolar episodes released by the DSM-III since the 1980s disseminates a more balanced metacode, which by catering to people's manic needs may legitimize moderate mood swings not only for privileged artists and poets but for all people needing immunization against their fears from the supernatural. One might begin the examination of the new metaphor of bipolar espisodes by picking at random a book published in the 1980s. Indeed, Demitri Papolos and Janice Papolos's (1987) optimistically entitled book *Overcoming Depression,* in which the term *illness* is scarcely mentioned, begins, for example, by citing celebrities from the Bible whose behavior was colored by mood swings, such as King Saul who needed King David's music to soothe his melancholy. It then goes on to mention the bipolar mood swings of King George III, Lincoln, Winston Churchill, Theodore Roosevelt, and writers like Balzac or Hemingway as well as composers like Berlioz and Mahler—all of which creates a picture that mood swings are not only normal but might be a gift reflecting *nobility* and creative *mobility.* But here we discover the broken link between the misunderstanding of ecstasy and the portrayal of mood swings, to which we ought to address ourselves next.

DIONYSIAN ECSTASY AND HEDONISTIC VIOLENCE

Does the new nonmedical metaphor of episodic bipolarity indeed signify a more balanced approach to mood swinging, which lifts the prohibition against the use of controlled doses of manic ecstasy needed to "overcome depression''? Is bipolar mood swinging no more a legitimate hallmark only for privileged poets, artists, and celebrities, whereas for the masses it still incurs a ''mark of Cain''? In short, has the ''manic panic'' epoch reached a new phase, or has it really come to an end?

Granted, by selecting at random such a popular book as the one entitled *Ecstasy* (Johnson, 1987), which attempts to market neo-Dionysian salvation,[7] one might obtain the impression that the ban against irrational creative folly has indeed been lifted in the West. One might also be led to believe that the new understanding of mystic ecstasy, with its balanced attitude toward deflated and elated moods implicit in the bipolaric metaphor, elicited a new call for recognizing people's needs for manic expressions hitherto largely oppressed. A closer examination of Robert Johnson's (1987) randomly selected handbook for ecstasy salesmen reveals, however, a consistent failure to connect the advertisement of ecstasy to people's needs to balance their bipolar mood swings for spiritual creative purposes. Although Johnson's yearning appeal to reinstitutionalize ancient Dionysian mythological rituals purports to introduce its language of joyful irrationality as a counterforce against the frustrating language of rationality, it does not spell out why people should engage in such nihilistic or hedonistic rituals in the first place. Here Johnson's how-to book on practicing Dionysian ecstasy in a modern country like the United States appears highly illuminating. On the one hand, he insists that Americans' eschewal of Dionysian irrational ecstasy stems from a basic misunderstanding because for them it evokes x-rated movies, but originally this ''term comes from the root *ex-stasis*—to stand outside oneself'' (p. 13). On the other hand, Johnson's interpretation of this Dionysian stepping outside one's daily life by drinking ''God's wine'' as an ''experience of spirituality'' (ibid.) seems to reflect a paramount evasion of facing the real meaning of irrational ecstasy so typical of Americans, who usually remain materialistic rationalists at heart.

One has only to follow Johnson's do-it-yourself marketing instructions for practicing Dionysian rituals to realize how the good old American rational advice is hidden behind this call for a Renaissance of the ancient practice of irrational mysticism. While thus no Americans would feel offended by Johnson's stating that ''football and baseball games certainly release a great deal of suppressed Dionysian energy'' (p. 92), they might have rejected Johnson's book (and hence discouraged their friends from purchasing it), had Johnson stated, for example, that shouting football fans express their irrational fears from the mystic world of the transcendental unknown.[8] Similarly, probably no American would mind if Johnson's ''Keep up with the Johnsons'' advice of giving a gift ceremoniously or of running and swimming were relabeled as an exotic Dionysian ritual by which to ''achieve spiritual release'' (p. 94). They would, however, react negatively if their physical (rational) activities were interpreted as being devoid of any spiritual meaning as long as they were not being performed with a religious or mystical intent. One must nonetheless realize that by dressing up ancient mythological and religious practices in modern secular clothing, which are so appealing to the average liberal American, the original meaning of such practices is grossly distorted. Indeed, if ecstasy is defined in the above secular nihilistic or rather hedonistic sense, I fail to see why violence caused by football fans shouldn't be labeled as Dionysian rituals. This is not to suggest that violence should be praised; but unless the issue of the deeper mystic need for manic expressions is raised, it is only the qualitative criterion that could distinguish between the bawling, shouting, cursing, and swearing described and condemned, for instance, by Canter, Comber, and Uzzell (1989) as violence and the football-watching interpreted by Johnson as a Dionysian unifying ritual.

However, if *ex-stasis* is understood in the ancient terms of the soul's desire to leave the body, then the next inevitable question is whether this process of leaving the body is succeeded by an act of entrance. Accordingly, if I am correct in assuming that this ecstatic "temporary death" (the soul's departure) functions as an immunization against the fear of death (by consuming small, temporary doses of death), then this "manic rupture" becomes meaningful only if one "has a book," that is, a belief about the transcendental world of spiritual souls from which one may return after the manic-mystic experience. Whereas Plato, Philo, Dionysus, and Erasmus as well as the Eastern shamans have a mystic book about the world of souls,[9] "Western Johnsons" elegantly avoid any association between ecstasy and mystic beliefs because of their own underlying taboo against irrational thinking.

Indeed, in his polemic essay on the Western "awareness craze" Edwin Schur (1977: 5) comments that "unlike the esoteric disciplines of the Orient, American adaptations need not involve a thoroughgoing commitment to any culturally grounded spiritual tradition." Thus, one might partially sympathize with this Western trend toward "irrationalization" if one realizes that irrational mysticism is usually associated with Eastern and ancient theosophies that tend to undermine material rationalism all together. If, however, mania and depression are understood as a dynamic force that may balance between the rational and the irrational languages, then indeed normative "bipolar mood swinging" may function as an immunizer against the more permanent state of psychotic-schizophrenic detachment from reality and rationality.

Let us hence review briefly the shamanistic functions in relation to schizophrenic states.

EASTERN SHAMANISM: THE UNBALANCED SOLUTION

Students interested in cross-cultural comparisons of altered states of consciousness have generally observed in comparing Eastern and Western psychotic behavior that "significant differences between acute schizophrenics and shamans are not found . . . [but] in primitive cultures in which such a unique life crisis resolution is tolerated, the abnormal experience [shamanism] is typically beneficial to the individual'' (cited in Pelletier and Garfield, 1976: 23). That is to say, behavior considered as deviant, schizophrenic, or otherwise dysfunctional in the West may be viewed in the East as a culturally accepted life crisis that can be resolved beneficially. Indeed, Mircea Eliade (1974), who defines the shaman as a ''master of esctasy,'' noticed that while most shamans come ''from particular families in which nervous instability is hereditary'' (p. 25), they enjoy a prestigious position in their societies because of their ability to control their ''schizophrenic-manic'' or even epileptic dispositions: ''It is not to the fact that he is subject to epileptic attacks that the Eskimo or Indonesian shaman, for example, owes his power and prestige; it is to the fact that he can control his epilepsy'' (p. 29). Similarly, J. Silverman (1967) noted in his comparative analysis of shamanism and schizophrenia that, although both schizophrenia and shamanism are ''the result of a specific ordering of psychological events,'' such as feelings of fear, failure, guilt, and estrangement,

> the essential difference between the two lies in the degree of cultural acceptance of the individual's psychological resolution of a life crisis. Thus, the same behaviors that are viewed in our society as psychiatric symptoms may, in certain other societies, be effectively channeled by the prevailing institutional structure or may perform a given function in relation to the total culture. (p. 23)

Moreover, according to Silverman's survey (1967) the shaman's prestige depends in part on his ability

> to be continually able to ''enter'' and ''return'' from the far-flung reaches of the cosmos . . . [whereas] similar kinds of ritualistic behavior when performed by a [Western] person in a schizophrenic state lead to absolutely nothing at all that has cultural significance, other than as verification of his insanity. (p. 29)

Joseph Campbell (1978: 215-16), who has found that the schizophrenic experience matches typical mythological themes and various mystical experiences, made an interesting observation in comparing the yogic and shamanistic practices to the LSD and the schizophrenic experiences:

> The LSD phenomenon . . . is to me . . . an intentionlly achieved schizophrenia, with the expectation of a spontaneous remission—which, however, does not always follow. Yoga, too, is intentional schizophrenia; one breaks away from the world, plunging inward and the ranges of vision experienced are in fact the same as those of a psychosis. But what . . . is the difference between a psychotic or LSD experience and a Yogic, or a mystical? The plunges are all into the same deep inward sea. . . . The symbolic figures encountered are in many instances identical. . . . But there *is* an important difference. The difference—to put it sharply—is equivalent

> simply to that between a diver who can swim and one who cannot. The mystic, endowed with native talents for this sort of thing and following, stage by stage, the instructions of a master, enters the waters and finds he can swim; whereas the schizophrenic, unprepared, unguided, . . . has fallen or has intentionally plunged and is drowning.

Following our short excursion into the Eastern world of ecstatic shamanism, we may conclude that the cultural factor seems to play a highly significant role not only in destigmatizing schizophrenic or manic ectasy but in using it as a controlling device for solving life problems. It remains to be determined, however, whether the practice of Eastern ecstasy within its mystic orientation functions as a substitute for the rational approach to life or for coexisting with it. In other words, the question that arises here is whether Estern shamanism may also be functional for Western people who intend to maintain their rational life perspective.

If in his cross-cultural surveys Ari Kiev (1972) found, for example, that in Kenya and in other African countries there is little depression, whereas the prevalence of mania is relatively high when compared to its incidence among whites, it is possible that this unequal mood distribution results from the Eastern and the African deemphasis on rationalism and its vicissitudes. In fact, in Kiev's (1972: 75) survey the suggestion was made that depression is to be found more among "individualistic, competitive, and aggressive striving Protestant cultures" because these rational, technical, achievement-oriented cultures produce unusual psychological stress and internal, sin-oriented guilt and self-reproach. As mentioned earlier, it appears that in the West it is only the "recognized and accomplished" artist, poet, or musician who is allowed to use the cyclic rhythm of "prepubic" depressions followed by orgiastic explosions of manic creativity.[10] To be sure, the natural cycle of oscillations between states of deflated pain and elated pleasure were also acknowledged by Western writers like Underhill, who was interested in the development of the mystic personality. Thus, in describing the phenomenon known as the "dark night of the soul," Underhill states (1974: 168) that "psychologically . . . the 'Dark night of the Soul' is due to the double fact of exhaustion of an old state and the growth toward new states of consciousness. . . . The great mystics creative geniuses . . . have known instinctively how to turn these psychic disturbances to spiritual profit."

However, since the Western mystic, like his Eastern colleague, usually relinquishes the rational way of life and since it is only the privileged Western "accomplished" master of art who may legitimately use the manic-depressive lifestyle, the problem of manic outlets for the ordinary Westerner remains unresolved.

As alluded to earlier, the attempts to ameliorate Western irrational fears of the transcendental world by adopting Eastern mystic philosophies, seem to have eventuated in the uncontrollable influx of psychedelic "overdose" explosions. Thus, neither a full "snapping,"[11] or switch, to Eastern irrational mysticism nor the nihilistic indulgence in hedonistic cultish practices of neo-Dionysian ecstasy seems to entail the promising remedy for Westerners' struggle with their irrational fears of the unknown. Now, if the schizophrenic response "I am the Messiah who redeems the world" constitutes the permanent,[12] no-exit answer to fears of the supernatural—for we are relieved of fear if we personify the Messiah who controls the transcendental world—then a manic-depressive system of socialization might comprise the necessary components for balancing between Western rational *deeds* and irrational *needs*.

It is with this balancing mechanism in mind that it is worthwhile to revisit now the ascent-through-descent book provided by Jewish mysticism.

CABALISTIC HASIDISM: THE MEDIATING APPROACH

I have argued at some length that it would be quite impossible to construe Westerners' popular use of the term *unconscious*, on the one hand, and their concomitant search for Easternlike mystic experiences, on the other, without acknowledging that both categories are by definition *irrational* systems that provide some responses to people's fears of the unknown. It may be suggested, further, that in spite of the increasing pressure for rational-technical achievements, which a Star Wars–style competition has exerted on the young Westerner, it is essentially not a complete switch to irrationality for which disillusioned Westerners yearn. It seems, rather, that the periodic disenchantment with Eastern and psychedelic practices indicates that it is the alluded to *balance* between the rational and the irrational languages the average Westener seeks.

In my study of the cabalistic-Hasidic paradigm of contraction (Rotenberg, 1983), I introduced the dynamic notion of ascent via descent and how material descent functions as a desensitizing mechanism of immunization against depression and how spiritual ascent may be understood as a reenergizing, mental rest phase. I further demonstrated how the Hasidic ideal of "uplifting sparks" may be conceived as a transformation procedure by which mundane, physical activities acquire the meaning and status of actualization much the same as the "uplifting of alien thoughts" acquires the force of spiritual-cognitive transformation. I then finally showed how spiritual ascent may be achieved in the Hasidic system via the individual dimension of the cabalistic meditative technique of *devekut*, whereas the engagement in Hasidic social and joyful ecstatic activities like singing and dancing may be understood as a material process of ascent.

I would like to suggest here that this ascent-via-descent paradigm also entails the components needed for balancing and mediating between the rational and irrational thought systems. Consider, for example, a key passage cited in the name of the Besht (the founder of eighteenth-century Hasidism), which might be perceived as a metacode for mediating between irrational mysticism and rational materialism. It could be thought of as a typical statement:

> From the Besht, blessed be his memory, the issue of life (*hachayut*) is "running and returning" (*ratzo vashov*); because, since the soul has been carved from a holy place, it should always be enthusiastic to [return] to its place of carving [creation]; and lest the soul cease to exist, it was therefore engulfed with materiality so that it will also be engaged in material matters such as eating and drinking and give and take [business], etc., so it wouldn't always be walking in the worship of God and in the secret of correction (*tikun*), and so it is in the rungs of the *sefirot* [the 10 cabalistic components of the world], smallness (*katnut*) and greatness (*gadlut*) through the running and the returning, since permanent pleasure becomes natural and is no longer pleasure, and therefore man is ascending and descending. (Besht, 1975: 27)

To consider the above passage as a Beshtian leitmotif and a metacode, one must take into account two facts: (1) that the Beshtian revolution occurred not in the Far or Near East but in eighteenth-century eastern Europe, which was already permeated with the ideology of rational materialism; and (2) that the Besht reached out to poor, frightened people who were still licking the wounds inflicted by pogroms and massacres and who were still bewildered by the smoldering trail left by the seventeenth-century false-messianic Sabbatean movement.

If indeed mystic ecstasy as a remedy against fear of the transcendental unknown connoted essentially an effort of the soul to leave the body, then the Besht's notion of ascent in terms of the "soul's enthusiasm to return to its source" referred to the irrational-mystic language. However, the Besht balances the soul's proclivity to ascent with the mechanism of "running and returning" between the depressive phase of *katnut* (which connotes the narrow-minded, depressive or oppressive concrete perspective) and the phase of *gadlut* (connoting the broad-minded, manic or ecstatic spiritual perspective), so that a great emphasis is put on descending to engage in material-rational matters (give and take). Thus, the human being is pictured as an ascending and descending creature who is urged to use joyful-ecstatic practices and irrational experiences of *devekut* as an immunization against the fear of damnation and death. He is warned, however, not to annihilate his self by cleaving permanently to God because "permanent pleasure is no pleasure." This balancing oscillation between ascent and descent, which I contend is possible only via self-contraction (see Rotenberg, 1983), but not through quietistic self-destruction, may consequently expound its paradigmatic attraction for Westerners, who consistently and persistently struggle with their self-imposed trap of rational-materialism.

The book of Exodus (19:24) says, "And the Lord said . . . get thee down, and thou shalt come up." "Descent for the sake of ascent" is an inherent part of the Jewish tradition at large, although it reached its epitomy and gained its major impetus in Hasidism. The Jewish *PaRDeS*, according to its Hasidic concrete interpretation, may now be understood not only as a hermeneutic system by which a *sod* (mystic) or a *peshat* (rational) explanation of Scripture is permitted. In the Hasidic *PaRDeS, sod* refers now to an ascending ecstatic experience of *devekut (unio mystica)* achieved through individual meditation or social rejoicing. Nonetheless, due to its general adherence to the cabalic book of *PaRDeS*, even the state of descent to terrestrial physical activities *(avoda begashmiyut)* like working, eating, drinking, or even copulating may not be conceived as Dionysian hedonism but as spiritual exercises, given that these performances are enacted with the proper divine intention *(kavanah)*. But how may this ascent-via-descent paradigm be put to work as a psychology of everyday life?

MANIC AND DEPRESSED GIVE OR TAKE VIA *DEVEKUT*

In a study of the cabalistic-Hasidic concept of *kavanah* (intention) a physician and a rabbi (see Bowers and Glasner, 1958) presented the argument that this technique of ecstatic concentration parallels the state of autohypnosis. I emphasize that the said study was conducted by a physician and a rabbi because in spite of the implicated theological background of the second author, this study, which focuses exclusively on equating the technical procedures needed for inducing autohypnosis with intention *(kavanah)*, seems to miss entirely the psychological *intention* inherent in the concept of intention *(kavanah)*. Since *kavanah* refers etymologically to the narrow process of doing something (usually praying) with the correct intention, and since the described techniques and the sources used by these authors essentially refer to the broader ecstatic process of achieving *devekut* (adhesion), I shall herewith use the term *devekut,* which to my mind encompasses *kavanah.*

True, *devekut* or *kavanah*, as Margaretta Bowers and Samuel Glasner contend, may certainly not be conceived as hypnosis or as psychosis because the former connotes surrendering or yielding to persuasion whereas the latter refers to a state that presumably "occurred spontaneously" (1958: 20). Bowers and Glasner conclude from this that self-induced autohypnotic *kavanah (devekut)* may be termed "experimental psychoses" because "these experiences [which] seem to have been deliberately sought out . . . were . . . apparently carefully cultivated . . . subject to the control of the mystic" (ibid.). Bowers and Glasner stress, also, that what they termed "experimental psychoses" appears "to be rather coherent, generally logical, and goal-directed, . . . personally uplifting and integrative . . . and socially acceptable and beneficial" (ibid.). Nonetheless, here it is important to stress that to describe *kavanah* as "experimental psychoses" because this mystic experience is "coherent and logical" would be a contradiction in terms, for psychosis is by definition incoherent and illogical, unless one accepts my immunization formula, according to which ecstatic *devekut* refers to a self-imposed, temporary death experience intended to help one overcome the fear of death.

Although this intention is expressed loud and clear in the sources they cite, like most Western rationalists Bowers and Glasner subtly evade this "irrational" focus, so that the ensuing technical discussion is devoid of the core psychological idea inherent in the cabalistic book of mysticism. Let me elucidate my point by citing from Bowers and Glasner's first and major source, the thirteenth-century mystic Abraham Abulafia, who may be considered to be the father of ecstatic cabala. Using Scholem's (1941: 133) translation, the authors' quotations from Abulafia's instructions to his disciples include the following:

> And when thou feelest that thy heart is already warm, and when thou seest that by combinations of letters thou canst grasp new things which by human tradition or by thy self thou wouldst not be able to know, and when thou art thus prepared to receive the influx of divine power which flows into thee, then turn all thy true thought to imagine the Name and His exalted angels in thy heart as if they were human beings sitting or standing about thee. . . . And all this will happen to thee after having flung away tablet and quill or after they will have dropped from thee because of the intensity of thy thought. And know, the stronger the intellectual influx within thee, the weaker will become thy outer and thy inner parts. Thy whole body will be seized by an extremely strong trembling, so that thou wilt think that surely thou art about to die, because thy soul, overjoyed with its knowledge, will leave thy body. And be thou ready at this moment consciously to choose death, and then thou shalt know thou has come far enough to receive the influx. And then, wishing to honour the glorious Name by serving it with the life of body and soul, veil thy face and be afraid to look at God. Then return to the matters of the body, rise and eat and drink a little, or refresh thyself with a pleasant odor, and restore thy spirit to its sheath until another time, and rejoice at thy lot and know that God loveth thee!

Abulafia, whose famous technique of letter combination may indeed be technically perceived as autohypnosis, stresses two intertwined processes that occur during *devekut*, without which this mystic experience would seem to remain psychologically meaningless. First is the endeavor of the soul to leave the body, during which the person is ready "consciously to choose death." Second is one's consequent readiness to receive the divine influx. After this autohypnotic experience of ecstatic *devekut* one is expected "to return to the matters of the body," restore the spirit, and *rejoice*.

I think it would be unduly overwhelming to the psychologically trained reader who is unfamiliar with the mystic lingo to cite additional cabalistic texts (which are abundant) in order to demonstrate how the expected departure of the soul during *devekut* is followed by one's absorption of divine influx. The psychologically oriented reader should, however, be interested to know more about the potential gains inherent in a meditative exercise of ecstasy that sellers of popular psychology urge him or her to practice through the many workshops and bookshops they market. For it is one thing to be asked to meditate in order to relax, merge with the cosmos, or empty one's self; and it is quite another thing to be taught not only how to immunize one's self against the fear of death but also how to strengthen one's being by learning to absorb cosmic influx. And it is precisely because conventional psychological discussions of ecstasy, autohypnosis, and the like analyze or even advocate these experiences without expounding their possible functions that I chose this comparative study on autohypnosis and *kavanah*.

With this understanding of the mystic experience of manic *devekut* as temporary death accompanied by an act of "taking" or rather "receiving" (absorption of divine influx), we may comprehend also its alternating psychological possibility of "giving." Indeed, the dimension of "giving" as another immunization device against the fear of death was similarly overlooked by Bowers and Glasner (1958) in the very sources they cited.

Quoting from the most famous cabalistic text, the book of Zohar[13], which describes how Rabbi Simeon, the son of Yochai, used the technique of bowing his head between his knees to induce an ecstatic experience, Bowers and Glasner present the following:

> When the day broke he lifted up his eyes and saw a light in the sky. He lowered his eyes, raised them again, and saw a light overspreading the whole sky, and discerned in it a house of many colours. Rapture seized Rabbi Simeon, but in that moment the light hid itself again. Meanwhile two messengers had come before him. They found him with his head between his knees, and addressed him saying, . . . "Master, the heavenly Academy seeks thy greeting, and know that we have been sent to thee." Many old lessons of the Torah were relearnt on that night. Rabbi Simeon said to the messenger: "I beg of you to give some discourse of Torah." They replied: "We have not received permission. It is for this that we have come to thee, that the new lesson this time may come from thee." (1958: 15)

Thus, if immunization against the fear of death may be apprehended now not only as an amorphic process of consuming small doses of death during the manic experience of *devekut* (via the soul's departure) but also as a dynamic act of giving to and/or taking from the Divine, then this optimistic *imitatio Dei* model may also better explain the Beshtian dictum concerning the earthy give and take in business and other activities during the depressed phase of rational realism.

Indeed, in his study about the Jewish mystical experience of *devekut*, Idel (1989b) shows how both trends, that of correcting Heaven, "giving" strength and adding to the Divine,[14] and that of receiving His influx during the experience of this mystical union were disseminated by various schools of Jewish mysticism. If mystical experiences involve receiving from or giving to the Divine, one may also better understand its affinity with the Hasidic imperative of rejoicing. Singing, dancing, and even drinking is accordingly, not a hedonistic catharsis,[15] but an act of ecstasy by which one may accomplish a give-and/or-take experience with Heaven in a fashion akin to Eastern expansion of spiritual consciousness via meditation because both processes are performed in accordance with a specific "book of mysticism."

Returning to the proposition introduced at the beginning of this chapter, we may now better understand the idea of using a controlled bipolar ascent-and-descent model of socialization as a preventative measure against the more permanent fall into the psychotic state of schizophrenia. The psychological meaning of "having a cultural book of therapeutic mysticism" may hence be conceived as an inculcated familiarity with a theory about the transcendental world that one is free to use when irrational fears of the unknown overwhelm him. This cultural "book" of preventative mysticism may also be understood in Campbell's (1978) terms as a theory for learning to enjoy the experience of swimming in the deep oceans. Indeed, Campbell's idea of "swimming lessons" purports to equip the modern person with a theory or an image of the universe and the transcendental world "not so that he lives in fear of it, but so that he recognizes that he participates in it" (p. 221). It is with this "rational" swimming-lessons approach to the irrational that I was able time and again to exercise in my therapeutic sessions the ascent-via-descent process of give and take.[16]

Ms. S., an intelligent woman in her early thirties who holds an M.A. degree and functions well as a professional consultant for correcting children's learning disabilities, emigrated during her childhood from one of the Near Eastern countries to Israel. During the two years of her coming to me for therapeutic help, my major goal was to help her rebalance her orientation between the Eastern mystic world she left behind and the rational Western world to which she switched so swiftly. That is to say, when she first came to my office, she was severely depressed, lonely, masculine, and very rational. Thus, any attempt on my part to discuss her cultural background, including the mystic orientation, was rejected by her until one day she met a young American professional whom she began to date. It was only after the discrepancy between her external pleasant, attractive appearance and her hard-nosed, "castrating" rational and masculine behavior seemed to threaten the endeared relationship with this man that I was able to begin practicing with her the give-and-take exercise. Ms. S. seemed to be trapped in a vicious circle of rationality and depression, which on the one hand enhanced her partner's revulsive reaction to her masculine, rational, depressive yet threatening disposition while on the other hand increased her fear of being abandoned to hopeless loneliness. The fear of loneliness seemed to precipitate her (Eastern?) fatalistic feeling of powerlessness and "social death," but at first she was reluctant to accept the idea that she could use her internalized "irrational" (circular) fatalism to break the spell of her depressive rationalism by reviving her latent

Eastern feminine spontaneity. We then resorted to discussing the mystic-cabalistic technique of *devekut*, which presumably empowers the believer through the process of giving (power) to and receiving (absorbing intellectual influx) from Him. Avoiding any explicit mention of our intellectual discussions of *devekut*, in subsequent sessions I then practiced with her ecstatic give and take whenever she felt completely powerless. I thus sometimes helped her to meditate and imagine how she receives (even physical) love and spiritual power, while at other times I urged her to imagine how she bestows love and spirituality on other people and particularly on her boyfriend. True, I did not practice with her ecstatic singing and dancing, but her meditative exercises, during which she imagined, for example, how she is forced to generate energy to help her father's simulated collapse, seemed akin to the autohypnotic state of *kavanah* (*devekut*).

In conclusion, by emphasizing that Ms. S. always felt more empowered after these "irrational" exercises, I am not trying to deceive or mislead myself or my readers to believe that this woman, who is today happily married to her boyfriend, found her salvation exclusively by rebalancing her bipolar mood swinging between the ascent-and-descent give and take. Nor am I attempting to suggest that a balancing dialogue between the ecstatic language of manic mysticism and the language of depressed realism is of a universal necessity. The point is, however, that if the bipolar ascent-and-descent paradigm is adopted as a dia-logic-balancing, socialization model, then the teaching of a specific cultural "book" of therapeutic mysticism must not be the exclusive domain of the true believer in the religious sense.

It is with this conception of having a specific "book" of mysticism, that is, a cultural theory about the transcendental world, that ecstatic meditation, singing, or dancing would become experientially more beneficial the more one is familiar with its functional meaning in the Hasidic or Buddhist milieu where it originated.[17]

In the next part the *PaRDeS* system will be presented as a balancing model for interpersonal give and take. Accordingly, the following chapter will examine the reciprocal nature of reading and writing, while in the final chapters the *derushic* act of recomposing biographies will be presented as the interpersonal pivot inherent in the balancing psychology of the *PaRDeS*.

NOTES

1. According to Gregory Zilboorg (1941: 23), in ancient times "the epileptic or the pathologically depressed or exhilarated man was looked upon as a superior person, endowed with powers, base or lofty but greater than those of the normal mortals." Moreover, George Rosen (1969: 51) adduced ancient documents showing how the prophetic possessed person was pictured as "a human figure in violent motion or epileptic convulsion." Indeed, some believe that the Scripture's description of the prophet Balaam as "falling into trance but having his eyes open"

(Numbers 24:4) in fact accentuates his authentic prophetic powers. One may therefore hypothesize that, ironically, in ancient times rulers like Julius Caesar might have faked their famous epileptic seizures in order to establish their immortal godlike status.

2. In my study about the impact of Protestant Calvinism on deviance (see Rotenberg, 1978), I discussed at some length the paradox of "predestinal free will" that emerged in Europe during the Renaissance. I demonstrated that this version of free will, which later corresponded to the Puritan convenant of work (i.e., salvation through work), was used only to blame people for their deviant conduct. However, the idea that free will should in theory have opened up new avenues of hope for deviants, who could presumably repent by using their free will, was subdued by the predestinal belief in innate damnation, which later corresponded to the Puritan covenant of grace. As alluded to, I have argued that perhaps subsequently the paradoxical notion of unconscious motivation—which in fact connotes a contradiction in terms because motivation as free will is incompatible with the deterministic unconscious—may be traced to the Renaissance use of predestined free will.

3. The antilabeling crusade that has spread all over Europe since the 1960s maintains that by the very act of diagnosing and labeling a person as deviant (whether as criminal or mentally ill), a self-fulfilling process is set in motion that eventuates in the irreversible internalization of the deviant tag by the labelee.

4. By wastebasket category I have in mind a temporary, undefined category, like "allergy" or "virus," that physicians use in their diagnosis until medicine discovers a more specific etiology of the physical suffering under consideration.

5. The pathogenic double-bind could, according to Gregory Bateson (1978), lead to schizophrenia if a person is repeatedly exposed to a no-win communicative situation. Although Western psychotherapists have warned parents against sending their children such double-bind messages, which can only be understood as "you're damned if you do and you're damned if you don't," Westerners usually fail to recognize their cultural double-bind metacodes. As suggested in the text, it is in this double-bind sense that one may perceive the Western imperative of controlled-depressed behavior as a damnation trap. One is damned as a psychopath if one overcontrols one's emotions, and one is damned as a psychotic if one becomes emotionally overdepressed if, for instance, a parent dies. However, since life is indeed comprised of paradoxes, I am not surprised that Bateson's double-bind theory of schizophrenia, so popular in the 1950s, was reformulated as a therapeutic method in the 1970s by Paul Watzlawick (1978) and others.

6. It is of interest to note that it was probably due to the unquestioned medical authority with which various mental illness categories were accepted that such a towering scholar as Gershom Scholem (1973: 125) stated unequivocally that "there is no doubt that Sabbatai Sevi was a sick man." After consulting many psychiatric textbooks Scholem made a detailed effort to describe Sabbatai's behavior and mood fluctuations as symptoms associated with the manic-depressive illness because "The sources suggest with almost absolute certainty that Sabbatai suffered from a manic-depressive psychosis" (p. 126). When during a private meeting with Scholem I once challenged his blind acceptance of this derogatory medical label in regard to Sabbatai Sevi, by pointing out the difference between the cabalistic-Hasidic notion of creative "ascent via descent" and the Christianized dogma of mania as a facade

against the predominant state of depression, he admitted that he accepted psychiatry as a medical given.

It would be quite intriguing to know how he would describe Sabbatai Sevi today, now that the DSM III has excluded this behavioral-phenomenon from the category "psychosis," since at the time he accepted its inclusion unhesitantly.

7. Dionysus, the god of wine in Greek mythology, is often identified with the Roman god Bacchus. Practically, however, he symbolized the propagation of ecstasy, madness, irrational wisdom of the senses, and the consequent transcendence of the soul. Marketing a neo-Dionysian spirit to Westerners without mentioning classic predecessors such as Nietzsche (1967) is not merely a matter of plagiarism; it reflects also a gross distortion and an essential misunderstanding of the Dionysian energy system. Although Nietzsche's Dionysus indeed symbolizes the ecstatic release of the instincts in primordial rituals, without the Apollonian counterbalance Dionysus contains a tragic element of self-destruction. Thus, Nietzsche's barbaric Dionysian "will to power" may not only create Zarathustra and its Nazi superman offspring but it may also instigate people to engage in orgiastic practices of self-annihilation. Thus spoke Nietzsche: "And what, then, is the significance of . . . the Dionysian madness? . . . Is madness perhaps not necessarily a symptom of degeneration, decline and the final stage of culture?" (p. 21)

8. It is amazing as well as amusing to realize how material marketing rules are used in America to sell antimaterial spiritualism. In this context Schur's (1977: 7) comments seem pertinent: "Far from inciting a break with our dominant patterns of competitive consumption . . . the 'new consciousness' has itself become a commodity. It is being heavily promoted, packaged, and marketed, much like any other commercial item."

9. In my endeavor to distinguish between the hedonistic or cathartic style of rational but meaningless (or valueless) ecstasy and the irrational-meaningful kind of ecstasy, I offer shamanism as a good case in point. Shamanistic ecstasy certainly belongs to the second category because it is structured according to a theory about the transcendental world of souls, which I call a "book of mysticism." Eliade (1974: 259) indicates, for example, that in the shamanistic world

> the universe in general is conceived as having three levels—sky, earth, underworld—connected by a central axis. . . . This axis . . . passes through an "opening," a "hole"; . . . through this hole . . . the gods descend to earth and the dead to the subterranean regions; [and] it is through the same hole that the soul of the Shaman in ecstasy can fly up or down in the course of his celestial or infernal journeys.

10. Unfortunately, it often happens that "unaccomplished," that is, unrecognized, artists are indeed labeled as mentally ill or psychopathic. However, if their work were all of a sudden discovered and hence publicly recognized, such people may be retroactively "rehabilitated" and destigmatized even after their death.

11. "Snapping" is a term used by Flo Conway and Jim Siegelman (1978) to describe a sudden, drastic alteration of personality resulting from a kind of electric shock that occurs in the brain when one's source of information about the world is changed too swiftly. The authors used this term to explain the mental disorientation and breakdowns that have characterized many Americans who have joined various cults since the 1970s.

12. As long as Western society will not legitimize the status of a part-time Messiah

or prophet, the permanent role of schizophrenia will persist even after one's need to control one's fears have ceased. The social belief in "once a schizophrenic Messiah or prophet always a messiah-prophet" could in theory be cancelled if, for instance, the person under consideration has found legitimate ways to control his life and predict his future.

13. Here it seems appropriate to point out that although scholars are divided as to whether the Zoharic categories of ecstasy qualify as "uniotive" *devekut*, in Isaiah Tishby's (1971, Vol. II: 303) analysis of the book of Zohar, this behavior is described as the mystic experience of union:

> In the doctrines of early cabalists . . . *devekut*, in its diversified forms, is an unequivocal mystic phenomenon: man's ascent toward a direct, intensive contact between his soul . . . and the divine to a point of fusion with it, and obliteration within it [the divine]; such a *devekut*, which is a direct consequence of the mystic intention, can also be found extensively in the Zohar.

14. Scholem's moderate interpretation of *devekut* as an experience of communion not requiring the complete obliteration of the personality has been challenged by Mosle Idel (1989b), who adduced ample evidence demonstrating how the *devekut* experience of *unio mystica* culminated in total self-annihilation. Since self-annulment would seem to contradict the cabalistic-Hasidic imperative of *tikun* (correcting Heaven via the active actualization process of "uplifting sparks" with *kavanah*), I think that only a give-and-take formulation of ecstasy could reconcile the two conflicting interpretations of *devekut*. If during one's temporary immersion in the Divine, he is expected to give to the Divine, his self is certainly not entirely obliterated because a nonbeing cannot give. Similarly, one's essential personality must at least be passively there to receive the Divine influx, if one considers *devekut* as such. I would suggest that the possibility of giving concurs with my (Rotenberg, 1983) understanding of the expansion phase and with Idel's (1989b) notion of integration, whereas the possibility of receiving is generally tantamount to my (ibid.) interpretation of the contraction stage and with Idel's (ibid.) idea of universalization. If, thus, integration during *devekut* constitutes the possibility of humans being enwrapped by other *sefirotic* elements, this expanded state of being facilitates giving. Conversely, one may understand receiving as a universalization process of absorption into and receiving from the universal influx via the process of opening up during the phase of self-contraction.

15. Indeed, Freud (1968: 81) understood the social institution of periodic festivals as a legitimized response to people's manic needs. "In all renunciations and limitations imposed upon the ego a periodical infringement of the prohibition is the rule; this indeed is shown by the institution of festivals . . . which owe their cheerful character to the release which they bring." Nonetheless, since Freud conceived manic festivals only in their hedonistic-cathartic sense and not as a give-and-take process operating according to a theory about the transcendental world people fear, his conclusions seem quite gloomy: "The Saturnalia of the Romans and our modern carnivals agree in this essential feature with the festivals of primitive people, which usually end in debaucheries of every kind and the transgression of what are at other times the most sacred commandments" (ibid.).

16. Here I would like to stress that although I fully agree with Campbell's (1978) mystic swimming-lessons conception for overcoming irrational fears of the

transcendental world of the unknown, I disagree with his Christian interpretation of the returning stage. Thus, "the inward journeys of the mythological hero, the Shaman, the mystic and the Schizophrenic" (p. 237), which culminates, according to Campbell, with the "twice-born" experience of rebirth, would, I believe, seem to contradict his own notion of swimming (which implies active control and not a passive birth) in the mystic ocean. I believe, therefore, that the manic experience must follow a Hasidic-cabalistic style of an ascent-via-descent process in which one's self-control is never entirely obliterated.

17. As a descendant of two major Hasidic dynasties, I must admit that when, occasionally, on festivals I join in with other Hasidim in an ecstatic dance, a meaningful feeling of exaltation permeates my being in spite of my usual intellectual stiffness. I attribute this feeling to my familiarity with the "Hasidic book of mysticism" because I never experienced similar feelings during secular dancing and feasting.

Part Three

INTERPERSONAL DIA-LOGISM

6

The Psychology of "Doing My Own Thing . . . for You"

In the previous chapter I have tried to show how induced exercises of controlled manic ecstasy may be understood as immunization devices against people's "ontological insecurity" (see Laing, 1978) or more simply against the fear of death. I have thus argued that by studying closely the sequence and logic of mystic experiences such as the cabalistic practice of *devekut*, such irrational processes become more rational. That is to say, by considering the cognitive-emotional receiving (of cosmic divine influx) or the giving (of power to correct Heaven) that presumably occurs during these experiences, one may understand the subjective feelings of empowerment that may imbue a person who has experienced *devekut*.

Since our Weberian (1970) point of departure posits that theosophic metacodes usually exert paradigmatic impacts on patterns of interpersonal behavior, I shall demonstrate in this chapter how the *imitatio Dei* model of giving in essence constitutes a misunderstood prerequisite for any form of effective interpersonal receiving.

Earlier I used Rabbi Ashlag's (1965) introduction to the cabalistic book of *Zohar* in order to explicate how the human desire to receive divine influx would be impossible without perceiving His equal or even greater desire or even need to give or bestow it on the human world. True, the theory of creation—according to which, in the cabalistic world, divine emanation and revelation (giving) is possible only if it is preceded by an act of divine contraction (*tzimtzum*)—is idiosyncratic to Jewish mysticism. But according to the cabalistic idea of divine *ayin* (nothingness), the monotheistic notion of *creatio ex nihilo* must be understood as creation from within God Himself, so that the first act of emanation refers to "the emergence of all things from the absolute nothingness of God" (Scholem, 1974: 95), which is to say practically that genesis meant giving. Thus, divine emanation and revelation as a paradigm people are urged to adopt as a model for their interpersonal giving requires contraction in terms of narrowing or dimming (if one uses the metaphor of light)[1] so that the receiver may be able to accept what is being conveyed to him or bestowed upon him.

Indeed, in my study of the Hasidic ethics (see Rotenberg, 1983: 84), I have maintained that the need for receiving and giving might better be understood if one examines the relevance of the cabalistic principle of contraction to processes of education or love relationships. I have thus argued that "the ultimate testing-ground for actualizing pleasure through interpersonal interaction . . . usually evolves from educational or love relationships, because it is in love or educational relationships that self-fulfillment is meaningless until the interacting partner provides the proper feedback signals that the educational/love message was indeed fully perceived." To visualize how in interaction between two unequal partners (child and father or student and teacher) one can fully convey what he feels or thinks only through narrowing and contracting the matter or theme to be conveyed, I have used the "funnel" metaphor provided by the Maggid of Mezeritz (1927: 47):

> When the Rabbi wants his student to understand his broad mind, and the student cannot apprehend it then the Rabbi-teacher contracts his mind in talk and letters. For example, when a person wants to pour from one container to another and he is afraid to spill, then he takes an instrument called a funnel, and by this the liquid is contracted . . . and he will not spill. So it is when the Rabbi's mind is contracted in talk and letters which he says to the student, and through this the student can apprehend the teacher's broad mind.

Thus, contraction in the maggid's sense, is not a one-time act of evacuation that leaves a vacuum.[2] Contraction is, rather, a prerequistic act of condensation for what I termed (Rotenberg, 1983) alter-centered revelation, or giving in the human and divine worlds. Divine contraction as a precondition for emanation and giving is best illuminated in Buber's (1963: 104) poetic words:

> How could the divine infinite (*ein-sof*) become a contracted God which roams the worlds to carry out His creation through acts of contraction? . . . Why did the infinite divine, as an absolute personality, vis-a-vis stands nothing, become a personality which stands vis-a-vis a receiver? . . . [It is] because of the desire to find a receiver, so that the divine will be able to bestow His light upon it.

I have begun my discussion of the need to give by using the cases of education and love relationships wherein the need for reassurance that giving was somehow received is relatively clear. At this point, no doubt, the Western reader, who shares the common moral vocabulary Robert Bellah and others (1985) termed the "first language of American individualism," grows impatient in his attempt to attend to my altruistic preaching. By "altruistic preaching" I have in mind the "good Samaritan" call to help (give) the other by ignoring or subduing our natural, self-centered underlying desire to receive. Although it is not my aim here to reiterate Bellah and his colleagues' alarming concern, which posits "that this individualism may have grown cancerous" (p. VII), I would like to argue hereinafter that (1) Western ego-centered, do-my-own-thing psychology encompasses a basic misunderstanding of the need to give, and that (2) a balanced, interpersonal give and take requires an acceptance and a mastering of a multilinguistic conception of interpersonal relationships.

My cabalistic analogy of God's need to give or to bestow influx may be understood on a human level by picturing an artist's cureless need to "give" the pictures he paints. I imagine that if an artist were locked up for life in his studio to paint as much as he desires but no human eye was permitted to glance at his work, he would eventually die[3] or attempt suicide. Consider only the self-endangering risks antiestablishment writers are willing to take in totalitarian states when they distribute (give out) underground copies of their work.

Thus, self-actualization guided by the "first language of individualism" would be largely self-defeating if it culminates in a simplistic psychology of "doing my own thing." If I follow literally the American "democratic" imperative of "doing my own thing as long as I don't hurt others," those others might still hurt me by obstructing "my own actualizing thing" if they refuse to receive what I want to give as an expression of my self-actualization. In this sense, then, the line between giving and receiving becomes considerably blurred because giving becomes ipso facto receiving. Indeed, reception theory (see Iser, 1978), which shifted focus from studying the text and its author to assess the role of the reader, suggests by its very definition that if there would be no reader to receive the author's writing (giving), his text would be quite meaningless. Similarly, the declaration "I am a therapist!" or "I am a teacher!" would be rather meaningless, a role theorists would claim, if there would be no one to receive the therapy or the teaching.

Giving, in the above dia-logic sense, is accordingly not a unilateral altruistic act of good Samaritanism but a reciprocal process of mutual dependency in which A might be willing to receive B's actualizing-giving under the condition that B or C is willing to receive A's actualizing-giving. Now if A is more talented than B but is still forced to shape or even limit his actualizing-giving because he is dependent on B's willingness to receive it, this dependency could either falsify and regress the process of creativity or enhance mutual growth of A and B if both succeed to transcend mutual jealousy or criticism. But still, how are we to envision the possibility of progress and creativity if this inevitable mutual *dependency* stands in diametric opposition to the "first language of individualism"?[4]

Before venturing to offer a new, balanced formulation of a give-and-take interdependency, let me elucidate from another angle the Westerner's eschewal of dependency.

THE DOUBLE-EDGED "SWEARING" IN "SELF-DETERMINATION"

The problem of dependency as a dirty word in the dictionary of the "first language of individualism" may be illuminated by observing how the idea of restrainment, whether by a community or by parents, has perplexed many Americans. In July 1989, *Newsweek* (Darnton, 1989: 66-68) published an alarming article about the growing number of youths admitted to mental hospitals. According to the author of this article, the startling manifestation in regard to this phenomenon lies in the shocking fact that the population under consideration is admittedly comprised of white middle-class and upper-class teenagers who display only minor behavioral problems usually defined as "defiant disorders," with no concurrent delusional symptoms commonly associated with psychosis. Illustrative examples taken out of a growing number of over 20,000 cases reveal that private hospitals structured like college dormitories are providing the restraining and caring atmosphere that parents who swore allegiance to the "first language" of noncompromising self-determination apparently fail to provide. Nina Darnton (1989), who wrote the article about the appalling phenomenon of committed youth:

> depicts concerned parents sitting around the kitchen table. "Where does he go?" asks the mother, "I don't know," replies the father. "He doesn't talk to me." "Do you know who his friends are?" "We are going to lose him if we don't get help," they agree. A reassuring voice then suggests calling the hospital: you owe it to your family. We bring families back together. (p. 67)

Since the cost of another dogma dictated by the "first language of individualism," which sanctions any form of generalization, that is, collectivization, usually culminates in saying nothing about anything, I shall risk my neck in suggesting the following generalization: If, indeed, parents (of a nonrepresentative sample of 20,000) need mental institutions to restrain their nonpsychotic, defiant offspring, then they must have taken the oath of not violating their children's right for absolute self-determination. If "lost families" therefore seek their "lost community" in mental hospitals, then Bellah and his associates (1985: VII) seem to be correct in drawing on Tocqueville's observation of American democracy when they say, "He [Tocqueville] also warned that some aspects of our character—what he was one of the first to call 'individualism'—might eventually isolate Americans one from another and thereby undermine the conditions of freedom."

In developing the theory of social contraction (1983) I have dealt at some length with this either/or "escape from freedom" into the communal "total institution" (including mental hospitals). I shall return later to tackle this dilemma of the "cursed blessing" of individualistic freedom, but I think the following case study might throw additional light on the problematic double-edged "swearing" into rugged self-determination.

THE SATTEMER WIG WOMAN AND THE SUICIDAL SOLDIER

During my sabbatical in 1986 I succeeded in obtaining an invitation to discuss with ultraorthodox Jewish therapists problems in working with ultraorthodox Jewish clientele in an ultraorthodox Jewish neighborhood in New York City. I emphasize my success in obtaining an invitation because it was only after they were convinced (by skimming through some of my books?) that I am both familiar and sympathetic with their heritage that they were willing to share with me some of their professional dilemmas. At this particular meeting, a spokeswoman-therapist described to me, during an hour-long session, how they have to use various delicate means to prevent "restless" youths from leaving the protective yeshiva college (where orthodox boys are expected to fulfill the commandment of studying Torah), although very often some of these boys seem simply unfit for studying all day. Then, after it appeared that I had gained the meeting participants entrance-fee confidence, one woman suddenly brought up the case of the "Sattemer wig woman." To familiarize the reader with the social meaning of belongingness to the community of Sattemer Hasidim, it would be imperative here to stress that this Hasidic sect is considered by most Jewish denominations to represent *the* most fanatic, ultraorthodox group—one that rejects Zionism and modernity (not including wealth and technical comforts). One example of this extremity is that a great number of Sattemer married women are not permitted to wear wigs, as other ultraorthodox women do, but must shave their heads and cover them with kerchiefs. The Sattemer woman under consideration came to the clinic allegedly because she felt somewhat constricted and depressed. The therapist stressed, however, that after a while it became quite clear that although this woman liked her family and social milieu, she felt somewhat confined and unfulfilled in terms of possible interests and activities. Then one day, after working with her for several weeks (no details were volunteered), the therapist was secretly told by the Sattemer woman that a day earlier she had dared to walk into a department store in order to put on a wig and look in the mirror just to remember how it feels to be with hair once again.

At this point I asked the therapist what her response was, and to my surprise she replied that naturally she had encouraged the Sattemer woman to exercise her rights and needs for self-expression. I then urged the rest of the workers in this ultraorthodox clinic to join me in a pre-biographic exercise of the "wig woman." Namely, I asked them to follow a possible scenario in which the wig woman, whose right for self-determination was now reinforced, will next come in and tell about a book she read or a movie she saw, until the pressure of her Hasidic group will force her either to give up her individualistic, recalcitrant behavior or leave the group. To challenge the American dogmatic equation between the ego-centered self-determination and alter-centered happiness, I shared with this group an experience I had encountered as a psychologist in the Israeli army. A soldier who had no family or friends in Israel was caught by his commanding officer when he was about to commit suicide. The officer reproached him vehemently by stating that he was going to bring him to trial for attempting to destroy military property. When finally the soldier was persuaded to believe that he was indeed not free to do what he wanted because he belonged to the army, he reacted with a spontaneous happy disposition that reflected the notion "Well, if I really belong to the Israeli army collectivity (which cares enough about my existence), then I am no longer lonely and in need of committing suicide."

The question I raised subsequently during this discourse, which was quite embarrassing for the workers in this clinic, was whether the doctrine of self-determination underlying American therapeutic philosophy would not stand in contradiction with another American "sacred cow," namely, the imperative of people's inalienable right to pursue happiness. In other words, I asked whether this woman would really be happy in the Jeffersonian sense of her human rights if she would be inadvertently encouraged to do her own thing at the price of being possibly excommunicated by her natural group.[5] As might be expected, any conclusive decision or self-reproaching following our session was skillfully evaded. However, when later, in various U.S. universities, I used the cases of the wig woman and the suicidal soldier in leading seminars on the problem of rugged self-determination in therapy, I became more and more convinced that the psychology of doing one's own thing is the first commandment every trained American therapist accepts without question, regardless of race, creed, or color.

To be sure, what is being questioned here is, not people's right for self-determination, but its applied interpretation into a dogmatic, Tocquevillian, self-isolating formula of human rights to receive that undermines people's equal right and need to give. Thus, both the therapists of ultraorthodox Jews and the parents of hospitalized youths accepted self-determination as an absolute doctrine apparently because imposing restraint or communal dependency would infringe on the Sattemer woman's or the offsprings' right and obligation to do their own thing.[6] Now, if self-determination in terms of doing my own thing formula disregards the give-and-take parameters inherent in the doing, then this "first language of individualism" is indeed "cancerously" isolating.

If, however, doing is understood as a need of the artist to give, then dependency on a community of receivers is an inevitable must. Consequently, the person who is doing (giving) his or her thing needs to be restrained by, and to depend on, some receivers who provide the feedback meaning to his or her doing. Nevertheless, doing my own thing could still foster isolating independency if it is translated into a tyrannic give or take. That is to say, one cannot impose giving to or taking from the other, unless doing one's thing is articulated in reciprocal terms that say, I receive your A-thing if you receive my giving you a B-thing. Tyrannic giving occurs, accordingly, when a reader or a therapist "missionarizes" or manipulates others to accept his or her interpretation of life and reality.[7] Similarly, despotic receiving occurs when an individual becomes a manipulative extorter or *shnorer* (see Rotenberg, 1983) who has indeed given up giving and has hence succumbed to exist as a receiving debtor.

In the following I shall explore the possibility of "give and take" as a nondespotic conceptualization of interdependency by construing the idea of multilinguistic interaction.

"RECIPROCAL INDIVIDUALISM" AND VERTICAL GIVE AND TAKE

So far I have claimed that the conceptualization of alter-centered giving might be rejected by Westerners as hypocritic good Samaritanism because of its inevitable association with dependency. Indeed, if Protestantism fosters achievement-oriented independency (see McClelland, 1967) as an ultimate goal of self-actualization, then its resultant norms of acquiring and possessing require a certain kind of taking rather than giving. Thus, giving to needy others[8] might in this sense be understood only as a vertical and unilateral process of altruistic contributions of "surplus goods"[9] left over after one's Calvinistic or, rather, Darwinistic ego-centered self-actualization (see Rotenberg, 1983). In the vertical form of altruistic giving the less talented receiver, whom I called "debtor" (ibid.),[10] becomes a dependent failure in a world that demands independent self-determination in the name of democratic egalitarianism.

By implying that Western egalitarianism *demands* independent self-determination, I come to say that one may understand why dependent people are exiled to dependency-fostering total institutions only if one assumes that people have not only equal rights but also equal ability and consequently also equal obligations to exercise their independent self-determination (ibid.). Thus, in the Western world of equality, only the infant has a right to be dependent on his parents but an adult may refuse the demands of others to activate the right to pursue happiness by being dependent on him. Consequently, in this vertical world of give and take, we might expect the following to occur: Freedom "refusniks" will be punished by being exiled to total institutions where, on the one hand, they will be released from their obligatory self-determination while, on the other, they will be deprived of their need to actualize themselves through giving. As a result of this sequence from now on however, any form of "giving" will always be conceived as a condescending, unilateral act exercised by a powerful creditor, whereas receiving will always be perceived as a degraded state of dependency.

How, then, are we to envision the possibility of give and take, not as a naive, utopian process of materialistic receiving according to needs and giving according to ability,[11] but as a horizontal circle of "reciprocal individualism" in which self-actualizing giving (in one area) is an integral part of legitimate receiving (in another area) (see Rotenberg, 1978). Reciprocal individualism, which concurs with Buber's I-thou stance, stands neither for massifying collectivism (in which one runs away from one's self into the mob) nor for isolating individualism (in which one runs away from the mob). In alter-centered reciprocal individualism the I and the thou may function as alternating givers and receivers because they converse in two different languages. But how does this egalitarian dialogue circumvent naive idealism?

READING AND WRITING AS HORIZONTAL GIVE AND TAKE

"And the Lord said, Behold the people are one and they have all one language . . . and now nothing will be restrained from them" (Genesis 11:6). If all people speak only the one materialistic language of the Babylonian tower, they "will be restrained from nothing"; they will destroy themselves through stagnation instead of restraining-contracting themselves to make room for each other. A horizontal dialogue is possible if the I, who masters the language of the Babylonian tower, gives materiality but receives spirituality from a thou who speaks the language of the Babylonian Talmud. Thus, one might be a reader-therapist in the rational language, while the other might be a schizophrenic-writer in the mystic-irrational language. Thus also, an interpersonal dialogue is possible in the tribal world (see Rotenberg, 1983) if "Zebulun," that is, one who speaks the rational language of materialism, gives technically while he or she receives spiritually from "Issachar," that is, one who speaks the irrational language of spiritualism or mysticism.

In biblical commentary dating back to the talmudic era, Zebulun, the tribal son of Jacob, is described as a merchant, and his brother Issachar is portrayed as a talmudic scholar. According to later hermeneutic legends these two brothers made a partnership or, rather, a contract between them. Zebulun, who dwells at the haven by the sea and goes out sailing in a ship laden with merchandise to earn his living, feeds Issachar, who sits and studies the Torah. Issachar is expected, in turn, to benefit Zebulun spiritually so that the division of labor between them will maintain an equilibrium between matter and spirit in the world. Although Issachar's spiritual language is, in its ancient sense, not synonymous with mysticism, it seems pertinent to stress here that in its later Hasidic formulation (see Besht, 1975: 57), the "spiritual type" refers to a person who behaves [speaks] in a super natural manner [language]." Therefore, from the present perspective Zebulunism and Issacharism could be understood as broad linguistic categories because the paradigmatic meaning emanating from their give and take refers to the dia-logic possibility in which A, the rationalist, contracts so that he or she may subsequently read what B writes in the spiritual or mystical language, and vice versa.

It is only via a dia-logic alternating contraction and expansion that the despotic, manipulative, vertical give and take in terms of a fundamentalistic reading or writing may be avoided in therapy, in literature, or other kinds of interactions. Indeed, in describing his (dia-logic?) method of dream analysis as an "exchange between two personalities," Jung (1978: 44-45) objects to any use of a mechanical technique (language) because in this situation "the therapeutic problem is reduced to the simple question: which of the two people concerned—the analyst or the dreamer—will dominate the other?"[12] Thus, for Jung dream interpretation might consist of a dialogue between the mystic language spoken by the dreamer and the realistic-rational language of the therapist.

The dialogue between the reader-therapist and the writer-patient as a process of contraction and expansion may be illuminated further by drawing on Laing's compelling analogy exploring the relationship between a contemporary expositor-reader and the ancient author of hieroglyphics. Drawing on many sources (among them Freud), Laing (1978: 31) suggests that the method of deciphering ancient texts, which depends to a large extent on the relationship between the ancient author and the contemporary expositor, "has been carried further forward and made more explicit . . . than the theory of the interpretation of psychotic 'hieroglyphic' speech and action." Certainly expositors of ancient texts or experts of art and poetry would hardly assume that the ancient author or the ancient or contemporary artist or poet was or is insane, even though they themselves may find the idiosyncratic texts or works of art incomprehensible, bizarre, or, most important, different from their perspective. Instead, they would undoubtedly blame themselves for lacking the talent, background, or understanding to decipher the language or explicate the meaning of the object or work in question. In attempting to overcome their narrow *Weltanschauung* and limited observational and interpretational skills, our expositors would then contract in order to seek in the observed object, not those properties that are strange and consequently incomprehensible to them, but those elements that evoke for them the commonalities between their own experience and the properties they are able to identify in the observed piece. By learning to identify in themselves the bizarre—or, rather unknown—characteristics of "the other," be it art or a person, they would then experience an inner growth and extension of their personality, which now includes a piece of "the other," as reception theorists would have it.

Laing's expositor-reader may thus be equated with a visitor in a foreign country whose sudden feelings of smallness and incompetency decrease the more he succeeds in understanding the local language of the people with whom he tries to interact. The possibility of a horizontal dialogue must, however, refer not only to an attempted conversation between a Frenchman and an Englishman who speak only their native language but also to discommunication between people who presumably speak the same language. That is to say, the impossibility of a horizontal dialogue may refer to an interpersonal clash that occurred because the interacting partners did not share a similar style of communication. In a visit to the People's Republic of China, our tour guide excused his poor English by telling us the following anecdote: Once an Englishman was about to purchase a horse from a Chinaman. They agreed about the price, but the Chinaman cautioned the Englishman by declaring that the horse did not look so well! Since the price was right, the Englishman disregarded the warning by stating that he needed the horse for working and not for a beauty contest. However, after this horse kept bumping into walls and trees, the Englishman wanted his money back. But the Chinaman said: I told you that the horse did not look so well, meaning to say that he was blind. Our Chinese tour guide, who through this anecdote reiterated a well-known linguistic principle, obviously implied that behind the literal translation of words there are cultural thought systems, with specific metacodes for speaking and reading. Accordingly, "does not look so well" may mean blindness in one culture and lacking in beauty in a different culture, although the same words are used.[13]

In my comparative assessment of training for assertiveness and "deassertiveness" (Rotenberg, 1983), I have adduced abundant evidence demonstrating how very often assertiveness training led to an I-*or*-thou breaking of partnerships and marriages because each partner refuses to speak in and listen to the other's language. I have stressed, accordingly, that the possibility of interpersonal growth must be sought in the I-*and*-thou principle of mutual emulation (see below), which means generally that Zebulun may grow when he contracts to learn (receive) Issachar's spiritual language and, conversely, Issachar grows when he contracts to learn (receive) Zebulun's material language. Learning to read and write in spiritual-mystical and material-technological languages may thus comprise the therapeutic possibility of "transaction" (Spiegel, 1971) in which the interpersonal process purports to engender reciprocal and mutual influences between the I-therapists and the thou-patient.

It is with this perspective of mutual emulation in mind that I would like to explore now the possibility of dia-logic reading and writing in the therapeutic situation.

EMULATING *TIKUN* (CORRECTION) AS READING AND WRITING

In my attempt to convert the Hasidic dictum of *tikun* (correction) into an educational-therapeutic theory of mutual emulation, referring to self-correction and mutual growth, I have shown how people's permission and obligation to correct Heaven also entails self-correction (see Rotenberg, 1983). If according to the cabala one is thus urged to restore or rearrange the world after the primordial "breaking of the vessels" by using the dictum of "uplifting sparks" and attributing divine meaning (*kavanah*) to every mundane activity,[14] one must also correct himself by rearranging (correcting) communication with the other.

To explicate the principle of mutual emulation (concerted self-correction for the sake of mutual growth) via a process which I termed "double-mirroring," I have used the following Beshtian imperative: "If a person had the opportunity to observe a transgression and he should feel [the need] to correct himself . . . then he will bring back the wicked person after he includes him through unification" (Besht, 1975: 21). Upon initial consideration of this imperative, one may wonder why the anormative behavior of "the other" should be casually related to the same anormative behavior in oneself and, further, how one's own correction of this particular behavior should simultaneously correct the other's behavior. To understand this process we should distinguish between the unidirectional modeling system of Albert Bandura (1969) or the passive, reflective looking glass of George Herbert Mead (1934) and the double-mirror model of the Besht, that is, the dynamic process of mutual emulation. In the one-way looking-glass model there are no assumptions as to whether and how an A, the role-taker in Mead's paradigm or the copier in Bandura's paradigm, affects B, the model or significant other, although it is possible of course, that the role-taker or copier, A, may serve as a significant model, B, during a different interactive situation. However, the mutual-emulating scheme proposes a situational dynamic and reflective process of double-mirroring in which both interacting partners are affected simultaneously. This active-dynamic, double-mirror concept assumes that if my interacting partner persistently repeats a certain kind of anormative behavior, then my performance in regard to this specific behavior must have been similarly anormative or insufficiently normative and persistent to serve its reflective modeling (mirroring) purpose. Hence, my correction of this behavior should reverse the process; for unlike modeling, emulation is a two-dimensional mirroring process. Indeed, Rabbi Yaacov Yosef (the Besht's disciple) (1963: 259) interprets the verse "who is a wise man; who learns from everybody" (Mishna Avot 4:1) by using the mirror metaphor (about 200 years before Charles Cooley) as follows: "A wise man is the one who learns from everybody like someone that looks in the mirror; and knows his own faults by seeing the faults of his fellow man." Similarly, Buber (1978: 241) related:

Once Rabbi Zusya came to an inn, and on the forehead of the inn-keeper he saw long years of sin. For a while he neither spoke nor moved. But when he was alone in the room which had been assigned to him, the shudder of vicarious experience overcame him in the midst of singing psalms and he cried aloud: "Zusya, Zusya, you wicked man! What have you done! There is no lie that failed to tempt you, and no crime that you have not committed. Zusya, foolish, erring man, what will be the end of this?" Then he enumerated the sins of the inn-keeper, giving the time and place of each, and his own, and sobbed. The inn-keeper had quietly followed this strange man. He stood at the door and heard him. First he was seized with dull dismay, but then penitence and grace were lit within him, and he woke to God.

A more common example of such mutual self-correction might be when a teacher suddenly lowers his voice to bring attention to the fact that both he and his students have been shouting over one another's heads. Likewise, a mother who notices that her child is eating in an unmannerly way while important guests are present attempts to correct her own eating habits in the hope that the child will emulate her behavior, rather than reprimanding him in front of the visitors.

Mutual emulation therefore also entails an operational definition of reciprocal or alter-centered (other-centered) individualism: Collective orientation in terms of alter's misconduct is reduced by enhancing ego's individualistic actualizing behavioral responsibilities toward self. Moreover, in theory at least, mutual self-correction should allow for mutual growth if indeed we believe that correcting one's multilinguistic ability enhances communication.[15] According to this categorical imperative, it is insufficient to act, as Kant declared, so that my action may or at most ought to become a general moral, natural law. Rather, the ultimate test of my actualizing personal behavior depends on how it actually affects my interacting partner or the others in my community. Thus, whereas Kant's moral autonomy by definition requires the absence of any social motivation to ethical conduct, alterism recognizes that self-actualization is possible only through its tested impact on others.

Taking together the examples provided by the Besht, Buber, and my own illustrations, we may return now to revise reception theory according to our dia-logic therapy perspective.

RECEPTION AND CORRECTION

To elucidate how receptionists concentrate on the readers, Terry Eagleton (1985) cites the first two sentences in John Updike's novel *Couples*: "What did you make of the new couple? The Hanemas, Piet and Angela, were undressing" (pp. 74-75). Since Updike does not answer the reader's immediate questions about these descriptive statements, Eagleton shows how the reader's assumptions about the meaning of these sentences must be tentatively guessed, and hence deferred (in Derrida's terms) until he reads on in the novel. Thus, the inference that Piet and Angela are a married couple because they share the same surname might reflect a cultural bias or be otherwise wrong and consequently quite frustrating if the reader will discover later in the novel that he erred in his initial guessing. By enumerating the following possibilities Eagleton then demonstrates how a multiplicity of meanings might be attributed by the reader to these two sentences: There might be two women, two men, or two tiger cubs called Piet and Angela. One cannot rule out the possibility that there is a group of people or a tribe called the Hanemas in addition to Piet and Angela. Piet and Angela might be liberated or incestuous brother and sister, father and daughter, mother and son, or simply two small children. And finally our biased assumption that they are undressing in sight of each other might be wrong because it is quite possible that they are shouting from one bedroom to another.

Now, although Eagleton illuminates how the reader must constantly defer his attribution and correct his assumptions about the others described by Updike, he cannot tell us what happens to the reader's self-actualizing giving. If we accept that the reader's (or critic's) need to give his interpretations (bestow influx) is frustrated either because the writer (e.g., Updike) did not respond to his reading or because the reader-therapist failed to correct his readings according to the patient-writer's responses, then we have a nonactualized or a despotic reader. If we agree that therapeutic reading and writing provide the tools for self-correction, which might prevent the tyrannizing interpretation by either the writer or the reader, then an egalitarian dialogue seems possible only if we accept (1) that reader and writer may speak in different languages and (2) that both may become alternating readers and writers all at the same time. We might, accordingly, equate the reader-therapist with our visitor in a foreign country (the land of schizophrenia) whose communicative ability improves the more he corrects his speech in the newly acquired language.[16] Thus, if the reader-therapist masters a mystic language and the writer-patient speaks a material language, or vice versa, then each of them can actualize himself by offering one or several creative interpretations of the text without imposing it on the other and without giving up his actualizing need to give (interpretations). Since these alternative interpretations are corrected according to the different "languages" spoken by the reader and the writer, and hence they do not imply that one of them does not know how to read or write, mutual growth may take place. Namely, if each one learns how to read the text in the language of the other and turn his self-corrected (contracted) reading into emulative and creative writing, then neither of them will feel that he "flunked" the reading course and a realistic *al-tikrei* (reading simultaneously two opposing possibilities) situation might ensue.

By depicting the coexistence of two alternative *al-tikrei* interpretations as a realistic possibility, I intend to account for the dia-logic need of both reader-therapist and writer-patient to give and to receive. This frequently overlooked, equal need would have been frustrated if one of them had to accept that the reading or the writing in only one language is to predominate the therapeutic dialogue. An example of fundamentalistic reading is the Oedipal language, and an example of writing despotism is the existential California language of "doing my own thing without hurting the other." Since both of these are presumably rational languages, let us return now to our dia-logo project in order to demonstrate how a therapeutic dialogue between the mystic and the rational languages was possible in our psychodramatic sessions.

DIA-LOGIC READING AND WRITING THROUGH PSYCHODRAMA

One of the more effective methods comprising the possibility of multiple text reading, which might turn into creative writing of a revised biographic text, seems to be therapeutic psychodrama. In role playing or psychodrama, readers act out a variety of possible interpretations in regard to a biographic problem enacted by a specific writer-patient. In dynamic role playing for both reading and writing usually only one rational or irrational language might be used, whereas the chances for a multiple choice between several languages increases in a psychodrama group if legitimations for mystic and realistic interpretations are equally reinforced by members of the group and their composing guide (i.e., the director or leader).

However, while the psychodramatic arena promotes an increased use of the mystic language of fantasy because of its affinity with the theatrical world of drama, in the West a legitimized application of this language to real life requires preliminary contraction exercises to ascertain acceptance of the mystical interpreter as an existential equal to the rational reader of reality. Thus, to maximize the dia-logic possibilities of more than one logos or language, we used in our group project the following sequence of contraction exercises: first dia-logic training, then self-corrective mirroring and finally psychodramatic interpretation. Let us follow this approach.

Dia-logic Training

In the first exercise group members are divided into dyads of A's and B's in order that the A's will tell the B's a problematic, disturbing experience they encountered. After telling the event, as instructed, in a factual-rational language, the B's are requested to recount the event as a mystic-irrational but meaningful experience. A and B are then requested to share with the group the impact of both readings by contracting, that is, by holding in abeyance, the particular reading mode (mystic or realistic) they believe predominates their thought system. Improvisations on this dia-logic exercise sometimes included mutual contraction in which B would contract

A's interpretation, or vice versa, by deemphasizing the significance of the partner's predominant approach to reading while overemphasizing the alternative possibility. Interestingly, since most Westerners tend to overemphasize the rational reading style, this role-reversing exercise, in which one side stresses the experiential meaning of a subjective-mystic reading of a personal event, often seemed to elicit confessions that this task in fact brought for the first time to the surface their covert irrational feelings, which they had been ashamed to express before. To enhance altercentrism, other modifications of this dia-logic technique included mutual contraction of ego-centered focus by deemphasizing the relative significance of the specific problem under consideration in relation to the family, community, or world at large. Additional hermeneutic improvisations included reading the problem as an exaggerated tragedy or comedy.

The Self-correcting Mirroring

If, according to the Besht's and Zusya's rule of organic unification, *brotherhood* means that the *other hood* is part of yourself, then indeed you may correct the other by correcting yourself. In this exercise the group is once again divided into A's and B's. The A's are asked to identify in their B partner's specific behavior patterns that appear to them deficient, dysfunctional, or in need of change and improvement. The B's are not allowed to listen to the instructions given to the A's, who are requested to attribute these deficiencies to themselves and consult with the B's about how to correct, change, or overcome these problems. When the B's are instructed separately how to offer advice to the A's, they are asked to include mystical solutions such as ecstatic exercises, whenever it seemed appropriate. Dyads are next asked to discuss among themselves the impact of these experiences and subsequently share them with the group. Here it seems of importance to note that while usually only about one-third of the B's stated immediately that these "deficiencies" apply equally to themselves, only after advising the A's how to correct their behavior did most stress that it would not harm them to correct simultaneously their own behavior in the specific area under consideration. Thus, self-corrective double-mirroring operated as a noblesse oblige mechanism; the cognitive dissonance caused by the B's advice to the A's triggered (mirrored) a reflective need for concurrent self-correction.

The Psychodrama of Mrs. F.

After exercising dia-logic reading and self-corrective mirroring, usually a natural situation evolved during which someone in the group volunteered to use a personal problem for psychodramatic interpretation. Here I shall present briefly the case of Mrs. F. because she and her husband (with whom she encountered communicative problems) seemed to speak in two different languages. Mrs. F. told us that she came from a poor, ultraorthodox Jewish family whereas her husband, who repented and presumably joined her way of life, came from a secular but well-to-do family. Mrs. F. believed that giving and doing for others entails the mystic promise that every giving, especially monetary, will enrich the donor so that his return will at least be duplicated. She complained that her husband refuses to accept this norm, although it is based on canonical exegesis of the Torah,[17] and although it is deeply entrenched in the Jewish mutual-aid tradition. Mrs. F. thus emphasized that it is not the fact that her husband's secular, well-to-do family abstains from helping while she and her nonrich family are constantly reaching out to help others that annoys her. It is, rather, her husband's silent alignment with his parents and his implicit consent with their attitude that troubles her.

Here I should insert that after such an ego-centered problem presentation elicited the group's sympathy, as happened in the case of Mrs. F., our group worker would usually shift focus from the protagonist to her "autistic" (quiet, nonpresent) partner. The worker therefore asked Mrs. F. to contract at this point but requested other group members to write on a piece of paper the husband's or his parent's possible responses to Mrs. F.'s "accusations." After reading and discussing briefly the written responses, the group worker asked Mrs. F. to participate in a series of psychodramatized scenes acting out different versions of her husband's and/or his parents' responses. Mrs. F. was then permitted to correct or disagree with the actor's version; and when a specific interpretation (or part of it) was somehow acceptable by her, she would be asked to reverse roles and enact the husband's parents' or her husband's "real" response in the way she perceived it. As a result of enacting-reading different versions of the husband's "writing," Mrs. F. learned for the first time (according to her own testimony) how to "read" her husband's rational language. Thus, the most dramatic breakthrough occurred when during the enactment of one proposed response Mrs. F. admitted that indeed her in-laws had offered several times to contribute a considerable amount of money needed for investment in an enterprise that would then assure a steady income, but her husband usually rejected it politely. It was only after an entirely new reading was proposed that the baffled feeling of Mrs. F. and of the rest of the group subsided in reviewing this puzzling situation as follows: Having relinquished the rational, capitalistic way of life in favor of a religious-mystic perception of the transcendental reality, perhaps the husband, it was suggested, felt that Mrs. F.'s way of reciprocal give and take was spiritually preferable.

A week later Mrs. F. came back all excited and told the group that after telling her husband what came up in the psychodrama, she learned to her surprise that indeed her husband evaded his parents' offers because he thought that this capitalistic patronage would desecrate the religiomystic aura of give-and-take that imbued their home. Mrs. F. subsequently admitted that only after she learned with the help of the group that in fact her husband was the one who contracted his rational reading of reality in order to learn her mystic language was she able to reciprocate by contracting her "righteous" mystic attitude; as a consequence her family life improved radically. Thus, *pardesian* therapy helped to rebalance this family's "paradise" by Mrs. F.'s learning to receive her husband's rational, Zebulunic giving (since they indeed took his parents' money), while Mrs. F.'s spiritual giving was not obstructed because she was still able to interpret the transcendental reality in her Issacharian language.

In conclusion, the divine need to give (bestow influx) and receive (human correction) as an *imitatio Dei* model may now receive its epitomized, concrete meaning on a human interpersonal level. Moreover, the present psychological perspective may throw new light on a debate among students of Jewish mysticism concerning the ecstatic experience of *devekut* (see Idel, 1988a, 1989b). Accordingly, the question as to whether this experience of mystic ecstasy involves the process of union or communion with God becomes secondary if not superfluous. For if one considers the psychological give and take that presumably accompanies such practices as a phenomenological experience, then the empowerment following *devekut* is far more significant than its original mystic state. It is hence the interpersonal reading and writing occurring during the therapeutic encounter that provide the testing ground for the *pardesian* dialogue. That is to say, it is only the living dialogue between the reader's and the writer's needs to give and to receive, occurring in therapy, that can testify unequivocally how despotic interpretations may be prevented. Therefore it is not the autistic dialogue between the reading receptionist and the dead writer, but the disputed living transaction during therapy that can demonstrate the possibility of egalitarianism. Thus, only the alternating *pardesian* contraction of either the rational (*peshat*) language or of the mystic (*sod*) language can facilitate the concurrent writing and reading without frustrating the self-actualization needs of patient and therapist to give and to receive.

NOTES

1. My student Baruch Kahana (1990) was able to show that in the Hasidic school of Chabad the alphabetic letters and the cabalistic idea of vessels were interpreted on the interpersonal level in terms of contraction (narrowing, dimming): He thus cites from the Chabad's founding father, who stated that

> the dimension of shedding light and influencing the other's mind or influencing and enlightening the other's morality . . . must come as a measure of contraction . . . since it is impossible to bestow on one's pupil the quality of mind as it is perceived by him . . . and so is drawn the quality of the mind's light through the letters which limit its qualitative light . . . and it is like a vessel, . . . through which water will be drunk. (Shneurson, 1976: 322)

It is thus possible that even if one accepts Chabad's extreme interpretation of the ecstatic state of *devekut* as an attempt to obliterate the self, (see Idel, 1989b) in regard to God, the norm of contraction predominates the interpersonal level in a deegoistic sense, which requires self-contraction to make room for the other.

2. In the Judeo-cabalistic world the possibility of a Godless vacuum would be considered blasphemous because "there is no space without Him" (*leit atar panuy miney*). Hence, unlike the neo-Platonic conception of evil as a vacuum or absence, in the Hasidic-cabalistic world what appears as evil is only a dynamic challenge for humans to overcome it.

3. By using the expression *dying* I have obviously in mind also a social death. In our dia-logic treatment project we worked intensively for about a year with an intelligent young man who at the time may have been described as having been "socially dead" in spite of the fact that he maintained a respectable position in a bank where he functioned as an economist. This young man's family moved when he was a child from an alter-centered (other-oriented) neighborhood permeated by a spontaneous religious (mystic) and Eastern atmosphere (his family came from one of the Near Eastern countries) to a European, ego-centered vicinity. Although our young man did well in the Western competitive school and in his subsequent academic studies in economics, he seemed to have lost all of his warm, spontaneous skills on the interpersonal level. He had never dated a girl, although he was already 28 years of age, and as a result his feelings of isolation and loneliness deepened so that in essence he had no social contacts with his autistic surrounding. Based on our notion that the best way to acquire a friend is to be one, that is, in order to be able to receive one has first to exercise a preliminary need to give, it was only after he agreed to become a big brother to a six-to-seven-year-old child that he was slowly able to open up and receive from others.

4. In exposing the self-defeating element inherent in such individualistic movements that advertise self-awareness or self-assertion, Edwin Schur (1977: 81) indeed links this self-contradicting propensity to Americans' abhorrence of any form of dependency: "Just as they isolate the self from all social context the new awareness prescribes that self-esteem should not depend on other people."

5. A good case study concerning this arbitrary application of individualistic-oriented therapy that clashes with one's right for happiness by belonging to a collectivity is provided in the following. Jona Rosenfeld (1980) was able to show how even the most caring and intensive individualistic therapy with Israeli young soldiers was often quite harmful if during war time, for example, they were separated from their social unit in the army, which provided and buttressed their essential collective identity and pride.

6. Another example of how the dogma of self-determination becomes socially self-defeating if one follows it *ad absurdum* to its ultimate possibility is the case of homosexuality. Although the average American, who usually shuns examining the limits of his or her precious individualistic rights and values, would most probably endorse without any reservation people's right for sexual preference, he or she would most probably evade the clash between homosexual self-determination and the problem of perpetuating the human race. That is to say, a certain measure of restraint would have to be applied in order to ascertain continuity of the human race or in order not to deprive a small minority's right for heterosexual relationships if, say, 98 percent of the population were homosexual.

7. In my study of hermeneutic pluralism in therapy (Rotenberg, 1987), I have equated fundamentalistic therapists to missionaries who manipulate other people to accept their religious belief system.

8. In studying the popular assertiveness training literature (Rotenberg, 1983: 92), I have cited sources warning people not to fall in the altruistic "unselfishness trap," which requires that one give part of one's income to needy others. One writer even reversed the "giving" slogan by paraphrasing it as follows: "Give to you. Support your local self!"

9. The idea that in the Protestant world altruism may refer only to giving unilaterally "surplus goods" is logically derived from the Calvinistic dictum that maintains that religious salvation and election is a direct function of egotistic economic success and the ability to display individualistic signs of possessing material goods. One might hence give out only the leftovers.

10. My differentiation between debtors (receivers) and creditors (givers) is borrowed from Nietzsche's (1969) use of contractual guilt. The ethical term *guilt* (which in German is *Schuld*) took its origin from the material concept *debts* (*Schulden*); and thus interpersonal guilt, according to Nietzsche and Martin Heidegger, is based on the contractual notion that someone "owes" something to another (*ist schuldig*). For Nietzsche and Heidegger, as for most other "man-centered" philosophers associated with the Protestant school of German idealism, interpersonal guilt is hence featured by mere material-contractual, universalistic, and instrumental relationships between people. Accordingly, salvation from guilt is not an interpersonal matter but a personal, ego-centered process associated with intrapsychic sin, to be reached when concerned only for oneself. Thus, if salvation is sought through ego-centric achievements, interpersonal relationships can be conceived only in material-contractual terms. In such relationships, the weak, deviant debtor will always remain beholden to the strong creditor, since it is not in the latter's interest to reduce his strength or to contract himself in order to create a contract of selves.

11. The collapse or revision of the communist "ideal" in most East European republics might testify that one needs more than an egalitarian ideology in order to motivate people to give according to ability and take according to need.

12. In this context Jung (1978) adds the following declaration, "I gave up hypnotic treatment for this very reason, because I did not want to impose my will on others." It is of interest to add here that in the dia-logic world of cabalic-Hasidism the idea of hypnotizing others does not exist. Although this concurs with the notion promulgated by the Hasidic founding fathers, who portrayed the Hasidic leader (the Zaddik) as a mediator (a pipeline) between matter and spirit, mesmerism seems to be practiced inadvertently by contemporary cabalistic holy men and Hasidic leaders because of their disciples' propensity for worshiping humans.

13. Although we witness how toward the end of the twentieth century the *iron* curtain separating East and West is being lifted, the *irony* concerning the differential meaning of how things are said in those two hemispheres might stay with us for quite a long time. The following joke might illuminate further how the differential intonations of the same words carry different meanings. Once an American and a Russian scientist met in neutral territory. The Russian expressed his curiosity about the United States by asking the American how life is in America. The American answered, "Well, I can't complain!" (that is, things are okay). "And how is life in

Russia?" reciprocated the American. The Russian answered, "I also can *not* complain!" (that is, I don't dare to, or there is no use in complaining).

14. Elsewhere (Rotenberg, 1983, 1987) I have derived the therapeutic principle of paradoxic rearrangement from the cabalistic notion of *tikun* (correction). I have thus shown how the cabalistic-Hasidic dictum of "uplifting divine sparks" to restore order (correction) after the primordial "breaking of vessels" (shattering explosion of divine light) became a guiding principle for rearranging paradoxically opposing elements. Accordingly, the rearranging of the letters of the word *nituk* (separation) into *tikun* (correction) may turn into a therapeutic guide for rearranging any seemingly contradictory elements.

15. Here it is appropriate to remind the reader that according to Mead's role-taking conception, the self-image emerges out of the individual's ability to imagine how significant others respond to his or her behavior. Bandura assumes likewise that a child grows (learns) by copying a model's behavior. Elsewhere (Rotenberg, 1983) I have thus stressed that Scholem's (1972) differentiation between restorative and utopian messianism is congenial with our distinction between modeling and emulation. Accordingly, modeling concurs with restoration because by copying, one reproduces the role model's behavior; whereas, emulation concurs with utopian messianism in which one restores the past or alters behavior but adds to it a future of one's own excelled behavior, which has never existed before.

16. We might learn a great deal from the world of art about multiplying criteria for beauty. If by learning the language of cubism or of impressionism one might learn to see beauty in what previously impressed him as ugly, not only a dia-logic situation of an egalitarian conversation is created but also new multiple criteria for determining human beauty are generated.

17. In the Hebrew version of the biblical dictum "Thou shalt truly tithe all the increase of thy seed" (Deut. 14:22), the words *aser teaser* are written. Since *teaser*, which means giving 10 percent of your income, can also read *teasher*, which means becoming rich, the Talmud (*Shabbat* 119:a) paraphrased this verse into a slogan that says, "Give a tenth so that you shall become rich" (*aser kedey shetitasher*).

7

Dia-logic Recomposing and Psychotherapy

Is the material world really nurtured by spiritual experiences, as most theosophical texts persuade us to believe? Does the literary text exert a real impact on the ontological text of living people? To explore these phenomenological queries and possibilities, I would ask the reader to accompany me in my excursion between two worlds, the real world of deviance with its therapeutic correction and the ideal world of literary texts. Let us begin our psychonarrative discourse with the following event.

I once watched a televised interview with 15- to 18-year-old American youths who served extended prison terms for murders they had committed during armed robbery. The most startling and appalling common denominator the skilled interviewer succeeded to elicit in these interviews was that whereas most of these youngsters admitted to a sense of failure or envy for not having succeeded like many others to put away at least part of the money they robbed, none of them expressed any feeling of regret or remorse about the very act of killing. When, subsequently, social workers and therapists were asked to explicate their potential or actual plans for rehabilitating such young killers, the most striking answer they gave evolved around the possibilities for teaching them the art of earning money respectfully.

The shocking echo of this televised program haunted me for days, and I felt bedazzled for not being able to explain to myself what it was in the rehabilitator's response that troubled me even more than the disturbing but not so surprising answers given by the young killers.[1] Since I have been associated for many years with therapeutic and research programs in prisons and institutions for treating young offenders, it was when all of a sudden I recalled the famous case of the young "umbrella man," which rocked the media and shocked the public in the early 1960s, that I knew what annoyed me in the rehabilitator's planned remedy for young "robbing hood" killers.

Very briefly, the umbrella man was, if I recall correctly, a 15-year-old New York City gang member who presumably had cold-bloodedly stabbed to death about three or four boys either with a regular knife or with his sharpened umbrella. The point is, however, that after he was sentenced to death, and hence isolated in a death-row cell, a totally new, rich spiritual side of his personality was discovered in the course of his contacts with priests, who at this stage constituted the only bridge between him and the outside world. It is insignificant here whether the death penalty was commuted as a result of the sentimental "sad tales" about the lost spiritual soul which appeared daily in the media. What seems instructive from the present perspective is that the uncovering of the spiritual-mystical criterion for actualization and success was possible in this extreme case only via a dramatic and complete isolation of the young lad from any material orientation as a desirable way of life.

A famous talmudic aphorism derides the Babylonians' stupidity because of their custom of eating "bread with bread" (*Nedarim* 49:b). A popular midrashic interpretation of this mockery explains that, metaphorically, bread means matter, and accordingly one may understand that it is senseless to heal matter with matter instead of balancing it with spirit. It is in this sense of healing matter with matter that the rehabilitator's prescribed remedy for "robbing hoodism" made less sense to me than the young killers' cruel but honest "congruent" response.

After all, the Protestant-Darwinian survival formula with its strict material success criteria dictates a certain cutthroat stepping on corpses. We all know the popular American "utilitarian" expression of admiration for the person who "made a killing in the stock market." The dispute between the young "robbing hoods" and the televised rehabilitators is thus one between metal and metaphor—that is, between those who use the concrete metallic pistol to kill and those who "make a killing" (those who make a lot of money). It is probably not accidental that the word *bread,* which among other things signified the Babylonian material tower, is still synonymous with the contemporary expression *dough,* which symbolizes money. Thus, the young killers who did not express remorse for their killing but only for their failure to "keep the dough," as they had been socialized to do, are simply an example of reification. They merely reversed the Western material success prescription of "thou shalt kill" metaphorically but "keep the dough" literally. Instead of being able to "put away the goods," they were nearly "put away for good."

It has frequently been pointed out (see Marcuse, 1966) that the Western world's tendency to produce one-dimensional, material people may be attributed to the Western exclusive emphasis on left-hemispheric socialization toward a rational-material orientation to success. Indeed, neurologists such as Oliver Sacks (1986) were able to describe how patients like Dr. P., a professor of musicology whom he treated, became so pathologically left-sided that their thinking in mere analytic, abstract terms was in this case manifested by a disability to identify buildings or put on a shoe, which required the activation of the right hemisphere. To be sure, although the responsibility for establishing the empirical connection between various hemispheric dysfunctionings[2] and specific treatment strategies remains, from the present perspective, solely the domain of neurophysiologists or neuropsychologists, the relationship between rational and emotional, mystical and intellectual, or material and spiritual orientations to life has occupied philosophers, psychologists, and theologists since time immemorial.

Dia-logic recomposing, which I will present next in this chapter, drawing heavily on juxtapositions with and extrapolations from a variety of humanistic disciplines, should hence be understood as a deconstructive-therapeutic language for balancing, or recomposing, these material-rational and spiritual-mystical opposing forces polarizing the human species.[3] Since impacts of material and/or spiritual orientations on human behavior are usually formulated by theosophically inclined writers, the focus of the present chapter is on studying the relationship between the ideal, *literary* theosophical text and the real, *literal* therapeutic text. It will be shown, accordingly, that by reading the therapeutic text, the metacode for socialization offered in a literary text might receive a more concretely applicable meaning. More specifically, the *pardesian* possibility for balancing matter and spirit by means of therapeutic reading will be introduced as two facets: (1) as a process of including the spiritual-mystical reading as part of the text and (2) as a supplementary process by which the spiritual-mystical reading is used as a nourishing device for growth on the interpersonal level.

RECOMPOSING VIA CONTRACTION AND DECONSTRUCTION

Let us begin by clarifying terms. *Recomposing* alluded to earlier, refers to a therapeutic method for rereading and rewriting parts of one's lifestory by contracting and deconstructing contradictory elements in the biographic text in order to facilitate the recomposition of an expanded, new, harmonic text. Psychotherapeutic recomposing thus constitutes not merely a situational reframing or rereading that either disregards or takes for granted the congruence between the *reframed* event and the social-cultural *framework* in which the new textual melody must resonate.[4] In fact, as a therapeutic reading-writing system that purports to encompass the possibility of progress, recomposing focuses on exploring how a new composition creates a new, meaningful melody that contains the intonations and the social echo by which the harmony between the individual's new song and its social resonance may be assessed. As such, recomposing should not be understood in structural terms according to which the reader-therapist concentrates on preexisting tonal-linguistic principles for deciphering signs and syntax or tunes that produced the melody of meaning.

By introjecting the notion of social echo, recomposing assumes, however, that unless rereading or rewriting of one's biographical composition is tuned up with the social orchestra in which it is to play, the new personal melody will discord. Recompositions may hence be therapeutic to the extent that the new, rewritten tunes concord with the religiocultural key or guiding metacode in which the new biographic melody is to be sounded. In other words, a recomposed lifestory or total history of a southern black man may be expected to echo harmoniously for this man's social band only if composed with a metacode or key for writing the kind of social jazz with which he and his friends are familiar. Such metacodes or master keys for decoding and writing texts or lives are usually acquired early in one's life in the respective culture or religious environment in which one was raised.

Thus, if deconstruction may be best understood in the context of critical reading, as Jonathan Culler (1987) suggested, then recomposing would comprise the other constructive-therapeutic side of deconstruction,[5] which encompasses societal reactions to reading and writing but is not structured by them. Moreover, if "to deconstruct an opposition such as presence/absence, speech/writing, . . . central/marginal, is not to destroy it . . . [but] to undo and displace it, to situate it [the opposition] differently" (p. 150), then recomposing focuses on the therapeutic potential inherent in centralizing the marginal by marginizing the central, which is possible in other words, only by contracting the central and expanding the marginal. Put in the terms of the *PaRDeS* system, the *peshat* (rational) interpretation and the *sod* (mystic) reading of the text employ equal positions.

To rephrase or incorporate deconstructive reading within the old cabalistic notions of contraction and expansion according to which nothing is erased from the original text but constantly rearranged to allow for an infinite creative recomputation and recombination of letters,[6] it would be useful now to juxtapose Derrida's concepts of graft and logocentrism with the cabalistic notions of contraction and expansion.

GRAFTING AND DIA-LOGIC THERAPY

In the ancient Jewish cabalistic tradition, the hermeneutic art of recomputing or recombining letters of words was used to assign new meanings to biblical texts. This technique practiced mainly by ecstatic cabalists (see Idel, 1988b) was based on the dia-logic principle (two or more alternating or complementary logical systems) in which the original text is never destroyed but contracted to allow for a coexisting discourse between the mystic and the intellectual, or between the material and the spiritual interpretations of the living text.

Derrida, the leading exponent of deconstruction, offers "grafting" as a model for an interpretive strategy by which the marginal text set aside by previous interpreters is given a more central reinterpretation. Derrida thus reverses the logocentric hierarchy characterizing Western thought, according to which the logical is prior or superior to the illogical, and concurrently nature is higher than culture, the literal precedes the metaphorical, and the spiritual is inferior to the material.[7]

In therapeutic terms grafting is thus not a dialectic process by which subconscious or mystic irrationalism must be negated or excluded and replaced by rational consciousness. Rather, grafted reading-writing, which includes the oral tradition of speech, retains the old text with its strict *peshat* (rational) reading known in Hebrew as *midat hadin* (the divine attribute of strict judgment); but it transforms and translates the text in the living, compassionate terms of *derush* or *sod* which could be classified under the category known in Hebrew as *midat harachamin* (the divine attribute of mercy and compassion). Indeed, states Derrida, grafting in

> deconstruction does not consist of moving from one concept to another but of reversing and displacing a conceptual order as well as the nonconceptual order with which it is articulated. For example, writing . . . entails predicates that have been subordinated, excluded, or held in abeyance by forces and according to necessities to be analyzed. It is those predicates . . . whose force of generality, generalization, and generativity is liberated, grafted onto a "new" concept of writing that corresponds as well to what has always *resisted* the prior organization of force. . . . It is to give everything at stake in the operation of deconstruction the chance, the force, the power of *communication*. (*Margins* cited by Culler, 1987: 141)

It is, then, this therapeutic power of communication, which excludes nothing from the "patient's" written text that expands the seemingly irrational silent utterances of this "patient" and gives them "the chance, [and] the force" that should interest the therapeutically committed reader of life as an oral text.

When Scholem began to graft the mystical Jewish cabalistic literature, considered before his time by the rabbinic establishment as esoteric *kwatch* (nonsense in German), as he phrased it, he in fact expanded and centralized marginal texts by assigning them a major regenerating psychological force in the history of Jewish revivalism. However, although Scholem contracted the role of nonmystical texts by considering them as rationalistic forces which were deficient as reenergizers of Jewish vitality (see Schweid, 1983), he nonetheless did not erase these texts but challenged their readers into a coexisting dia-logic discourse that would fit a *PaRDeS* system of hermeneutics.

After our short deconstructive detour, an illustrative case from our dia-logic therapy workshop[8] might help to demonstrate how the dia-logic alternating between the two thought systems is used by contracting the intelligible and rational biographic "facts" in order to *include* (i.e., graft) or to expand and legitimize the mystic-irrational experiences for the sake of giving them "the chance, the force [and] the power of communication."

MR. M.'S COMMUNICATION WITH PLEASANT "VOICES"

Mr. M., who was in our project's intensive care from December 1987 until October 1988, was at the time an unmarried, 26-year-old diagnosed schizophrenic who lived with a foster family in Jerusalem. M. was the fourteenth child of a Jewish ultraorthodox (*chareidi*) family residing in New York. His late father's family came from Austria-Galicia and his mother's family immigrated to the United States from Lithuania. M. described a normal, happy childhood growing up in a Hasidic community, in spite of the fact that due to his psychiatric problems he had resided for extended periods with his married sister and with one of his older brothers. Living with the foster family in Jerusalem was arranged so that he would be able to work mornings in a sheltered workshop and study in a *yeshiva* (talmudic college) in the afternoons.

I shall not dwell here on additional psychiatric background information because my intention is to focus mainly on the way we attempted to transform his irrational symptom of hearing voices into a mystic part of the text to be grafted into a dia-logic power of communication to be included in the main text. When M. first described to our psychonarrator (commonly termed *therapist*) the voices he heard on a daily basis, he seemed to be alarmed at two facts: (1) that they degraded him by addressing him as a "profane" person or by telling him to go to hell, and (2) that they were not real because nobody else could hear them.

Although our first successful task—to identify the voice of his dead father (who passed away in 1987)—should have at least partially "normalized"[9] the very phenomenon of hearing voices by convincing him that everybody is capable of reproducing in "his head" familiar voices, his paranoic feelings persisted mainly due to M.'s conviction that the voices, which were derogatory in nature (even if they were his father's), had a controlling effect over him.

Nonetheless, our dia-logic treatment plan for the months ahead consisted of the following facets and steps. First, an attempt was made to elicit also voices that were encouraging or pleasant. Second, M. was encouraged to examine whether the voices made him feel more lonely or less lonely. Third, M. was taught how to maintain a dialogue with the voice by reinterpreting the content. Finally, M. learned to produce the voice by free will in order to challenge it and control it as every person would do when he wants to ponder over some important issue with his own inner voice or with some significant other who may not necessarily be alive.

Here is a verbatim record of the first dia-logic phase, when dia-logist A. (our psychonarrator) helped M. to recall favorable voices and identify the feeling of pleasant companionship.

A: M., can you tell me a bit about the voices?

M: I don't know . . . They just come.

A: How often do they come?

M: Sometimes a lot, sometimes less.

A: Every day?

M: Yes, every day. But sometimes there are hours without them, and then they come only for a few minutes.

A: Do they bother you?

M: Yes, it's not good. I mean there are no voices. I know it's not real but I feel them. Sometimes they tell me things like [addressing me with] profane names (*tome*) or by telling me to kill myself.

A: Can you tell me a little more about what it's like?

M: It comes all of a sudden. Sometimes I'm alone, sometimes among people. I think it's like my father or sometimes it sounds like my brother-in-law who lives in Lakewood.

A: What do the noises mean?

M: It's like talking to me, telling me things like how to walk with my feet out or to take bigger steps.

A: How does it make you feel?

M: It gives me a headache and bothers me. It comes and goes.

A: What makes it come and go?

M: I don't know. It just comes, sometimes just after hours of quiet.

A: Are the voices only bad?

M: What do you mean?

A: Do the voices ever mean good things?

M: Well, I don't know. It could be.

A: How could it be? Are they interested in you?

M: Maybe they are interested in me. Like sometimes I hear a voice "bmmmm," and it, like, says to me good. Like I walked nicely.

A: It tells you, like, something good?

M: Well, not really good. Well, maybe good.

A: How could it be good in a way?

M: Well, if it tells me something good, it likes me and cares about me.

A: That's an interesting point.

M: I never thought about it that way, but it sometimes says, like, good things. It still doesn't make me feel good, but sometimes I smile when it tells me something good.

A: Does the smile give a happy feeling?

M: Maybe, like, a little happy. Like my father is showing or telling me I did something good.

A: Like he's interested in you?

M: Sometimes, like it shows he cares about me and maybe it makes me feel a little good.

A: Sometimes it's, like, a little good?

M: It's better without the voices, but it could be a little bit that it tells me good things. Sometimes I think, like maybe it's telling me like I'm important.

A: It's interested in you and it's special for you?

M: Even if it's not real, it's like real and it's interested in me.

A: Sometimes it's with you?

M: Yes, like it can make me feel I'm not alone, that somebody cares about me.

A: It cares about you?

M: Sometimes in a good way. It's not only always telling me bad things; it can mean good things too. I never really thought about it in a good way, but it could be good sometimes, a little bit.

A: So you said it can make you feel not alone and sometimes tells you good things?

M: Yes, it can be that way.

A: Maybe we can talk about this more next time. It is interesting that you can now see a good side to the voices.

M: Alright.

I think that the reader will easily agree that the most striking repetitive theme in the above dia-logic dialogue is the process of normal or normalizing mysticism in the sense that gradual increasing legitimation was given to the pleasant, encouraging side of hearing voices. By making space for a dia-logic (alternating, complementing) meaning of heard voices, one may notice further how M. was able to admit that in fact they often made him feel less lonely as well as important and loved (''somebody cares about me'').

A few months later M. seemed to be able to maintain an increasing control over these voices by learning to argue, talk back, and legitimize the strengthening effect available in the dialogue with the mystic voice of the dead father.

A: Good evening.

M: Good evening. I was feeling maybe a little better but then the voices started again. It wasn't any different; noises like ''zmmm and nm.''

A: It bothered you a lot?

M: Yes, even when it's good things like telling me I walk nicely or that I'm smart. Why does it have to come? It makes me different and that isn't good. It's better to be regular.

A: You said it often sounds like your father.

M: Yes, usually. Sometimes it can sound like maybe my brother or brothers-in-law.

A: Did you ever talk back or answer the voices?

M: Not really. The voices aren't real. How can I talk back to them?

A: The voices tell you things. You can respond to them.

M: But my father is dead.

A: Yes, but you seem to say sometimes that he is still close to you. Like he's telling you things.

M: Yes.

A: Did you ever try to talk to him at the cemetery?

M: I came after the funeral, and they were already sitting *shiva* [seven days of mourning]. After the *shiva* I went to the cemetery and then another time and a third time at the *shloshim* [mourning ceremony after 30 days] when we put up a stone. I didn't like to talk to him—well, sort of I did. Like he should be a good advocate (*meilitz yosher*) for me. I thought like he is in paradise (*gan eden*), and I wanted to know exactly where he is. Maybe he is near the angel (*malach*); that would be good. When I was at the cemetery I also went to the old Sattemer Rebbe's [Hasidic leader's] grave.

At my father's grave I asked for forgiveness (*mechila*). Like if I ever wronged him he should forgive me.

A: For what sort of things?

M: Well, if I ever said bad things to him, like if the voices say to me "damn him" (*yemach shemo*), so I answer back "damn him," and maybe once I yelled at him and said I wanted to kill him. I was young, maybe ten years old, and he shouted at me and said he wanted to change my school and I should come back to Williamsburg after being with my sister for four years in Monsey. I remember only that it was good in Monsey and I didn't want to leave. I shouted at my father, "I'll kill you!" Maybe I could burn in hell for that.

So at his grave I asked for forgiveness.

In the last years he was sick and in bed or a wheelchair and he didn't yell at me so much. At his grave and at the Sattemer's grave I also asked that someday I should have a good *shiduch* [arranged marital match].

A: It's acceptable to talk at the graveside?

M: Yes.

It is quite acceptable especially in religious circles to ask forgiveness, health, and blessings from a dead parent. But it is important to point out here that by being a psychiatric patient for about ten years, M. was trained like most Western schizophrenics to consider the hearing of voices only as a symptom of the illogical thinking characterizing the psychotic state of mental illness. His religious Hasidic background appears instrumental, however, in his learning to reinterpret the mystic voices into concretizing, strengthening terms, as seems evident in the following excerpt.

M: Today I heard a voice. It sounded like my father. It said: "I will lift up mine eyes unto the hills, From whence cometh my help; my help cometh from the Lord who made heaven and earth."

A: From *Tehilim—Shir Hamalot* [Psalms 121:1-2].

M: Yes, I think so.

A: What did it mean?

M: It means like the Almighty takes care of me. He is all over. Wherever you go to look he is there.

A: What kind of a feeling did it leave you with?

M: Sort of a good feeling, like I have *hashgocho* [guidance, protection] and am being taken care of. It even made me smile a little.

A: It's a big message for you from far away—as though you'd looked to the faraway hills.

M: Yes, like from my father; he's dead but he is, like, telling me things still. It's better not to hear the voices but sometimes like this it's good.

A: Does it mean that the Almighty is always watching over you?

M: I think so.

A: Is this only good.

M: What do you mean?

A: Is it only good for you? Does He see everything?

M: It's only good for me, but maybe it's not so good he sees sometimes—not good things; but it made me feel good.

A: Do you chant Psalms much?

M: Sometimes.

A: Sometimes, you can see in the words the feelings of a troubled person?

M: I guess so; but in that *posuk* [passage], it gave me a hopeful feeling. Like once I thought that in the morning prayer "He who always renews with His goodness the deeds of Genesis" like it gives hope.

A: Do you mean every day is a new day?

M: Yes, maybe even every second.

A: So you can always start again?

M: I don't know from the beginning, but everything each day is like new.

A: You can see it in a new way?

M: Maybe so. The voices about becoming a *goy* (gentile] didn't come again, so maybe now I'm a little better.

I have overburdened the reader with texts reporting the dialogues between the reader A., who may be termed now the psychonarrator because he introjects narrative remarks into M.'s script, and M., the patient and writer, to elucidate how through mutual contraction the dia-logic alternation between the logic and the mystic thought systems was used to transform the hearing of voices into pleasant, "de-lonelyizing" communicative forces that M. learned to produce and use.[10] I could indulge further in this dia-logic text to show how M. was able to carry over the energy gained from his inner dialogue with the voices to the interpersonal level of communication. Thus, M. learned first to argue with his brother's voice, then to "fight" it out and settle things with his roommate, and later he was able to acquire a *chavruto* (companion) for everyday learning. More importantly, however, the case of M. illustrates how a dia-logic, open approach to such concepts as the *bat kol* (daughter of a heavenly voice), discussed earlier, may be used in practice for normalizing a mystic-schizophrenic experience. Thus, having a "book" that permits one to conceive the hearing of a voice either as a divine *bat kol* or as an inner normal echo, in terms of a discourse with oneself or with an alter ("another"), diminishes the threat of excommunicating and stigmatizing as damned psychotics those people who hear voices.

Returning to our discussion of Derrida's concept of grafting, the above text illuminates also how a consensus of what is important, central, and hence true is challenged. That is to say, although according to Western pragmatic logocentrism truth is established by consensus[11] and convention that determines that whatever is validated by a specific method is true, whereas truisms derived via other means are excluded, our text shows how the marginal mystic text may contribute to a different or even broader understanding of truth if one includes the phenomenological reading of the irrational-mystic as part of the text comprising the experience of truth. If, thus, scholars adhering to the historical method centralize primary sources while marginizing or excluding secondary sources (see Introduction) because they are interested only in what they believe to be the original truth of the text's author, then still the phenomenological impact of secondary sources might produce a different yet widely accepted truth to which these historians may be quite oblivious. Moreover, since most ordinary people do not read the original Greek text of Plato and since most people depend on secondary interpretive sources to understand the complex primary texts of such writers as Heidegger or Lacan, a definition of truth would be possible only within a culture producing a metacode that legitimizes a dia-logic reading of primary and secondary sources.

Accordingly, if deconstruction is interested, as Culler (1987) suggested, "in what has been excluded . . . to keep alive the possibility that the eccentricity of women, poets, prophets and madmen might yield truths about the system to which they are marginal" (pp. 153-154), then recomposing may be understood as a therapeutic reading-writing method for producing a dia-logic (alternating) truth by incorporating and assigning the irrational, mystic *sod* the same communicative power of therapeutic truth as is usually assigned to rational *peshat*, as demonstrated in the case of Mr. M.

But are we talking only about the dia-logic possibility of *alternating* between the two thought systems, intellectual *peshat* and mystical *sod*, or are they to complement and *supplement* each other? Whereas the first interpretation of dia-logic recomposing assumes a structural rearranging play by which one thought system is contracted for the sake of expanding the other, a dia-logic definition of recomposing in supplementary terms would entail the possibility of growth and progress that goes beyond the original structure of the text. Let us scrutinize this possibility via another clinical case.

THE "PSYCHOTIC" METACODE FOR THERAPEUTIC GROWTH

I have said that if deconstructive reading gives the marginal, irrational, or secondary text the power of communication, not by destroying dialectically the rational and/or primary source of the text, but by maintaining a dialogue between them, then recomposing may entail also the possibility of therapeutic growth and progress. That is, if critical secondary reading does not replace the previous primary text, a combined *al-tikrei* reading of two versions of the text should enrich the text in a developmental sense.

In his critical reading of Foucault's *History of Madness,* Derrida (1978: 33) commits himself first to "follow as faithfully as possible Foucault's intentions in reinscribing an interpretation of the Cartesian Cogito" before offering his own interpretive reading of those texts. Accordingly, we would say that Derrida uses a dia-logic (*al-tikrei*) reading metacode, which attempts to present both the primary and the secondary interpretations of a text.

Nonetheless, from Derrida's deconstructive reading we still do not know whether Derrida's readers perceive his interpretations as a broadening, expanding understanding of Foucault's and Descartes's texts or as a new, substitutive understanding of truth. Thus, it is again therapeutic recomposing that can demonstrate how the inclusion of a mystical or a secondary interpretation of a text broadens the perception of truth and enhances the possibility of growth and progress because the therapeutic reading of the text includes the writer's response. However, if therapeutic recomposing is to include not only the author's response to the reader's interpretation but also the cultural echo to the new melodic reading of one's biography, how are we to assess this cultural echo? The question here is whether recomposing is interpersonal in the sense that it must consider also the dia-logic relationship that evolves between the text and its living context, between a critical reading and its readers in a specific social milieu. Here we come back to the concept of social key or metacode, introduced earlier. To assess properly the impact of a specific reading we need to identify cultural linguistic keys or metacodes that facilitate the dia-logic reading in terms of intrapersonal and mainly interpersonal growth possibilities.

Thus, in order to demonstrate how the mystic (*sod*) reading nourishes the intellectual (*peshat*) reading of a text, we should first introduce a socio-religious metacode that possibly nurtured such a dia-logic reading of texts and lives. This metacode for reading reality through the combined double spectacles of rationalism and mysticism may be identified, as I have often indicated, in many facets of the Jewish *PaRDeS* socialization system.

From early childhood the Jew is trained to repeat three times daily the biblical verse of "*Shema Yisrael*" ("Hear, O Israel . . ."): "And thou shalt love the Lord thy God with all thy heart and with all thy soul and with all thy might. . . . And thou shalt teach them diligently unto thy children" (Deut. 6:5-6). Thus, the ordinary Jew is exposed since childhood to what could be termed the two linguistic structures of compassionate "loving with the heart" and of scholastic "teaching" through the brain. Indeed, from time immemorial to this day one could find this ordinary Jew in the synagogue either listening to sermons (*derashot*) delivered by preachers (*darshanim*) or studying by himself multiple commentaries of the Scripture,[12] which include both Maimonides's kind of rational-philosophical explications of biblical verses and Nachmanides's style of cabalistic-mystic interpretations of the Torah.

This hermeneutic orientation may, of course, be understood as an either/or system because prima facie it allows a person to choose either the mystic or the intellectual interpretation of text and context, yet it tells us little about how this double and even contradictory[13] understanding of Scripture may affect the reader psychologically. We may assume, however, as alluded to above, that our understanding of the text as a metacode for our living contexts may expand if the irrational and the rational *al-tikrei* readings of a reality are to enrich and nourish each other rather than be used as two alternative orientations. Our Aristotelian-Socratic problem of establishing truth in a cultural sense may be illuminated by using two popular anecdotes. One is about a woman who is told blatantly by a psychiatrist that after examining her he finds her to be crazy. However, when the woman insisted on her right to obtain a second opinion, this psychiatrist added that he finds her also to be ugly! The second anecdote is about a matchmaker who tried to convince a young man that besides being a little pregnant, the potential bride he offered him is perfect! Whereas pregnancy must be established via an Aristotelian either/or metacode of truth, the tacit metacode encompassed in the first anecdote might insinuate that one cannot be irrational-crazy and beautiful all at the same time. In other words, it is only a dia-logic (*al-tikrei*) metacode that can teach people to perceive the possibility of being an ugly rationalist or a crazy, beautiful utopist. To be sure, what we are seeking now is to identify an example of a religiocultural metacode that trains people to perceive the mystic-irrational apprehension of texts and contexts as forces that nurture the concrete-rational explanations of texts, or vice versa.

Indeed, one finds in early Jewish midrashic sources that God first considered creating the world with a capacity only for rigorous judgment (*midat hadin*) and that not until later did He decide to let the world function by *combining* the attributes of rigorous, rational judgment (*din*) with the attributes of irrational emotionalism and mercy (*rachamim*) (see *Genesis Rabba* 12:15). According to the major cabalistic text, the book of *Zohar*, the rational quality of rigorous or stern judgment (*midat hadin*) is pictured on God's left side while God's quality of love, mercy, or compassion (*midat harachamim*) is aligned on His right side. However, the state of redemption, which from our perspective may be conceived as a realization of therapeutic growth and social progress, is symbolized through the idea that the right side will eventually contain the left side (see Wolfson, 1986). Thus, the possibility of therapeutic progress, in terms of the ideal state of redemption, may be attained by combining the mystical and rational approaches, which are to contain or nurture each other rather than function as two alternatives.

In Chapter 2 I have shown how the midrashic metacode of *al-tikrei* (don't read it thus, but read it *thus*) provides the guide for therapeutic progress by demonstrating how a secondary narrative reading of a text (*derash*) may be added to the understanding of one's true psychological reality derived merely from reading the primary rational text (*peshat*). This complementing, dia-logic relationship between the written Torah (*peshat*) and the oral Torah (*derash*), which constitutes the *PaRDeS* system of hermeneutic pluralism, could now be compared to the way Derrida (1976) portrays Plato's and Rousseau's conceptions of writing as a *supplementary* form of speech. Thus, along with Plato's condemnation of writing as a finite, tyrannic form of communication that distorts the infinite form of oral speech, we have seen in previous chapters how in the therapeutic oral form of midrashic communication the speaker and author of his biographic text gains an expanded conception of his reality because of his ability to refute or dispute with the reader-listener-therapist the primary reading (*peshat*) of his lifestory. Although the presentation of oral speech (*derash*) as an expansion of the written word (*peshat*) somehow reverses Rousseau's concept of writing as a supplement to speech, in both models there are no specifications about the ways the mystic-irrational form of speech or reading is to supplement or nourish the rational primary text.[14]

However, a metacode for using the mystic-irrational "craziness" to strengthen and nurture the concrete-rational "prettiness" that seems applicable to therapeutic growth is, quite surprisingly, articulated by both a rational philosopher like Maimonides and by leading ecstatic cabalists like Abraham Abulafia and Isaac of Acre. This dia-logic coexistence indeed concurs with our therapeutic interpretation of the *PaRDeS* system. Idel (1988b: 74) in his study of the mystical experiences of Abraham Abulafia asserts that the ecstatic thought system of this thirteenth-century cabalist was dominated by the concepts of intellect and imagination. Thus, in his attempt to intepret his personal experiences of vision in terms of the possibility of prophecy, Abulafia followed Maimonides, who believed that "prophecy is impossible without the imaginative faculty through which the flow of the intellect is transformed into visual images and sounds."

It is of great interest within the present context to stress that the twelfth-century Maimonides, who is considered *the* most rational philosopher in Jewish history, depicts the possibility of attaining the desired state of prophecy through what would be today termed epileptic or psychotic experiences. Thus, upon describing the process of becoming a magician, Maimonides states in *The Book of Commandments* cited by Idel (ibid.) that

> it is impossible for those possessing these imaginative powers not to perform one of those acts by which this power is actualized and brought to light. And among these are those who strike upon the ground many times with a stick which is in their hand, or scream out in strange cries and abandon their thoughts and gaze at the earth a long time until they find it, as in the matter of falling sickness, and will relate what is to occur in the future.

While the above descriptive procedure for becoming a magician contains a clear admission (though not an approval) in regard to the causal connection between psychotic ecstasy and prophecy, elsewhere Maimonides (*Yesodey Hatora* 7:2) relates unequivocally that "the prophets are on different levels . . . and. . . while they prophesize, their limbs shake and the power of the body fails and their faculties become crazy and the mind is clear to understand what it envisions."

The dia-logic idea that these psychotic imaginative or rather mystic emotional experiences are to nourish and strengthen the intellect, rather than be dialectically replaced by the latter, is then developed by Abulafia, who frequently uses the metaphor of the rider to elucidate this metacode. Thus, contends Abulafia (1580), if one attains ecstasy through "the fire of desire . . . and his intellect is stronger than his imagination, he rides upon it as one who rides upon his horse and guides it by hitting it . . . to make it stand in the place where his intellect will wish" (quoted by Idel, 1988b: 143).

To be sure, this *dia-logic pardesian* metacode, according to which the mystic schizophrenic or imaginative powers are to nurture and strengthen the intellect, differs from the *dialectic* metacode, according to which rational consciousness is to replace the irrational subconscious or according to which the latter force of desire is to be transformed or sublimated into an intellectual power. Thus, in the *al-tikrei* metacode "mad can be beautiful!" Indeed, the absence of asceticism[15] from Jewish ecstatic mysticism may be understood here in terms of a dia-logic metacode because it portrays the imaginative, sensual forces as strengthening devices for spiritual, intellectual growth. Thus, Idel (ibid.) contends that

> radical asceticism is a widely used method for attaining ecstatic states in many mystical systems, the purpose of such afflictions being to weaken the power of the body or of matter to enable the intellect to act without interference. Such an approach is widespread in Neo-Platonic literature, in which matter is understood as evil in its very essence; a struggle was carried on between the intellect and the body, and at times between the intellect and the soul, which is portrayed as the representative of the bodily powers. As Abulafia understood man's inner struggle as taking place between the intellect and the imagination, one cannot find in his writings extreme ascetic instructions necessary for one who seeks to attain

"prophecy." His approach is rather that, in order to attain "prophecy," one must act in the direction of strengthening the intellect rather than that of suppressing the body, the soul, or the imagination.

A most radical imaginative force that permeates Abulafia's texts and cabalistic literature in general expounds how erotic images may strengthen the intellectual faculties. Indeed, Idel (1988b: 185-186) cites a text that uses the image of intercourse to explain that in regard to

> the nature of prophecy . . . the human mind has not the power to apprehend . . . until it is attached to the Divine intellect, in a connection similar to that of the body and the soul, or the connection of form and matter, similar to the union of male and female, the best and sweetest of which is the first—that is, a virgin groom with a virgin bride. . . . At the time of their union they attain the pinnacle of their desire . . . and the movement of their desire is from then on a calm one . . . neither excessively rapid nor excessively slow, but as fitting: and after the two minds settle on one matter . . . they will attempt to guide their actions with the intention of impregnation. . . . The matter of those who seek out "prophecy," . . . is similar to what I have said concerning . . . the groom and bride.

In another text cited frequently in the name of the late thirteenth-century cabalist Isaac of Acre (see Piekarz, 1978), the image of carnal desire is portrayed as a major source of energy for spiritual desire. Rabbi Isaac of Acre is thus quoted as having used the tale about a street-corner idler whose passion for a princess whom he saw coming out of the bathhouse turned into spiritual passion, in order to inculcate the metaphor of carnality as a metacode of energizing spirituality.[16] Indeed, his aphorism declaring that "a person who does not desire a woman is lower than a donkey" (p. 209) became a slogan designed to signify how sensuality is to nurture spirituality.

Now since testimonies of personal ecstatic experiences, which are quite rare in Jewish mysticism (see Idel, 1988b: 77), at best describe the emotional state of the practical mysticist but not how it affected his rational powers of the intellect, it is again the therapeutic text that can teach us how such psychotic experiences and/or erotic imaginations may be used to strengthen and nourish one's intellectual functioning and not only replace them. Here is an illustrative dialogue between our psychonarrator, N., and the author-patient, E.

THE PSYCHOTIC-EROTIC ENERGY OF MR. E.

Mr. E. is an Israeli male lawyer with a European middle-class background who was 32 years old when he began his intensive treatment in our dia-logo workshop. In addition to his legal training, he acquired a B.A. degree in psychology and philosophy. While preparing for his bar exams Mr. E. began to consume about six or seven valium tablets per night to reduce strain. He had been divorced for the past ten years and ever since had been under the care of psychiatrists who "did not understand him" and who disregarded the problem of drug addiction. He had experienced delusions and aspired to be a spy in the Israeli Mosad (secret intelligence agency) but instead was hospitalized for two months in a *mosad* (in Hebrew the word *mosad* also signifies a "total institution," such as a mental hospital).

When Mr. E. began his dia-logic treatment, he was depressed, suicidal, out of a job, very sarcastic, and skeptical about his chances to be normal once again because a psychologist had once told him that he would never cease to be schizophrenic. He told N., his psychonarrator, that he is corresponding with a dead person, and he incessantly interrogated N. about various medical symptoms of mental illness he read about.

It was our feeling that the "dead person" referred to the normal, logical lawyer he once had been and who was dead now because he had entered the forbidden rose garden of the schizophrenics, from which there is no return. It also became gradually apparent that after having tasted the wild, free, schizophrenic fruits growing in the excluded "rose garden" of creativity and unreason, he lacked the energy and desire to return to the legal land of reason where his parents resided. This burned bridge, between living in the central, rational world of *uptight* lawyers and the *tieless* land of irrational creativity, which he mentioned time and again, was thus the first target for our dia-logic attempts. The following is a typical statement from E. about the impossibility to shake schizophrenia, after which N. asked E. to maintain a dialogue between the old (normal lawyer) E. and the new (psychotic) E.

E: I'll never be well. Don't you see? A person who's been beyond the edge will never be a person again. He's seen it. He's seen the horror.

N: It depends on what happens afterward. It can sometimes be a necessary learning experience. I'd like you to try and have a dialogue between these two parts. It's not acting, . . . it's kind of connecting those parts of yourself, having them talk to each other.

E: O.K. [reacting out of a sense of compliance] . . .

(Old): You are the ruins of the noblest man.

(New): Oh . . . What the hell!

(Old): You were burnt for glory.

(New): You're dead!

(Old): I don't know you any more.

(New): What can I do, brother? That's the way I am. I ain't happy [all said with a lot of painful affect]. I am experiencing hell because I don't know what's the right rhythm of life. What's the state of mind, that's the question of questions. The state of mind a person should have. Once I knew. Now I suffer. Don't judge me. It's a matter of sickness, not useless. That's it.

N: Good. Do you often find yourself having that inner dialogue?

E: Yes.

N: Confusion?

E: [Starts to sing.]

N: You couldn't be open, crazy with your family?

E: They wouldn't allow it. In fact, you are the only one where I speak like this.

N: I think that's one of the values of what we're doing.

E: That I'm making a fool out of myself?

N: Not at all. That you're able to be yourself . . . or express different parts of yourself and learn how to relate to those different parts. You're very judgmental of yourself.

E: I do a lot of watching, listening. I don't do much. I hold back.

From these kind of inner dialogues we ascertained our assumptions that the "dead" person was the old lawyer E. and that his family would not accept the new "crazy" E., who actually enjoyed singing and acting out fantasies.

Our next dia-logic goal was not only to legitimize and centralize the "crazy" E. while also grafting and reviving the "dead" E. but also to use these irrational energies as new, creative, strengthening powers for communicating with the rational lawyer. Our psychonarrator N. thus encouraged E. to accept a job as a lawyer, which he did. However, the bizarre, sexual-pervertive experiences or fantasies about which E. concomitantly reported first bedazzled N. because, given his own Western background, he expected E. to speak once again in the logical, legal language of lawyers. When we decided to interpret E.'s fantastic or fantasized erotic experiences as positive-creative energizers for his spiritual growth, it seemed not only to attenuate his previous tantalizing Waspy either/or conception of life but also to enable him to maintain his job as a lawyer and finally develop a more "normal" relationship with a woman. If thus E. would brag that he never had so many women making passes at him or if he would tell N., as he once did, that a woman who works in the government and earns 1,500 Israeli shekels per month "made a sexual offer to turn him on in the perverted manner he likes," N. was urged to interpret these experiences as evidence for the new life, love, and spirituality that arose in him. Indeed, after several months of steady work, when E. told N. that he had a new girlfriend who was a medical student, he stated spontaneously: "I'm now at a different level—not only sexual; something spiritual. We can talk. . . . Can you believe that she has a medical problem and can't do it in the [perverted] way." And when N. said that evidently there is a God in heaven (because he is now forced into a nonpervertive phase of spirituality), E. responded, "That is the proof of it, isn't it?"

True, E.'s deterministic feelings, according to which someone like him who was once a schizophrenic will always be a schizophrenic, persisted and kept coming up in his dialogues with the psychonarrator N. for a long time;

and his delusions about being a spy for the Israeli Mosad did not evaporate either. It seems, however, that precisely such a therapeutic text validates what happens in the intersection between the literary text and its literal context. Does the imaginative power, be it erotic or psychotic, obstruct the intellect's growth? Has it been dialectically transformed into an intellectual-spiritual force, or do the "imaginative," mystic forces of *sod* strengthen the intellect of rational *peshat* by coexisting dia-logically with it?

It is hence only the empirical fact that E. not only kept his job, received a raise in salary, and aspired to eventually becoming a judge, while being able to control his psychotic thoughts, that may enlighten us about the phenomenological state of affairs prevailing between the intellectual and the imaginative power presumed to strengthen it. Consequently, it is also such therapeutic discourses between N. and E. that may verify the ontological validity of such conclusive extrapolations derived usually from declarative rather than from phenomenological texts when Idel (1988b: 113) states, for example, that a certain "passage epitomizes Abulafia's awareness of the need to connect between the intellect and the imagination— that is, to bring the intellect to rule over the imagination." Indeed, it was E.'s eventual spontaneous assertion that his "psychotic thoughts aren't really psychotic because they don't go up in my head. I don't act accordingly" that may thus demonstrate the presumed possible relationship between text and context—that is, between the intellect that is to rule over the imagination that strengthened it.

It remains, nevertheless, an open empirical question whether the new recomposed melody of Mr. E.'s life—or of anyone else's life—will eventually concord with his social echo or discord with the musical metacode of his cultural milieu. It is apparently easier to tame individuals than to reframe their societies.

NOTES

1. For the psychologically oriented reader I find it appropriate to point out here that I am not oblivious to the professional tradition of discussing in psychopathic terms the "robbing hood" killers' lack of remorse. This psychiatric "bastard" term has been eliminated from the official mental health nomenclature, although it has been continuously used under the counter as a wastebasket category to refer to incorrigible criminals. I have nonetheless studied and described this phenomenon elsewhere (see Rotenberg, 1978) in the reconceptualized term *differential insensitivity* to refer to behaviors fostered via a desensitization process in various normal sections of the population. From this perspective there might be no qualitative difference between the nurse's and the killer's insensitivity at the sight of a corpse; however, a discussion of the moral distinction between the two is beyond the present interest.

2. The most important findings related to the lateralization of the cerebral hemispheres are usually those deduced from research with animals and humans who

had their corpus callosum and anterior commissure sectioned to prevent the interhemispheric spread of epilepsy. According to these studies the left hemisphere was indeed found to produce speech and rational-analytic thought that processes temporal units, and it was claimed that the holistic right hemisphere organized the spatial, tonal, and other sensual and affective percepts, including those that constitute the emotions. Although this neurophysiological research orientation is beyond the scope of the present perspective, the problem of drastic and dangerous switching between a mystic and a rational orientation to life, which I have discussed at some length previously (see Rotenberg, 1987) is relevant also to the present dia-logic model for the psychotherapeutic reading of experiences in emotional-mystical or rational-material terms.

3. Although the present orientation maintains a close affinity with therapeutic formulations offered by humanistic and existential psychologists, it is set out to examine possibilities for balancing spiritual-material forces via the dia-logic interchange between the rational-material (*peshat*) and the mystical-spiritual (*sod*) thought systems rather than by an either/or blocking of one linguistic hemisphere, as phrased, for instance, by Paul Watzlawick (1978).

4. Here is the place to stress that my critical comment on the futility of reframing without considering the cultural framework is intended to reexpose, as I have often done before, American hopeless ethnocentricity. Accordingly, psychotherapeutic reframing or its commercialized school (see Bandler & Grinder, 1982) known under the heading of Neuro-Linguistic Programming (NLP) appears to entail clever and efficient techniques for reinterpreting disturbing life events that might work for Californians, but it is highly questionable whether such situational-existential reframings mean anything to Iranian Shiites or even to Mexicans. While this is not intended to impute to American "reframers" the use of uncanny syllogisms, I would like to stress that keen rehabilitation of identities impinges upon the cultural context of total biographies.

5. In addition to the melodic and cultural echo the term *recomposing* contains, it is the *de* in the term *deconstruction* that seems to sound disharmoniously to the ear that is sensitive to therapeutic texts. It is thus acknowledged here that the replacing of the *de* with a *re* (in *re*composing) is due only to semantic sensitivity. However, deconstruction per se is certainly not a destructive process of decomposing but rather a very creative philosophy of rereading.

6. The cabalistic ideal of de-egoistic contraction, which is derived from the process of recombining the letters of the Hebrew word *ani* (I) to form the word *ain* (naught), is but one example of a rich tradition embedded in Jewish mystic belief. Accordingly, the letters that constitute the Torah were purposely not divided into words (presumably, in the ancient Hebrew text there is no word spacing or punctuation) so that people might infinitely recombine them into new words in order to always find new meanings and endless ways to interpret the Scripture.

7. In essence, most Jewish sources claim also that in the process of creation, matter preceded spirit. But matter, for that matter, was never seen as superior to spirit. The Hasidic literature is permeated with multiple dicta instructing, for example, how to transform matter into spirit (see *Yaacov Yoseph*, 1963).

8. In our dia-logo therapy workshop, mentioned in my preface to this book, we used the cabalistic notion of contraction so that people were helped to make space for including their schizophrenic-mystic thought system in their biographic texts by contracting the rational reading of their life events.

9. It is only proper to point out here that this normalization of schizophrenic mysticism has been advocated also by Laing (1967), Sarbin (1969), and others. Laing argued, for instance, that according to his existential diagnosis, understanding why a person would see himself as nonexisting or as part of a machine creates a bond between doctor and patient that normalizes the patient, since these two people are not qualitatively different because the doctor, also, has good reasons to feel sometimes as if he does not exist. Similarly, contends Sarbin, when a person labels himself Napoleon, he engages in "attention redeployment" in order to reduce strain, as most people do at one time or another. Indeed, Sarbin (1967) cites a case of an elderly spinster whose hearing of voices was normalized after she admitted that she actually recalled a voice of a man she had loved 30 years ago in order to deploy attention from her present feeling of loneliness.

10. K. Stewart (1969) has shown, for example, that in some Eastern societies, such as the Senoy of Malaya, children are taught to control their periodic dreams of falling into an abyss, by learning to transform the dream of falling into a dream of flying, which they control and enjoy.

11. Indeed, it is a great question whether in some instances academic methodological consensus, which provides for its adherents the safe feeling of "insiders," does not in fact produce a covenant of mediocrity by which creativity is excluded and progress is hindered for the sake of collective self-protection.

12. Elsewhere (Rotenberg, 1987) I have demonstrated how this midrashic system, according to which there are "seventy faces" (ways) to interpret the Torah, in fact creates a multiple hermeneutic circle diametrically opposed to any fundamentalistic mode of interpreting the Scripture.

13. The midrashic idea of hermeneutic choice may be identified also in its trend to propose contradictory interpretations for one biblical passage (see Rotenberg, 1983, 1987).

14. The interrelationship between the rational and the irrational, which is to nourish the rational, was also formulated by Rabbi Nachman of Bratzlav, the great grandson of the Baal Shem Tov, the founder of the eighteenth-century Hasidic movement. The "engulfing" intuitive mind that encircles one's head entails, accordingly, a Bergsonian element of creativity that is to nurture the rational "inner mind" (see Weiss, 1974), which has indeed penetrated one's inner mind by being processed through the criterion of logical consistency. Within the present context it may, however, be useful to differentiate between the intuitive, semirational mind and the irrational, mystic-schizophrenic thought discussed here.

15. The very fact that Nazarites were considered sinners according to Jewish law (Numbers 6:11), is an illustrative testimony to the way asceticism was essentially condemned by the Jewish sages (see Urbach, 1971). By contrast, in Christianity one may become a monk or reach the state of sainthood only by subjugating the body, which is the seat of evil and the root of carnal corruption (see Porter, 1902).

16. Although it is unclear whether Isaac of Acre's metaphor of carnality should be understood as a libidinal energy that might be transformed or sublimated into mystic spirituality or rather nourish it on an ongoing basis, Abulafia's erotic image of the impregnating intercourse touches upon a religious dilemma. Namely, how can a person use the intercourse image as a device for "strengthening the intellect" without violating the talmudic dictum that teaches "Contemplating transgression is worse than [committing] transgression" (*Yuma* 29:a)?

8

Derush: The Pivot for Re-biographing and Pre-biographing

Derush is the narrative element that occupies the axial role in the *PaRDeS* multiple hermeneutic pendulum. As such, it regulates one's intrapersonal and interpersonal fluctuations between choosing a rational-realistic interpretation of life as *peshat* or the irrational-mystic understanding of *sod.*

The word *narrative* is defined in dictionaries, as C. G. Prado (1986: 23) asserts, "in terms of the recounting of a sequence of events." Thus, as a recounting story-telling method, narration operates on the intrapersonal level of time because we recount or organize sequentially rational and/or irrational experiences or events that did occur in the past or that we hope will happen in the future. As a story-telling activity it also functions, however, on the interpersonal level of space because, after all, we tell stories to other people. Psychologically, narration becomes, then, a major tool for adjusting ourselves to the changing world surrounding us. Indeed, Prado (1986: 36) observes that

> one of the first things we must notice is that some narratives work and others do not. We constantly adjust our stories in light of new experiences. We seem quickly to come to feel that things will go well with us only if we get our narrative *right*, only if they match something external to them. We are, in other words, launched on the search of truth, for correspondence between our narratives and a putative reality.

Before we tackle the apparent contradiction between our "need to adjust our stories" and our "search of truth," let us consider Prado's assertion that narration as an adjustment tool seems to integrate or hold together our fantasies with our concrete reality. Accordingly, narration may be conceived not only as a method for *describing* one's past but also as an instrument for *prescribing* our future. In other words, narration embellishes and enriches our gloomy reality by providing some fresh breathing air and living colors for our grey life events. Consequently, it follows that if the narrative *derush* is the pivot that bridges between rational *peshat* and mystic *sod*, then the art of re-biographing and pre-biographing is its axis. After all, it is our own lifestory that we need to tell and retell to ourselves and to others in order to make it in this world. But how do we search for truth by adjusting our lifestories? How may facts and fictions relate as a packaged (self-contradictory?) combination to our physical and our metaphysical world all at once?

I shall deal first with the problem of narrative *derush* and its relationship to rationality and truth and then address myself to the possibility of narrative re-biographing as a pivotal element in the *PaRDeS* therapy system.

THE NARRATIVE BETWEEN THE RATIONAL AND THE NONRATIONAL

What is the relationship between rationalism, truth, and realism? Alibis may elucidate the possibility of rational *lies* while narrational *ties* (connecting events) may be realistic if they help to recount experiences.[1] Our excursion into or excavation of the nature of narrativism, which I claim pivotizes and epitomizes the *PaRDeS* therapy system, might well begin by defining the concept of *derush*. What is the phenomenological meaning of the word *midrash?* The term, which is derived from the Hebrew word *darash* (searched, derived, interpreted) is a verb, that is, a function or activity; a noun, referring to biblical and talmudical expositions; and an institution, referring to the *beit hamidrash* (house or school) where the actual work of studying or interpreting is done. As far back as the talmudic era (the first to sixth centuries), when the oral law became the normative vehicle for regulating the entire spiritual and terrestrial activities of Jews, a continuous need emerged to apply the Torah (the written law) to all conditions of life, with its vicissitudes and changing circumstances. This was done partly through the continuous process of lawmaking (*halacha*) and partly by midrashic expositions (see Strack, 1969: 202) that, according to Yom Tov Zunz (1974: 21), "maintains the transmitted word but at the same time changes it."

Although experts differentiate between the terms *derush, midrash,* and *derasha,* by and large the *midrash,* or *aggadah* (although these are not quite synonymous terms), refer mainly to the use of symbolic legends, stories, and parables which contain, according to Hermann Strack, two major forms: the tannaic or halachic midrashim and the homiletic midrashim. The former are more closely connected with Scripture because of their regulative, legal function, whereas the latter, which refer mostly to compiled sermons delivered in synagogues and public places during the Sabbath and festivals, allowed a more freely creative, concretizing interpretation of Scripture because its function was "to bring Heaven nearer to the congregation" (1969: 202).

Although the custom of delivering public midrashic sermons has, in practice, never ceased, the compilation of midrashim believed to be part of the transmitted oral law continued only until the eighteenth century, and there is great dispute as to how much normatively binding significance should be attributed to various later midrashim, especially to those that are moral-ethical and not halachic. However, there seems to be a more general consensus that the midrashic method, with its open-ended symbolic parables and with its legal expositions, often allowed for a dia-logical coexistence of seemingly contradictory interpretations of Scripture by relying on the talmudic dicta such as the one stating that "these and those are God's living words" (*Gittin* 6:b). In effect, the midrashic method with its constitutional paradox offers a priori divergent and often contradictory interpretations of laws and events to be used differentially according to temporally changing circumstances.

Now, should we conclude that as a multiple interpretation system that uses parables, stories, and legends to embellish perception and foster acceptation, *derush* fails to qualify as an Aristotelian establisher of truth? Should we suggest apologetically that the parabelic applies mainly to the homiletic or that midrashic pluralism should be understood as a *hermeneutic* past that must become a *hermetic* present?

Before tackling the broader problem of narrative truth, it is instructive to note at the outset that the Talmud provides clear answers in regard to both of these questions. Thus states the Jerusalemite Talmud (Sanhedrin 4:b): "Had the Torah been given as one cut [without possibilities for divergent interpretations] we could not stand on our feet. . . . It is necessary that the Torah be capable of forty-nine ways of interpretations of affirming an opinion and forty-nine ways of opposing it." While this answer settles the question of legal pluralism, we find another passage propagating the infinite seventy-faces approach of *derushic* narratology. Thus, in regard to the biblical passage "The words of the wise are as goads, and as nails well planted are the words of masters of Assemblies, which are given from one Shepherd" (Eccle. 12:2), the Talmud (Hagiga 3:a-b) offers, for example, the following interpretation: "But should you think that just as the nail diminishes and does not increase, so too the words of the Torah diminish and do not increase; therefore the text says 'well planted'; just as a plant grows and increases, so the words of the Torah increase." Accordingly, it seems that following such beliefs as "the words of the Torah increase and grow like a plant," the seventy-faces notion of finding infinite ways for interpreting the Holy Scripture according to changing needs appears prima facie to be the norm regulating apparatus of Jewish mundane life.

What we have now is a paradigmatic, multiple, open-choice-based narrative system termed *derush* or *midrash* that appears to be instrumental in helping people to adjust the text to their lives and their lives to the text.[2] But how could a narrational adjustment code justify a nonrational life mode?

Although authoritative commentators like Maimonides (1977: 15) have established that "one does not question haggadah" (*midrash,* legend), one may indeed apprehend its implications for narrative truthfulness and usefulness if one understands *derush* as a metacode for re-composing biographies.

"HUMPTY DUMPTY" AND THE CONFESSION METACODE

In the literature known as reframing therapy (Watzlawick, 1978) or paradoxical therapy (Weeks and L'Abate, 1982), and especially in what is termed cognitive therapy, emphasis is put on helping people "to change their irrational beliefs, to 'shift' their perceptions from those that are unrealistic and harmful to those that are more rational and useful" (see McMullin, 1986: XV). Thus, if a client complains, for example, that her husband said she had fat legs and she felt that her legs are indeed grotesque, she would be urged to choose one of the following alternative interpretations about the husband: "1. He's an idiot! 2. He was angry for not having dinner ready. . . . 3. He is going through his midlife crisis. . . 4. He has fat legs and he's projecting" (p. 13). In order for this woman to experience a perceptional shift by internalizing one of the alternative interpretations, she would be encouraged, we are told, to rehearse the interpretation most appealing to her so that eventually she would be able to differentiate between this new "true" interpretation by rating the others false (p. 82).

Since, admittedly, "the accuracy of the alternative interpretations is not crucial" (p. 14), the question that arises is why do such therapists train people to deceive themselves? Why make that woman believe that her husband has fat legs when in reality she might indeed possess a fat pair of legs? In answer to my queries these therapists would probably suggest that if the new belief is useful in that it is less damaging to the patient's self-esteem than is her previous interpretation, then this new belief becomes phenomenologically part of her subjective truth. Accordingly, in cognitive-reframing therapy rationality qualifies as *truthfulness* if it passes the test of *usefulness.* We could further defend the phenomenological doctrine of subjective truthfulness by positing the possibility of falseness inherent in the following anecdote.

A rich king invited a selected group of guests to a voyage on his private yacht upon the occasion of his young, beautiful only daughter's birthday. In the midst of their joyful journey, a terrible storm erupted, threatening to sink the yacht. While the sailors were busy in their strenuous attempt to save the boat, a huge wave swept the princess into the sea. The desperate king promised enormous amounts of money to anyone who would dive into the sea in order to save his princess, but no one would budge. Finally, when he declared that he would take his daughter's savior as his son-in-law and bequeath him with half his fortune, all of a sudden an elderly, short, and ugly maintenance person was seen jumping into the stormy sea, and the princess was saved by him in a most mysterious way. When eventually the king had to keep his promise in spite of himself, and envious people kept pressing the elderly man to reveal how he generated the courage for his noble act, the maintenance man was said to respond by asking, "All that I want to know is, who pushed me overboard?"

Here the objective fact, that the old man dived to save the princess, is false if one considers the subjective aspect of his intentions. Indeed, in considering the hermeneutic problem of true interpretation, John Thompson (1985: 143) states similarly that "one can imagine a case in which the act of shooting a prince could be equally . . . described as the overthrow of a monarchy, even though the assassin had no revolutionary intentions whatsoever." Hence, if the subjective intention of the old man or of the assassin determines the truth of factual events, then so-called scientific positivism seems to depend on nonscientific phenomenology more than we like to admit. And returning to our criterion of phenomenological usefulness, if the old man's or the assassin's identity changed subsequently because the objective "false" interpretation of their acts as saviors of a princess or a state created their new integrated biography, then this new reality becomes true by its consequences. Thus, cognitive reframing constitutes a *derushic* therapy system that offers a multiple choice among alternative interpretations of the text in order to adjust it to people's lives.

We may suggest, even further, that cognitive reframing encompasses a dia-logic *al-tikrei* possibility because in theory both a husband and his wife may have fat legs. But here we must insert our "Humpty Dumpty" metacode as a basis for our thesis claiming that there is essentially no difference between a personal truism based on a schizophrenic-irrational Humpty Dumpty myth, and the so-called rational-realistic cognitive lie that trains a fat-legged woman to believe that it is in fact her projecting husband who has fat legs. The Humpty Dumpty myth, or metacode, refers, as will be elaborated below, to a psychotic "disintegration anxiety" which draws on the belief that if Humpty Dumpty breaks, no one could put him together again.

To establish my thesis I shall urge my readers to drag their thin or fat legs to the biographic territory because it is, not in the fragmented reframing situation, but in the global biographical domain where people might suffer from what Heinz Kohut (1984) termed "fragmentation anxiety" about their identity. It is, consequently, only the total arena of the re-biographic and pre-biographic process that one should scrutinize in order to verify how people acquire the beliefs determining their elating or deflating feelings about their fat legs. It is because of this global nature that evolves from our effort to re-biograph our identity that I proposed the term *recomposing* as a substitute for the more technical term known as *reframing*. Recomposing, which creates a new melody out of an old tune, includes also the social echo that applauds the revived music imputed to one's new identity. Biographic recomposing as a buffer against identity fragmentation might be best understood when one considers how "political rehabilitation" is used by powerful members of society (Rotenberg, 1987).[3] It is, accordingly, from such politicians that one could learn how the "new leaf" approach offered by many therapists to ex-social failures would seem insufficient for reharmonizing one's total identity melody. Consequently, the possible styles of identity recomposing would depend largely on specific cultural or religious metacodes. Hence, if a linear original-sin metacode functions counter to people's efforts and hopes to rehabilitate their failing past, then only a sad, biographic recomposition that describes the carrying of one's guilt-cross would seem permissable.

The pivotal role of *derushic* re-biographing or recomposing as a liaison between rational *peshat* and mystic *sod* might be illuminated now by exploring first the relationship between the Humpty Dumpty metaphor with Augustine's classic confession metacode. I tend to agree with Lonnie Kliever (1986: 102) that in general "the *Confessions* of St. Augustine furnishes the paradigm for this effort to use certain life experiences as 'parables' both of the whole of a person's life and of an era's religion."

In analyzing Augustine's *Confessions* as a pioneering autobiographic metacode, Volney Gay (1986: 66-67) uses Kohut's self theory to explain how Augustine found in God the self object (significant other) he lacked in his childhood. To explicate how people might simply disintegrate if their need for loving others (self objects) remains unfulfilled, Gay uses the Humpty Dumpty myth as a preface to his thesis. He thus asserts that

> pre-Oedipal anxieties are often variations of "Humpty Dumpty." As we know, Humpty took a great fall and no one could put him together again. Kohut terms such fears fragmentation anxiety. It appears directly in the psychotic's fear of going to pieces. . . . Like castration anxiety, fragmentation anxiety defines one dimension of the human condition. Hence . . . great cultural institutions, including religion, have addressed fragmentation anxiety and in many ways contained it.

It is not necessary here to reiterate Gay's Kohutian analysis, but it is important to consider his conclusion, which is relevant to the present perspective: "Given his immense talent and culture, which seems to have offered every opportunity for self-debasement, Augustine's struggles and solutions are remarkable" (p. 69). In other words, what Gay seems to suggest is that although Augustine's parents were apparently incapable of handling Augustine's Oedipal (or pre-Oedipal) original-sin guilt feelings (p. 71), which are inevitable in a culture that conceives of childhood pleasures as sins, his ability to adopt religious figures and God Himself as his self objects surely saved him from a Humpty Dumpty disintegration. Now, although Gay's observation concerning the pre-Oedipal fragmentation anxiety is unacceptable as a generalization describing a universal phenomenon, which "defines the human condition" at large, three observations may be derived from Gay's Kohutian analysis. The first is rather general in that it suggests that if a person is unable to attain and retain a coherent biography, he might disintegrate like Humpty Dumpty. The second indicates, more specifically, that since confession as a metacode for re-biographing is idiosyncratic because it signifies by definition a Christian admission of sin or guilt, then other religions might produce different metacodes for re-biographing. The third observation implies that fictitious Humpty Dumpty stories are often being used not only as a metaphor that helps elucidate the human condition but also as a metacode that dictates the process of re-biographing.

I shall return to deal with the two first derivations but address myself presently to the relationship between fictitious myths and the presumably factual process of autobiography. I shall begin by wondering why people believe that they write what Paul Murray Kendall (1985) has termed a "pure" biography or autobiography when they use such culturally or religiously biased metacodes as Humpty Dumpty's disintegration, Job's suffering, or Don Quixote's naivete, which are by definition fictitious myths.

Here again the answer would probably be that such metaphoric stories qualify as Kendallian (1985: 13) "pure" biographies because they are "eschewing all extraneous purpose."[4] In other words, the claim would be made that since such Humpty Dumpty metaphors elucidate only the "human condition," the "purity" of the biography is not defected by a rational and culturally biased factor of fantasy. But knowing that such narrative myths are not merely metaphoric descriptions but also cultural metacodic prescriptions, we must insist that there is no qualitative difference between using Humpty Dumpty's or Don Quixote's rationalized fable for re-biographing and one's cabalistic or incarnational and hence irrational-mystic interpretation of his lifestory. In both cases the fables are being used as narrative *derushic* metacodes that help people maintain a coherent biographic identity. In both cases also the fable or parable bridges between one's explainable natural world and his unexplainable supernatural experiences. It is, consequently, in these linking terms, which bridge between the unknown world of mystic *sod* and the known world of rational *peshat*, that one should understand the axial role I assign to the *derushic* function of re-biographing in the *PaRDeS* system.

Thus, let us examine now the function of *derush* as a pivotal factor in the process of recomposing total biographies. As alluded to earlier, I am inclined to agree with Kohut (1984: 18) that the psychotic fear of identity fragmentation or "disintegration anxiety" that might possess a person "because of the unavailability of the psychological oxygen, the response of the emphatic self objects . . . is closer to what people call fear of death" than to any other adversive experience. On the basis of studies (see Yaker,

1972) showing that Western schizophrenics often suffered from a ruptured, inner linear time conception that reflected their inability to relate their present to their past and future, I have then questioned the wisdom of the therapeutic "new leaf" approach to people's future if they suffered from a failing past (see Rotenberg, 1987). I have thus claimed that while the linear original-sin metacode advocates a deterministic closed-book conception of one's failing past, the midrashic-cabalistic contraction metacode propagates an inner cyclistic time conception that allows one to re-biograph his past by contracting its failing sting in the light of his expanding corrected present.

Accordingly, if someone is raised with an unshakeable, linear Oedipal original-sin metacode, his biographic identity might disintegrate unless he adopts a confessional (self-blaming) mode for his autobiography. Comparatively, however, the "born again" or "born twice," or more simply new-leaf, paradigm for re-biographing represents in theory an identity-rupturing model that might intensify one's "disintegration anxiety." After all, a born-again, new-leaf perception of one's life requires a schizophrenic divorce from one's failing past unless one internalizes a confessional, self-blaming conception of one's total identity.[5]

To demonstrate how the midrashic paradigm might help people to reintegrate their total biographic identity, I have used such role-modeling cases as the biblical King David. As it is well known, King David was described in the Bible (2 Sam. 34) as an adulterous sinner, but the Talmud (*Shabbat* 56:a) states unequivocally that "whoever maintains that David sinned is nothing but mistaken." I have then shown that in order to convert King David's re-biographing into a re-biographic model of repentance, the Midrash takes heed to stress that David's sin was not erased but retroactively contracted or reconstructed (i.e., minimized via reinterpretation) only after he repented in a later stage in his life.[6] Studying ex-convicts, I was then able to show how those who adopted a *hermetic* conception of their past suffered from a ruptured identity whereas those who used the *hermeneutic* approach to their past were able to reintegrate their biographic identity.

In conclusion, then, in the *PaRDeS* system the narrative *derush* is indeed used as a bridge between one's realistic *peshat* and one's metaphysical experience of the unknown coming from the world of *sod*. *Derush* functions, accordingly, as a mediating or buffering service for preventing a cognitive dissonance or a rupture in the biographic identity because it connects the unreal with the real. Indeed, Prado (1986: 28) contends that according to the Platonic expectation, "it is the conformity of narratives to an extranarrational reality that gives them integrity and progressiveness." And so *derushic* narrativism as a method for "the recounting of a sequence of events" (p. 23) constitutes a *pragmatic* and *paradigmatic* metacode for ontological re-biographing that may be derived from biblical stories about role models like King David. More specifically, re-biographic contraction patterned according to King David's *derushic* role model may be used now in two ways: For those who suffer from "fragmentation anxiety" due to overexpanded feelings concerning their failing past, contraction may be used to minimize that past in light of present corrective behavior. In cases where the past is overexpanded by feelings of self-pity and complacency, King David's role-modeling contraction may be used to deflate one's *vanity* for subsequent elation of his rebalanced *sanity*. In both cases, however, King David's *derush* provides an ascent-via-descent axis for recomposing biographies.[7]

In the following, I would like hence to demonstrate how King David's contraction metacode is being used by a contemporary role model for combating identity disintegration.

THE RE-BIOGRAPHIC CONTRACTION OF REB OSHER

Jerusalem, Zafath, and other old-new religious towns in Israel are imbued with a mysterious, mystic aura that even the most sensitive and trained eye of a professional tourist will be unable to capture. In various corridors, courts, or open alleys of old or lower-class neighborhoods, rich and poor, modern and traditional, or European and Eastern, people may be seen day and night waiting for hours in an egalitarian and nonstigmatizing fashion near a dilapidated entrance to a run-down flat. Inside the besieged room or apartment there is a simple Eastern or European holy man who gives advice to people in trouble. This holy man might respond to the title rabbi and in most cases would use cabalistic ideas as recommended remedies but will, however, rarely claim to be a rabbi or a cabalist. The nature of help given by these holy men might range from common-sense advice, prescribed magic rituals, charismatic warmth, and even financial or other material assistance. Money for services is usually not collected, but donations are welcomed and received by improvised secretaries, assistants, or family members who usually take care of the waiting list. Interestingly, these holy men operate in Israel alongside and very often in collaboration with professional mental health services from all denominations.

One of the most fascinating, humble figures constituting a one-man welfare organization whose legendary 40-years-helping story awaits to be documented by a gifted author is Reb Osher. Reb Osher, who is in his eighties, and who is indeed a simple, religious man who allegedly discovered his magic ability to help people about 50 years ago, resides in an old Jerusalemite neighborhood that borders the center of ultraorthodoxy. This rather neutral location makes it accessible to people from all walks of life who wait on their feet in the open courtyard in the cold rain or in the hot sun during all hours of the day and late into the night from both sides of his old-fashioned flat with the hope that one of the two assistants might let them sneak in for a moment's glimpse or for short-sentenced advice.

Although I intend to limit my description to that of a psychological role-modeling contraction method, I owe the reader at least a telegraphic or a photographic image of Reb Osher's all-encompassing, private welfare organization. It must be those rich people, including some who cross oceans to seek help from him, who donated astronomical amounts of money to establish the organization called Yad Ezrah (A Helping Hand). These helping institutions, which are all controlled personally by Reb Osher, include medical and dental clinics, a printing press for mentally disturbed males and a sewing factory for mentally disturbed females, discount food stores, a block of apartments for cheap rental, a yeshiva plus a dormitory, an agricultural project, and a private bus service for transporting pupils (and for visiting holy graves).

It was in the beginning of the 1980s that students and friends began to whisper in my ear such statements as, "If you are really interested in *contraction* you should see Reb Osher in *action*." When a few years later I finally generated sufficient energy to begin my hunt for an interview, I was told that Reb Osher was sick (allegedly he suffered from a dislocated disc) and that I would have to try my luck by coming and waiting with the crowd because Reb Osher does not believe in prearranged appointments.

Thus, for several months I came periodically, sometimes twice or thrice a week, to wait and to observe how people received medical and psychological advice, which was sometimes delivered through one of the assistants and sometimes given directly by Reb Osher himself to those whom he accepted in person according to criteria unknown to and unquestioned by the public. As the only professor who expressed interest in his operations, I was, however, invited by one of the assistants, who would meet with me regularly in order to describe Reb Osher's activities and convey to me his philosophy. The selected assistant, Reb K., assured me that Reb Osher, who by that time knew about me, was sincerely embarrassed and sorry for constantly having to postpone our meeting because of people's pressures and his sickness.

The yearned-for meeting became more and more intriguing and challenging for me, however, the more I became convinced by Reb K.'s case descriptions and explanations that it was indeed *derushic* contraction that guided Reb Osher's life and his approach to people. For time and again Reb K. mentioned King David's personal suffering descent after his adulterous sin and his subsequent joyful ascent acquired via repentance, which he expressed in his poetic psalms and vocal harp music.

Then one day I was suddenly told that Reb Osher would see me in the late afternoon. After coming twice and waiting for two more hours, I talked with Reb Osher in a brief meeting that turned into a preface for our long interview the next day.

I would like to focus now on Reb Osher's role-modeling contraction behavior, which I witnessed during these two personal meetings. Thus, after I overheard how Reb Osher responded to businesslike and emergency telephone calls and after I observed how he gave guidance to people through the window or to those who came in crying, I was able to interview Reb Osher uninterruptedly for several hours. Reb Osher, a white-bearded, traditionally dressed old man with a beaming face and a radiating look, sat on the bed in a simply furnished room heated via an old-fashioned gasoline heater (it was mid-winter). He mocked me first by asking, "What can a professor learn from a simple person like me?" Our conversation (which I was allowed to record) was tedious and long, but since I aimed to get at the heart of Reb Osher's method, I shall report here only how I attempted to use a paradoxical technique in order to verify whether and how Reb Osher used *derushic* contraction as a role-modeling metacode for re-biographing.

I proclaimed at the outset: "Reb Osher! I have a real problem with you. Here is what is happening to me. It has now been several months since I began my hunt for an interview. Paradoxically, however, the more I wait, the more I am told to chant psalms or to come or go before or after I visit the Wailing Wall, the more I admire you not only because of the commotion around you but due to my own growing excitement and almost redemptive expectation. Is this what you want to convey to me?" Reb Osher smiled and asked if I felt like a rag (*smartut*, a nothing). He did not answer me but instead delved into a long autobiographic monologue that began somewhere a quarter of a century ago when he, a petty merchant, discovered his gifted powers to help people.

"Imagine," he said. "Once a wealthy man came to me crying that he lost all his money, which amounted to more than 900 million dollars and that he is left with the choice of committing suicide or leaving the country because the banks will ruin him, and I had the *chutzpa* [nerve] to tell him that his creditors will be afraid to touch him and that he'll get back all his money even if he stays in the country; and believe it or not, the man listened to me and became richer than before. I felt that God trusts me."

"Moreover," he went on, "once during the High Holidays I went to pray in Meyron [at the grave of a holy cabalist], and I wanted to be left alone, but a bitter woman nagged me and begged me to help her because she had tried everything but she couldn't bear children. And again, to get rid of her, I asked her how many children do you want and she answered, twelve! And I, Osher, said, 'You'll have twelve children.' This woman," exclaimed Reb Osher excitedly, "bore twelve children, no more and no less. These are facts which may be verified. Thus, how do you think I felt? I felt that God loves me. Two weeks ago, however, I got this thing in my back. First I tried to continue business as usual, but then I fell flat on my back and with that I sank into depression. I felt here is my nakedness, my nothingness. I lost all my belief in a split second because I was demobilized. Professor Rotenberg!" he screamed, "I am a *Kakker!* [full of shit]. Where is my faith? Where is my righteousness?"

And so he went on for over an hour until the urgency of pressing matters, which were waiting behind the door, brought him back to reality.

It was only days after my experiences with Reb Osher that all of a sudden it dawned on me that by contracting his achievements in an ascent-via-descent pattern, he had in fact answered my initial question. I began my interview by stating that I admired him. His response was: What is there to admire? his nothingness? his loss of faith the moment he was inflicted with the slightest uneasiness? Slowly I put the cases about which I had heard together with the cases I had observed, and they all fitted the role-modeling contraction metacode.

Thus, King David's human weakness, his adultery, which was exposed to the whole world and which therefore must have haunted him his entire life, as Reb Osher stressed repeatedly, may be seen as a role-modeling contraction descent. However, King David's ability to ascend and thank God by singing and chanting *because* he is still alive is used by Reb Osher to teach his people to descend and contract their vanity and then to ascend with joy back to life. Indeed, Reb Osher's favorite slogan used by him repeatedly in order to anchor his King David contraction metacode in the Scripture was expressed in the following way. Six times during our interview Reb Osher stressed (as did his assistant Reb K.) that only King David enjoyed the status of an everlasting King of Israel because he was the only King who ascended with joy to success and to victories from a perpetually descended (contracted) state because he always stated, "I acknowledge my transgression; and my sin is ever before me" (Psalms 51:3). Time and again Reb Osher described dramatically how King David lost no strength by including his human weakness (the adultery that was exposed to the whole world) in his biography.

When, subsequently, I asked Reb Osher's "clients" to tell me parts of their lifestories, they seemed to fit the *derushic* re-biographing pattern. Most of these people tended in a natural way to recompose their life stories by reinterpreting their *peshat* reality in mystic *sod* terms. To be sure, those people did not lose touch with reality. On the contrary, they seemed to have learned to enrich their natural world by incorporating supernatural images into these empty spaces of their biographies, which previously had comprised the basis for their "fragmentation anxiety." These people did not lie about their failing past. They did not erase or replace facts but learned to contract the known real in order to regain contact with the unknown ideal. Thus, contraction seems indeed to comprise *PaRDeS* in action.

Reb Osher's *axis mundi* contraction method may thus elucidate the possibility of *derushic* role modeling for recomposing biographies. As implicit from the above, it is not necessarily the whitewashing of the failing past that helps a person to reintegrate his identity. Reb Osher's role-modeling emulation of King David's contraction has indicated that the resonance of one's personal melody does not depend on the elimination of sad tunes from his past but only on its recomposition into a harmonious piece of music that will accord with the social milieu in which it is sounded.

As such, this identity melody, which recomposes mystic and realistic tunes into one biographic symphony, must also incorporate voices of the future.

For us to clearly see *derushic* rebiographing as a buffer against identity fragmentation, some case documentation illuminating the possibility of linking the world of mystic *sod* with the reality of materialistic *peshat* is in order. In seeking case material demonstrating this process of re-biographing and pre-biographing, numerous examples from our dia-logo project came immediately to my mind. A compelling case of re-biographing was that of the rabbi's widow, the old Mrs. F., who suffered from guilt feelings for not having visited her husband during the last six months of his life while he was dying of cancer. At first nothing seemed sufficiently effective for changing the gloomy dialogue she maintained with her deceased husband, who would not see her before his death; then her *derushic* recomposition began. Thus, after helping her to tell and retell how it was in fact she who saved the family in Europe, and how it was in fact she who helped her husband to found a yeshiva in Israel, Mrs. F. all of a sudden volunteered a *derush* about a verse in Psalms that seemed instrumental for recomposing her identity melody. Quoting the passage "He giveth snow like wool" (Psalms 147:16), Mrs. F. stated that since wool and snow are both white, snow in terms of sufferings may sometimes warm a person like wool. Mrs. F. was thus able to hear a new melody in her biographic composition in which her husband's reluctance to see her was reinterpreted as his gratitude and wish to save her the suffering that would ensue from seeing him in his decaying position.

An instructive case of pre-biographing was Ms. S., with whom I role-played for months countless scenarios she might encounter after moving with her boyfriend (who eventually became her husband) to the United States. It was, however, only when I looked into the bosom of my own family when all of a sudden I discovered the epitomizing role model for re- and pre-biographing grounded in the *derushic* narrative necessary for bridging between one's fear of the mystic world of *sod* and the realistic life of *peshat*. It is hence with the drama of my youngest son who dared to enter the *pardes* but unfortunately did not come out that I choose to close this book.[8]

THE RE-BIOGRAPHIC AND PRE-BIOGRAPHIC SCRIPT OF BOAZ

Throughout this book I have stressed that ecstatic practices like singing and dancing may be understood as immunization exercises against people's natural fear of death. Thus, ecstasy, conceived as a process during which the soul endeavors to leave the body, is generally tantamount to taking small doses of temporary death experiences because it operates as a desensitization mechanism. Accordingly, if the court jester, shaman, or

Hasid has been up there in heaven but returned, he has a good reason to rejoice and feel safer on earth. In other words, a "Hasidic court jester" may suffer less from fragmentation anxiety the more he is desensitized or indifferent to petty, mundane needs or to social-status symbols.

Moreover, popular *derushic* slogans such as the one stating "This world is like a corridor for the world to come" (*Fathers* 14:21) may hence be seen as precipitating desensitizers to identity fragmentation because it inculcates an indifference to material needs and the like. As a device against identity fragmentation, such *derushic* desensitizers also become instrumental for rebiographing because memories about one's failing past may be contracted, that is, minimized or reinterpreted, or conceived as a necessary descending phase that may be recomposed into new, resonating tunes. A consistent, integrated identity requires, however, the recomposition of a melody in which the tunes of the past accord with the voices of one's future. Thus, rebiographing is the sounding board and the springboard for healthy prebiographing because it harmonizes one's new trust in one's past with one's messianic hopes for the future,[9] as indicated by Scholem (1972).

When my youngest son, Boaz, began his studies in a highly prestigious yeshiva high school, he felt physically and intellectually inferior to some of the charismatic figures in his class. Since he was a class leader in grade school, despite his being the youngest in the class, this new "weakness" first troubled him to the point that he lost motivation to study. He then tried to play the court jester in his class, but only to realize that his classmates didn't laugh with him but at him, that in fact he was mocked as someone who had no personality or style. Although he gained the reputation of being a courageous "man of truth" who would not hesitate to expose his teacher's hypocrisy even at the cost of being several times expelled from school, he had to learn the facts of life about his classmates' cowardliness the hard way. It was only toward the end of high school, when he grew to be a tall, broad-shouldered, handsome young man, that he was able to reconquer his status as a leader by first challenging and then aligning with another charismatic leader, who then became his best friend. When Boaz subsequently joined a most prestigious elite unit in the paratrooper division of the Israeli army, after passing very difficult physical and mental tests, his qualities of leadership became firmly established. The inspiring exaltation with which he helped his comrades through extreme hardships consisted of the two elements described in this book as bridges between the fears of the unknown world and their concrete, cruel reality in this commando unit. On the one hand, Boaz consistently mocked terrestrial hardships by referring to this world as a "corridor," while on the other, he would sweep his comrades into ecstatic, Hasidic-style singing that would help everybody to overcome the everyday fears that permeated their dangerous existence.

It was only many months later, when we began to read his naive and honest autobiographic movie script, which he entitled *The Prophesy*, that we realized how Boaz had spontaneously adopted King David's or Reb Osher's ascent-via-descent re-biographing method to reintegrate his failing past with his successful new leadership identity. Boaz, whose unfinished script of life in the yeshiva dormitory could potentially be made into a classic documentary, does not erase or replace his failing past. Instead of adopting a convenient new-leaf identity, Boaz, at the age of 17, knocks and mocks ruthlessly his past social failures as if he were a wise old man who can afford to reminisce about his youthful foolishness at the age of 71. Selected scenes from the dramatized encounter with his friend E. will suffice to illuminate how this re-biographic descending and self-abnegating contraction through condescending and condensing his ego was used for the sake of subsequent pre-biographic ascent and identity reintegration. Boaz, who used the pseudonym D., described the encounter with his friend E., that took place when he returned after being kicked out of school for a whole month. They meet in a secret room controlled only by his friend E.

D.: Hey, what's that? I never knew about this room.

E.: Obviously you did not. What do you know, D.?
(D. looks at E. but doesn't yet understand)

E.: Ya D.! Tell me, what are you—smart or stupid? good or bad? What are you? You can't answer this! Take cognizance of the facts! You are a zero whom everybody succeeds in navigating.

D.: (in a defensive tone) What do you mean?

E.: (mimics classmates) Hey D., come and make me laugh, I am bored in class. (A small pause in the conversation during which D. begins to understand.) You see these D.? (E. displays a set of keys.) That's possession! I can open and close doors! This gives me power! . . . This room is an old visitor's room of the yeshiva; it has better equipment than a regular room; *we* have a shower and a kitchenette and an exit to the roof.

D.: Who are we?
(E. mentions a few names)
(D. begins to understand how foolish he was. . . .)

E.: Don't worry! I was exactly like you when I arrived. . . . I found a way to survive here.

D.: God! I was so stupid. . . .

E.: It's too bad that only now I realize that you could be one of us. . . .

D.: Okay, I'll go now.

(Rotenberg, B., 1987: 13-16)

The script goes on to describe how D. (Boaz) made his way back as a leading figure first through self-pitying tears, which he stopped at a split second the moment he used determination and persistency.

Boaz, whose courageous, noncompromising truthfulness became a spiritual guiding legend and a legacy for his friends, family, and this book, often referred to himself as God's court jester, whom God loves, wants near Him, and therefore pardons him when he occasionally neglects some of the rituals.

Although, unlike the "Hasidic court jester," he did not return from his far-flung ecstatic and devout volunteering mission because he was killed in action at the age of 18, his unfinished life symphony will, I hope, always rekindle our messianic faith in a better recomposed future as promised in his re-biographic script *The Prophecy*.

NOTES

1. A more extensive discussion of alibis in terms of an a priori or an a posteriori model of rationalized criminal conduct may be found in Rotenberg, *Re-biographing and Deviance* (1987), Chap. 8.

2. In view of the element of dynamic adjustment inherent in the midrashic and even in the halachic legal system, one may wonder about the roots and tacit intentions of various fundamentalistic, fossilizing interpretations of Judaism. On the one hand, it appears that Hegel and especially Kant apparently ignored the midrashic self-renewing adjustment system. Hence, in explaining Jewish survival as a mere "barren legalistic" (fossilized) system, they disqualified Judaism as an ethical-moral religion (see Rotenstreich, 1984) because of its presumed passive obedience to halachic frozen laws that were formulated and externally enforced on the Jews 2,000 years ago. On the other hand, it also appears that various Jewish sects periodically adopt a monopolistic and karaite (fundamentalistic) interpretation of the Jewish law, which seems to be diametrically opposed to the pluralistic "seventy faces" tradition that the very idea of the Jewish oral law presumably promulgates.

3. The case of "political rehabilitation" provides a compelling demonstration of how powerful members of society demand a new reading and writing of their past and deserves a separate treatise that is beyond the scope of the present study. A systematic study of such re-biographic struggles would most probably reveal that people's hope to have in their future a "good past" is a vital need for their identity reintegration. It would, then, be on the basis of such a study that we would question the effectiveness and wisdom of a historicistic treatment model that trains ex-criminals and ex-mental patients to redeem themselves by erasing their failing past in order to adopt a new-leaf approach to their future. From the selected cases which I adduced (Rotenberg, 1987) and analyzed I learned that in spite of the here-and-now or from-now-on credit that some ex-failures were given, their incessant hunt for a new, favorable reading of their disenchanted past often continued till the last days of their lives. One may thus wonder what happens to the identity of powerless ex-failures when they are asked to confront reality and carry the unshakeable Oedipal-original-sin guilt-cross that stronger people succeed in shedding.

4. In his prologue to Kendall's book on the art of biography, Stephen Oates equates the various approaches to writing biographies to a stage production. Oates contends that if one adopts the historical-democratic approach in which

> the author . . . presents the life of his subject virtually day by day, often moment by moment . . . [and] if we are still around when the curtain falls . . . because of the deluge of information, we may have no clear picture of the subject and probably little sense of him as a living person. [Whereas] a pure biography, on the other hand, is a living drama in a manageable length. . . . In pure life-writing, the biographer allows his subject to occupy center

stage, with just enough historical backdrop for us to understand the subject in proper context. (see Kendall, 1985: VI)

It is remarkable to note here that Levi-Strauss (1966) criticized the biased fallacy inherent in the so-called objective method of historiography due to the inevitably arbitrary choice of coding units that may be significant for one code and not for the other. Similar to Oates he thus states that

it is thus not only fallacious but contradictory to conceive of the historical process as a continuous development, beginning with prehistory coded in tens or hundreds of millenia, then adopting the scale of millenia when it gets to the 3rd and 4th millenium, and continuing as history in centuries interlarded, at the pleasure of each author, with slices of annual history within the century, day to day history within the year or even hourly history within a day. (p. 20)

To me it seems nonetheless quite presumptuous to call Kendall's professed subjective method pure biography.

5. Here Ruth Benedict's (1972) classic distinction between the Eastern "shame cultures" and the Puritan "guilt culture" appears helpful in explaining the possibility of harmonious self-blaming identities. Thus, in contrast to the Eastern identity, which might disintegrate by "losing face" incurred by shame on the interpersonal level, the integrity of a Western identity depends on how it is trained to handle inner guilt. It is therefore possible that if a person has internalized the unshakeable metacode of original sin and man's fall, that a self-blaming life via periodic confessions would paradoxically enhance identity integration. Indeed, Benedict states that in guilt cultures

a man who has sinned can get relief by unburdening himself. This device of confession is used in our secular therapy and by many religious groups which have otherwise little in common. We know it brings relief. Where shame is the major sanction, a man does not experience relief when he makes his fault public even to a confessor. (p. 223)

6. This point that corrected behavior in a specific present must precede the contracting reinterpretation of one's failing past is a crucial part of the present model. In essence, this reversed-causality paradigm, wherein the present affects the past, makes it impossible for one to whitewash or psychopathically rationalize one's sinning past because one's present corrected behavior constitutes the basic status of one's identity.

7. Here it is noteworthy to emphasize that the contraction model (see Rotenberg, 1983) is comprised of a dynamic relationship between contraction and expansion on the interpersonal and intrapersonal levels. Thus, the Hasidic notion of ascent via descent may be understood as a therapeutic device that like a spring coil or a springboard enables one to ascend higher the more one descends, that is, the more one contracts or depresses one's state of being (or even becomes depressed).

8. The reader is reminded that according to the original talmudic source on which the fourfold exegetic *PaRDeS* system was constructed (Hagiga 14:b), not all four sages who entered the mystic orchard *(pardes)* came out alive.

9. For a more detailed analysis of how messianism comprises a metacode for a future-oriented psychology of hope and pre-biographing, see Rotenberg, 1987.

Appendix

Pardes and PaRDeS: Towards a Psychotherapeutic Theory*

A cardinal question that should concern mental health workers is: What is the major deficiency in modern socialization that may explain the psychological need of Western youth to seek salvation in Eastern mysticism and/or cults? Max Weber considers that since the rise of Protestantism in the sixteenth century, we are witnessing in the West the gradual predominance of rational, calculated thinking as the sole criterion and evidence for salvation and divine election.[1] Similarly, Michel Foucault has claimed that until the Renaissance, "[M]adness and non-madness, reason and non-reason [were] inextricably involved: inseparable...," while "[T]he end of the eighteenth century, affords the evidence of a broken dialogue...in which the exchange between madness and reason was made [because] the language of psychiatry, which is a monologue of reason about madness, has been established only on the basis of such a silence."[2]

It follows that Protestantism has driven the irrational thought system out of bounds. If Western Protestantism has excluded the mystic-irrational language from its text, one may wonder what has happened to people's eternal irrational fears of the transcendental unknown, and the unrationalizable predicaments that forever haunt people in an "imperfect world."[3]

It may be suggested that the social pressures for rational-technical achievements serve to increase irrational anxieties of Western youth. Among the available options, two extreme stands are available. One calls for a *flight* to mystic or psychedelic cultism, while the other proposes to *fight* irrationalism by categorizing it as unconscious drives that must be converted to conscious rationalism via psychoanalytic methods.

It has been argued that a sudden switch to a non-rational mode of thinking may cause a dangerous "snapping"[4] in the mind and that the practice of Eastern mystic salvation methods is unsuitable for Westerners.[5] Conversely, by

* For a short version of this theory, see *Israeli Journal of Psychiatry* 31, no. 3 (1994):162-169.

adherence to a strict rational way of thinking (here termed the fight response, i.e., transforming the non-rational unconscious to consciousness by psychoanalysis), we discover a tantalizing approach to life due to its deterministic philosophy in which the despotic control by the unconscious of our consciousness leaves little room for free will, hopes, and efforts to combat irrational fears (see Freud's "writing pad" analogy[6]).

It seems that Western youth sought a balance, not an either/or choice between their physical and metaphysical worlds. To bridge these two polar "flight vs. fight" positions, which seem to provide Westerners with poor remedies for dealing with non-rational fears of the transcendental unknown, in the present appendix two meanings of the Jewish concept of *pardes* will be presented as a phenomenological theory which comprises a psychotherapeutic bridge between the rational and non-rational approaches to life.

PARDES AS A LEGEND REFLECTING LIFE

The early use of *pardes* refers to a famous legend appearing in the Talmud (Hagiga, 14:b) concerning four sages of the second century who engaged in esoteric-speculative studies. Here the word *pardes*, which according to its Hebrew and Greek origins means literally paradise, was used to stress that, by their daring attempt to "enter Paradise," the four risked their lives because they stretched the limits of the human mind to explore hidden and forbidden mystical territories beyond the human world. These four sages were Rabbi Akiva, Ben Zoma, Ben Azai, and Elisha Ben Avuya (referred to in the Talmud as Acher, meaning the "other," the "outsider").

According to the Talmud, "One saw and died, the second saw and lost his mind, the third laid waste the young plants [i.e., referring to Acher, who became a heretic and corrupted the young], only Rabbi Akiva entered in peace and came out in peace."

Although "the exact meaning of the *Pardes* [entered by the four sages] has long been an object of speculation,"[7] this legend seems to reflect the dangerous pitfalls and abysses that await people who venture to immerse themselves in deep meditation and mystical practices. The later and more popular use of *pardes* converted this concept into a fourfold hermeneutic system.

The possible connection between the two meanings of *pardes* has been overlooked. I shall introduce briefly the second use of this term and then propose a psychological theory combining the two.

PaRDeS AS A HERMENEUTIC SYSTEM

According to the usage of the term *pardes* attributed to thirteenth-century Kabbalists, especially Moshe DeLeon, "Each consonant of the word PaRDeS denotes one of four (in Hebrew the a and e vowels are not needed) possible levels for interpreting the scripture. P stands for *peshat,* the literal meaning, R for *remez,* the allegorical meaning, D for *derash,* the Talmudic and Aggadic interpretation, and S for *sod*, the mystical meaning."[8]

The main idea that followed from the hermeneutic notion of *PaRDeS* was that it is not only permissible to interpret the Torah and other sacred texts according to these four different thought systems, but that people are in fact urged to shape their Torah *Weltanschaung* by choosing a suitable interpretation compatible with their personality makeup. Indeed, Scholem cites sources indicating that the four exegetic categories that came to be known under the acronym *PaRDeS* "served only as a general framework for a multiplicity of individual readings...which...was expressed in the widespread belief that each single Jew approached the Torah by a path that he alone could follow."[9]

I have described earlier in this book how the concept *of PaRDeS* seems to encompass a psychotherapeutic model if this multiple hermeneutic system for interpreting written texts is applied to the behavioral domain of interpreting life contexts. *Derash* (which includes the allegoric philological techniques attributable to *remez*) may be used as a pivot category for bridging the rational cognitive language (*peshat*) and the mystic-non-rational thought system (*sod*). By using clinical examples and historical case studies, I have demonstrated that *derash*, which is connected on the one hand to factual and real biographies, may act as a balancing pivot between the corporeal rational world and the mystic world that relates to people's mystical experiences.

By using *derashic* analogic stories and parables that broaden and change the meaning of our life stories, we may perceive *PaRDeS* as a psychotherapeutic bridge between the rational and the mystical. In a clinical project using this model we attempted first to treat people on a rational-cognitive level (*peshat*), and only in experiences that would be considered irrational, such as "hearing voices," would we use the mystic language (*sod*) that conveys the feeling that one will not be excommunicated as a schizophrenic, as *sod* is a legitimate thought system.

In support of this approach, the famous saying "The essence is not the *midrash* but the *maaseh* [act or fact]" (*Avot*, 1:17) may be rephrased as, "the essence is not the *maaseh* [act] but the *maasiya* [story]." This reversal means that there are no facts, only interpretations and stories about facts of life.

How could this *PaRDeS* model be related to the legend about the four sages entering the *Pardes*?

PARDES AND *PaRDeS*: TOWARD A COMBINED PSYCHOLOGICAL THEORY

A straightforward moral derivation from the story about the four sages would suggest that, considering the dangers people will encounter in their attempt to experience and understand the nature of life and death, only one quarter (the "Akivas") stand a chance of entering "paradise." In other words, if the actions of forefathers and ancient rabbinical role models are to be understood as "signs for the sons," that is, as guidelines for normative behavior, then three out of four ways symbolize an entry into an irreversible disastrous state. The irreversible nature of their fate seems incompatible with the Jewish cyclical notion of *teshuvah* (literally "return," i.e., repentance, or the possibility of recuperation).

The Baal Haturim, one of the mainstream commentators on the Torah, has interpreted the verse "and thou shalt choose life" (Deuteronomy, 30:19) by stating that the letters of the word *bachayim* (literally, "*in* life") make up the number seventy and "this comes to say that there are seventy faces [ways] to search [understand] the Torah." Thus, the imperative of choosing life contains the notion of hermeneutic pluralism, that is, the idea of choosing an individually suitable interpretation for life. Consequently, if indeed "the four ancient scholars...came to denote speculations concerning the true meaning of the Torah on all four levels," as Scholem suggests,[10] then these four approaches to life may be best understood as signifying symbolic psychological states in people's lives.

Accordingly, these four psychological states may refer to four different phases that one person may experience during various stages in his or her lifecycle. This is not to suggest that each one of us must experience all of these phases, but it would represent a radical point of departure to propose that the *pardes* legend may also be understood as psychological phases and not just as symbolic personality types according to which each one represents an absolutist approach to life.

The fourfold experiences presented below entail two mystic and two rational phases of psychological struggles in one's life. These phases will be introduced here in a concise format of general propositions.

It should be noted that I do not claim that the proposed interpretation of the original terms is derivable from the available texts. Indeed, many may find fault with viewing Akiva (as will be argued below) as representing a bridging paradox, or that Acher symbolizes a reaction to the rational. Our "deconstructive" perspective comes to emphasize that, if indeed this legend has stimulated and preoccupied the minds of thinkers for hundreds of years (including the formulators of the *PaRDeS* system), then it most probably comprises more basic psychological forces characterizing people's inner struggles, which may constitute a useful paradigm for socialization and psychotherapy. From this vantage point it would seem inconceivable to accept a historic-philologic position attributing, for example, Ben Zoma's punishment to his disrespect for Rabbi Joshua,[11] while the Hasidic Lubavitch interpretation, applying *PaRDeS* to expand the meaning of the morning prayer *modeh ani* (thanking the Creator upon awakening), appears as a phenomenological case in point that encompasses cumulative paradigmatic components.[12]

THE FOUR SAGES AS PSYCHOLOGICAL STAGES

Acher as Rational *Peshat* (The Rebellious Phase)

If *peshat* is understood as a rational-literal interpretation of the text, it carries a "fundamentalistic" message of sticking to the letter. This stage occurs usually during early adolescence, when the mind of the young tends to question strict interpretations of texts, especially if they are applied to living contexts as normative expectations.

Thus, a fundamentalistic interpretation (*peshat*) may trigger a heretical response. Accordingly, the meaning of Acher may be understood as estrangement, or feeling as an "outsider." This rebellion against the *peshat* may be understood also as a moralistic revolt against apparent social and divine injustice that is likewise characteristic during adolescence. Indeed, this perspective seemed to constitute the essential nature of Acher's sin as indicated by Libes.[13] Alternatively, it could be conceived as a temporary state denoting the impossibility of accepting a ready made world of "absolutes."

If this reactive position is misunderstood by oneself and by one's significant others, one may indeed remain an excommunicated *acher*—as an estranged "outsider." It is hence only a misleading external or inner voice that turns the Talmudic statement "return naughty children except for Acher" (Hagiga, 15:a) into an irreversible exit.

The need to have a significant other, or a "self object," providing the questioning youth with an introduction to a life of contradictions and paradoxes has been well documented by clinical studies.[14] To elucidate this point, here is one clinical example: A young man was sent to a mental institution as he had a compulsive need to ask questions about every mundane activity he had to perform. Consequently, he could not eat, drink, sleep or engage in any behavior without asking questions. This compulsion was triggered by a teacher who would conclude each class with the invitation: "Are there any questions?" His psychiatrist traced this compulsion to the fact that during the crucial "questioning phase" of childhood, he did not have a mother or any other "self object" who could answer his queries about life.

It is insignificant here whether one accepts the causal relationship between early childhood deprivation and the subsequent compulsion. What seems important from the present perspective is that even blasphemous questioning of the written letter—one's natural need to rebel against seemingly dogmatic demands—may turn a person into a permanent *acher*—outsider—or leave him in the other world of the *sitra achra* (literally, "the other side," the domain of evil in Kabbalistic terminology), if no accepting sounding board is available during this vital phase in life.

We may summarize this phase by suggesting that the Talmudic allegation that "Acher laid waste the young plants" (Hagiga, 14:b) means that his antinomian rebellion against a *peshat* interpretation characterizes the young plants and their corruption. During adolescence one is vulnerable to such estrangements due to the natural need to rebel heretically against the written dictating *peshat*.

Akiva as Rationalizing *Derash* (The Paradoxical Response)

If Rabbi Akiva entered in peace and came out in peace (or rather came out "in one piece"), then his entrance and exit may also be understood as a symbolic role-modeling phase in life. Rabbi Akiva began his studies at the age of forty, that is, in a later, more mature stage of life, and was the one who laid the foundation for the Midrashic system in terms of its "seventy faces" notion of hermeneutic pluralism.

A well-known Talmudic story (Menachot, 29:b) relates that when Moses ascended to Heaven to receive the Ten Commandments, he found God attaching crownlets to many letters of the Torah. When Moses inquired about this peculiar activity, God is said to have answered that one man—Rabbi Akiva is his name—will, in the second century CE, interpret mountains of laws and ideas on the basis of these crownlets. To understand how the Midrashic system of paradoxical interpretation evolved from the encounter between Moses and Akiva, the Talmud states that God allowed Moses to skip ahead a few hundred years and visit Rabbi Akiva's Beit Midrash (Talmudic college). However, Moses was unable to understand what Rabbi Akiva taught his students and felt very aggrieved until a student asked Rabbi Akiva, "How do you know that your interpretations are correct?" Rabbi Akiva's answer that "This is the law given to Moses on Mount Sinai" epitomizes the Midrashic principle of paradox, demonstrating how the Midrash may contain contradictory interpretations *ad absurdum*. Thus, Moses may not understand how his own teachings are being interpreted although this very interpretation is traceable to Moses who received it at Mount Sinai.

According to the Talmud (ibid.), Moses went on to ask God why he and not Rabbi Akiva was chosen to receive the Torah. We may assume from this story that 1) the Midrashic principle of the coexistence of contradictory interpretations was an established norm of Jewish hermeneutic pluralism, and 2) Rabbi Akiva may be seen as the founding father of Midrashic hermeneutic philosophy of paradoxical thought.

It is the ability to live with contradictions, to bridge between mystic idealism and rational realism, that symbolizes the possibility of entering and returning in peace and in one piece from the *pardes* paradise. It is the *derash* phase of the forty-year-old mature Akiva that may be seen as a resolution of the earlier stage of the heretic rebellion of Acher, the outsider, against the fundamentalistic *peshat*.

If Acher and Akiva represent the two relatively comprehensible sequential phases of negative and positive rationalism, let us turn now to examine the two more complex mystical phases of sod comprised in the *Pardes-PaRDeS* combined formulation.

The two mystic phases of *sod* will be divided into what may be termed the passive-theoretical approach and the active-ecstatic techniques of Kabbalah.

Ben Zoma as Passive *Sod* (The Psychotic Break)

It is noted of Ben Zoma's style of entry into *pardes*, that when he ascended to the heavens, he became immersed in the possibility of measuring the space between the upper waters (heaven) and the lower waters (seas) during the first or second day of creation. When Ben Zoma did not reply when questioned about his well being, Rabbi Joshua is said to have exclaimed, "From whence are the feet?" (Tosefta to Hagiga, 2, 6). This term is thought to express the danger of ascent to the lofty mystic worlds where one may loose touch with reality, that is, the ground where one's feet are to stand. Perceiving the *pardes* legend as a parable, Ben Zoma may symbolize people's eternal danger of being caught in an unresolvable position dealing with the non-rational mystic world of transcendence.[15]

Western mental health workers would be forgiven for diagnosing as psychotic the visions described in the *Hekhaloth* mysticism or *Merkavah* literature that emanated from mystic experiences akin to Ezekiel's prophetic visions. Consider the following description of gatekeepers in the Heavens: "Angry and warlike, strong, harsh, fearful, terrific, taller than mountains and sharper than peaks. Their bows are strung and stand before them, their swords are sharpened and in their hands. Lightning flows and issues forth from the balls of their eyes, and balls of fire from their nostrils, and torches of fiery coals from their mouths. They are equipped with helmets and with coats of mail, and javelins and spears are hung upon their thews...the horses upon which they ride stand beside mangers of fire full of coals of juniper and eat fiery coals from the mangers, [taking] a measure of forty bushels of coals in one mouthful."[16]

Such visions may be seen in paranoid hallucinations during psychosis or confusional states, but they could also be understood as reflecting one's fear of death. These fears are accepted in cultures in which visions are legitimized by mystic texts and practices in their everyday lives.

Joseph Campbell has suggested that the psychotic, the LSD addict, the Yogic, and the mystic all plunge "into the same deep inward sea...the symbolic figures encountered are...identical.... But there is an important difference.... The mystic...enters the waters and finds he can swim; whereas the schizophrenic...is drowning."[17]

If Ben Zoma symbolizes the danger of drowning in the deep psychotic ocean when facing the natural fears of the unknown world of transcendence, then in Ben Azai's death we may see the active response inherent in ecstatic Kabbalah.

Ben Azai as Active *Sod* (The Ecstatic Response)

If the *pardes* legend is seen as phases, then Ben Azai's death during his mystic ascent need not be seen as a failure and a punishment. His death may be considered as a righteous act reserved only for God's most favorite sons. Indeed, Libes states that "Ben Azai was a pure mystic who was not interested in theurgic activities but in his soul's *devekut* [literally, "clinging" to the Divine, akin to *unio mystica*]. And therefore he peeked and died because such a death constitutes the soul's desire of every mystic."[18]

From a psychological perspective, Ben Azai's death may symbolize the danger inherent in the mystic's efforts to reach *devekut*, which comprises the main activity of ecstatic *sod.* The Midrash (Vayikra Rabba, 16:4) relates that when they informed Rabbi Akiva that "Ben Azai sits and studies and the fire burns around him," Rabbi Akiva asked Ben Azzai, "Perhaps you are dealing with the rooms of the *Merkavah*?" (literally, the Chariot, referring to Ezekiel's vision of God). The fires referred to here are the heavenly fires and, according to Kabbalistic tradition, bringing down such fires is one of the main activities attributed to those mystics known as "the descenders of the *Merkava*." Ben Azai's art of dying may symbolize the ecstatic *sod* response to fears of death as also expressed in hallucinations of Heaven's gatekeepers as creatures whose eyes and nostrils spit fire (passive *sod*).

We shall now consider how Ben Azai's art of dying may be understood as a therapeutic device against the natural fear of dying. Ecstatic *devekut* may be understood as a small temporary dose of death. If the state of death is perceived as a process during which the soul leaves the body, then ecstatic *devekut* might be understood as an immunizing act of temporary death.

During clinical work I conducted using the *pardes* model—discussed in this book—people reported how ecstatic *devekut* exercises functioned as a fear reduction device of a contrived experience of a calamity they were asked to imagine. We were able to observe in many cases that ecstatic *sod* helped to reduce paranoid hallucinations and fears not only of people with a Hasidic orientation. It is in this therapeutic sense that we may understand active *sod* as a technique of ecstatic kabbalism that, like the Akiva response, may be learned only after the mature age of forty.[19]

Accordingly, we may understand the more complex mystic *sod* as containing two dangerous responses to our need to deal with fears of the transcendental world: becoming a passively psychotic Ben Zoma or becoming an ecstatic Ben Azai.

NOTES

1. Weber, M. *The Protestant Ethic and the Spirit of Capitalism*. London: Unwin, 1970.
2. Foucault, M. *Madness and Civilization*. New York: Random House, 1967.
3. Weber, M. *The Sociology of Religion*. Boston: Beacon, 1967.
4. Conway, F. and J. Siegelman. *Snapping*. Philadelphia: Lippincott, 1978.
5. Suzuki, D. T. *An Introduction to Zen Buddhism*, chapter on Jung. New York: Grove, 1964.
6. Freud, S. "A Note upon the Mystic Writing-Pad." *Standard Edition*, Vol. 19. New York: Hogarth, 1955, 226-232.
7. Scholem, G. *On the Kabbalah and its Symbolism*. New York: Schocken, 1965.
8. Ibid.
9. Scholem, G. *Kabbalah*. Jerusalem: Keter, 1974.
10. Scholem, *On the Kabbalah and its Symbolism*.
11. Libes Y. *Chetoh shel Elisha* (Hebrew). Jerusalem: Academon, 1990.
12. Schneerson, M. M. *On the Essence of Chasidus*. New York: Kehot, 1978.
13. Libes, *Chetoh shel Elisha*.
14. Kohut, H. *How does Psychoanalysis Cure?* Chicago: Chicago University, 1984.
15. Urbach, E. E. "Hamasoret Al Torat Hasod Bitkufat Hatanaim." *Mechkarim BaKabbalah UbeToldot Hadatot Mugashim LeGershom Shalom* (Hebrew). Jerusalem, 1968.
16. Scholem, G. *Jewish Gnosticism, Merkabah Mysticism and Talmudic Tradition*. New York: The Jewish Theological Seminary of America, 1960.
17. Campbell, J. *Myths to Live By*. New York: Bantam Books, 1978.
18. Libes, *Chetoh shel Elisha*.
19. Idel, M. "Letoldot Haisur Lilmod Kabala Lifney Gil Haarbaim" (Hebrew). *American Jewish Studies Review* 5, 1980.

Bibliography

Albee, G. "Psychopathology, Prevention and the Just Society." *Journal of Primary Prevention* 4 no. 1 (1983): 5-40.

Arieti, S. *Interpretation of Schizophrenia.* 2nd ed. New York: Basic Books, 1974.

Ashlag, Y. *Mavo Lesefer Hazohar* (Introduction to the Book of *Zohar*). Tel-Aviv: Kedma, 1965.

Bandler, R., and J. Grinder. *Reframing.* Moab, Utah: Real People Press, 1982.

Bandura, A. *Principles of Behavior Modification.* New York: Holt, 1969.

Baranover, Y. *Haderech Chazara* (The Way Back). Tel-Aviv: Maariv, 1984.

Bateson, G. *Steps to an Ecology of Mind.* New York: Ballantine Books, 1978.

Bauman, Z. *Hermeneutics and Social Science.* London: Hutchinson, 1978.

Beck, A. T. *Cognitive Therapy and the Emotional Disorders.* New York: New American Library, 1979.

Becker, H. S. *Outsiders.* New York: Free Press, 1963.

Bellah, R., R. N. Madsen, W. M. Sullivan, A. E. Swidler, and S. M. Tipton. *Habits of the Heart.* New York: Harper & Row, 1985.

Bellak, L. *Manic-Depressive Psychosis and Allied Conditions.* New York: Grune and Stratton, 1952.

Benedict, R. *The Chrysanthemum and the Sword.* Tokyo: Charles E. Tuttle, 1972.

Berg, S. P. *Gilguley Neshamot* (The Transmigration of Souls). Jerusalem: Hamachon Lecheker Hakabala, 1986.

Bergman, S. H. *Dialogical Philosophy from Kierkegaard to Buber* (Hebrew), Jerusalem: Mosad Bialik, 1974.

Besht, I. *Keter Shem Tov* (The Crown of Shem Tov). Jerusalem: Rosen, 1975.

Bettleheim, B. *The Uses of Enchantment.* New York: Vintage Books, 1977.

Bilu, Y., E. Witztum, and O. Van Der Hart. "Paradise Regained: 'Miraculous Healing' in an Israeli Psychiatric Clinic." *Culture, Medicine and Psychiatry* 14 (1990): 105-27.

Bloom, A. *The Closing of the American Mind.* New York: Penguin Books, 1987.

Bowers, M. K., and S. Glasner. "Auto-Hypnotic Aspects of the Jewish Cabalistic

Concept of Kavanah." *Journal of Clinical and Experimental Hypnosis* 6, no. 1 (1958):3-23.
Buber, M. *Bepardes Hachasidut* (In the Orchard of Hasidim). Tel-Aviv: Devir, 1963.
______. *Pointing the Way*. New York: Schocken, 1974.
______. *Tales of the Hasidim: Early Masters*. New York: Schocken, 1978.
Buss, A. H. *Psychopathology*, New York: J. Wiley, 1966.
Buss, A. R. "Development of Dialectics and Development of Humanistic Psychology," *Human Development* 19 (1976):248-60.
Calvin, J. *A Compend of Institutes of the Christian Religion*. Edited by H. T. Kerr. Philadelphia: Westminster, 1939.
Campbell, J. *Myths to Live By*. New York: Bantam Books, 1978.
Camus, A. *The Stranger*. London: Penguin Books, 1968.
Canter, P., M. Comber, and D. L. Uzzell. *Football in Its Place*. London: Routledge & Kegan Paul, 1989.
Cohen, S. *Visions of Social Control*. London: Polity Press, 1985.
Conway, F., and J. Siegelman. *Snapping*. Philadelphia: Lippincott, 1978.
Culler, J. *On Deconstruction*. London: Routledge & Kegan Paul, 1987.
d'Aquili, E. G., "The Myth-Ritual Complex: A Biogenetic Structural Analysis." *Zygon* 18, no. 3 (1983): 247-69.
Dan, J. *Encyclopedia Judaica*. Jerusalem, 1972.
Darton, N. "Committed Youth." *Newsweek*, July 31, 1989, pp. 66-68.
Derrida, J. *Of Grammatology*. Baltimore: Johns Hopkins University Press, 1976.
______. *Writing and Difference*. Chicago: University of Chicago Press, 1978.
Dewey, J., and A. F. Bentley. *Knowing and the Known*. Boston: Beacon Press, 1949.
Diagnostic and Statistical Manual (DSM). Washington, D.C.: APA, 1958, 1968, 1980.
Dov Baer, Maggid of Mezeritch. *Maggid Devarav LeYaacov*. Lublin, Poland, 1927.
Eagleton, T. *Literary Theory*. Oxford: Basil Blackwell, 1985.
Eco, U. *Foucault's Pendulum*. New York: Harcourt Brace Jovanovich, 1989.
Eisenstein, J. D., ed. *Otzar Yisrael* (The Treasure of Israel). Vol. 2. New York: Encyclopedia Ivrit, 1906-1913.
Eliade, M. *Shamanism: Archaic Techniques of Ecstasy*. London: Routledge & Kegan Paul, 1974.
Ellenberger, H. *The Discovery of the Unconscious*. New York: Harper & Row, 1970.
Fachler, M. "A Seminar for Repenters: Participant Observation." The Hebrew University of Jerusalem, 1988.
Feder, L. *Madness in Literature*. Princeton: Princeton University Press, 1980.
Feitelsohn, M. M. *Selected Works* (Hebrew). Tel-Aviv: Massada Ltd. 1970.
Felman, S., ed. *Literature and Psychoanalysis*. Baltimore: John Hopkins University Press, 1982.
Fingarette, H. *Self-Deception*. London: Routledge & Kegan Paul, 1971.
Foucault, M. *Madness and Civilization*. New York: Random House, 1967.
Frank, J. D. *Persuasion and Healing*. New York: Schocken, 1961.
Frankl, V. *Man's Search for Meaning*. Tel-Aviv: Devir, 1970.
Freud, S. *The Basic Writings of Sigmund Freud*. New York: Random House, 1938.
______. "A Note upon the Mystic Writing-Pad." *Standard Edition*. Vol. *19*, 226-32. New York: Hogarth Press, 1955.

______. *Group Psychology and the Analysis of the Ego.* New York: Bantam Books, 1965.

Friedman, M. "Philosophical Anthropology and Dialogue as Keys to the Integration of Human Sciences." Sixth International Human Sciences Research Conference, University of Ottawa, 1987.

Funkenstein, A. *Intellectuals and Jews.* Tucson: University of Arizona, 1989.

Gay, V. "Augustine: The Reader as Selfobject." *Journal for the Scientific Study of Religion* 25, no. 1 (1986): 64-76.

Goffman, E. *Asylums.* Chicago: Aldine, 1956.

Goleman, D. *Vital Lies, Simple Truths.* New York: Simon & Schuster, 1985.

Gordon, D. *Therapeutic Metaphors.* Cupertino, Meta Publications, 1978.

Green, A. *Tormented Master.* Alabama: University of Alabama Press, 1979.

Grinker, R. R., H. MacGregor, K. Sellan, A. Klein, and J. Kohrman. *Psychiatric Social Work: A Transactional Case Book.* New York: Basic Books. 1961.

Habermas, J. "The Hermeneutic Claim to Universality." In *Contemporary Hermeneutics,* edited by J. Bleicher. London: Routledge and Kegan Paul, 1980.

Haley, J. *Uncommon Therapy.* New York: W. W. Norton, 1973.

Harman, W., and H. Rheingold. *Higher Creativity.* Los Angeles: Jeremy P. Tarcher, 1984.

Heineman, Y. *Darchey Haagada* (The Ways of Haggadah). Jerusalem: Magnes Press, 1974.

Hertz, R. *Death and the Right Hand.* New York: Free Press, 1960.

Hospers, J. "What Means This Freedom?" In *Free Will and Determinism,* edited by B. Berofsky. New York: Harper & Row, 1966.

Idel, M. *Kabbalah: New Perspectives,* New Haven, CT: Yale University Press, 1988a.

______. *The Mystical Experiences in Abraham Abulafia.* Albany: State University of New York Press, 1988b.

______. "Rabbi Karo: Between Autobiography and Historiosophy." Paper delivered at the Tenth World Congress of Jewish Studies, Jerusalem, 1989a.

______. "Universalization and Integration: Two Conceptions of Mystical Union in Jewish Mysticism." In *Mystical Union and Monotheistic Faith,* edited by M. Idel and B. McGinn. New York: Macmillan, 1989b.

Iser, W. *The Act of Reading.* Baltimore: Johns Hopkins University Press, 1978.

Ish-Shalom, B. *Rabbi Abraham Isaac Kook: Between Rationalism and Mysticism.* Tel Aviv: Am Oved, 1990.

Jacobs, L. *Jewish Mystical Testimonies.* New York: Schocken, 1978.

Johnson, R. A. *Ecstasy.* New York: Harper & Row, 1987.

Jung, C. G., ed. *Man and His Symbols.* London: Picador Pan Books, 1978.

Kadushin, M. *The Rabbinic Mind.* New York: Bloch, 1972.

Kahana, B. *The Chabadic Personality Theory.* M. A. Thesis, The Hebrew University of Jerusalem, 1990.

Kaiser, W. *Praisers of Folly.* Cambridge, MA: Harvard University Press, 1963.

Karo, J. *Maggid Meysharim* (Hebrew). Jerusalem: Ora, 1960.

Kaufmann, W. *Critique of Religion and Philosophy.* New York: Doubleday, 1961.

Kendall, P. M. *The Art of Biography.* New York: W. W. Norton, 1985.

Kiev, A. *Transcultural Psychiatry.* New York: Free Press, 1972.

Kliever, L. D. "Confessions of Unbelief: In Quest of the Vital Lie." *Journal for the Scientific Study of Religion* 25, no. 1 (1986):102-115.

Kohut, H. *How Does Psychoanalysis Cure?* Chicago: Chicago University Press, 1984.

Kurtzman, H. S. "Deconstruction and Psychology, An Introduction." *New Ideas in Psychology* 5, no. 1 (1987):33-71.

Kurtzweil, B. *Masot Al Sipurey S. Y. Agnon.* Jerusalem: Schocken, 1970.

Lacan, J. *Ecrits.* London: Tavistock, 1966.

______. "The Insistence of the Letter in the Unconscious. In *Structuralism,* edited by J. Ehrmann. New York: Anchor Books, 1970.

Laing, R. D. *The Politics of Experience.* New York: Ballantine Books, 1967.

______. *The Divided Self.* Middlesex, England: Penguin Books, 1978.

Leavy, S. A. *The Psychoanalytic Dialogue.* New Haven, CT: Yale University Press, 1980.

Lemaire, A. *Jacques Lacan.* London: Routledge & Kegan Paul, 1977.

Levi-Strauss, C. *Structural Anthropology,* New York: Basic Books, 1963.

Liberman, S. *Greek and Hellenism in Jewish Palestine.* Jerusalem: Mosad Bialik and Yad Ben-Zvi, 1984.

Maimonides, M. *Teshuvot Harambam* (Responses of Maimonides). Jerusalem: Mekitzey Nirdamim, 1960.

______. *Guide of the Perplexed.* Translated by S. Pines. Chicago: Chicago University Press, 1965.

______. *Moreh Nevuchim* (Guide of the Perplexed). Jerusalem: Mosad Harav Kook, 1977.

Marcuse, H. *One Dimensional Man.*Boston: Beacon Press, 1966.

Margaliyot, R. *Sheelot Uteshuvot min Hashamayim* (Questions and Answers from Heaven). Jerusalem: Mosad Harav Kook, 1989.

Marx, K., and F. Engels. *The Communist Manifesto.* New York: Penguin Books, 1978.

McClelland, D. C. *The Achieving Society.* New York: Free Press, 1967.

McMullin, R. E. *Handbook of Cognitive Therapy Techniques.* New York: W. W. Norton, 1986.

McNeil, E. B. *The Psychoses.* Englewood Cliffs, NJ: Prentice-Hall, 1970.

Mead, G. H. *Mind, Self and Society.* Chicago: Chicago University Press, 1934.

Meklenburg, Y. Z. *Haketav Vehakabala* (The Written and the Cabala). Nurnberg, Germany: Bulka, 1924.

Melamed, E. Z. *Bible Commentators* (Hebrew). Vol. I. Jerusalem: Magnes Press, 1978.

Merkur, D. "Unitive Experiences and the State of Trance." In *Mystical Union and Monotheistic Faith,* edited by M. Idel and B. McGinn. New York: Macmillan, 1989.

Myers, F.W.H. *Human Personality and Its Survival of Bodily Death.* 1903.

Newman, L. I. *Hasidic Anthology.* New York: Schocken Books, 1975.

Nietzsche, F. *The Birth of Tragedy and the Case of Wagner.* New York: Vintage Books, 1967.

______. *On the Genealogy of Morals.* New York: Random House, 1969.

Norris, C. *Deconstruction.* London: Methuen, 1982.

Otto, R. *Mysticism East and West.* New York: Macmillan, 1976.
Page, J. D. *Psychopathology.* New York: Aldine Atherton, 1971.
Papolos, D. F., and J. Papolos. *Overcoming Depression.* New York: Harper & Row, 1987.
Pelletier, K. R., and C. Garfield. *Consciousness East and West.* New York: Harper, 1976.
Philo. Vol. 4. Cambridge, MA: Harvard University Press, The Loeb Classical Library, 1949.
Piekarz, M. *The Beginning of Hasidism.* (Hebrew). Jerusalem: Mosad Bialik, 1978.
Polsky, H., and Y. Wozner. *Everyday Miracles.* New York: Jason Aronson, 1989.
Porter, F. C. "The Yecer Hara." *Yale Bicentennial Publications.* New York: Charles Scribner's Sons, 1902.
Prado, C. G. *Rethinking How We Age.* Westport, CT: Greenwood Press, 1986.
Rank, O. *Truth and Reality.* New York: W. W. Norton, 1978.
Ricoeur, P. *Hermeneutics and the Human Sciences.* New York: Cambridge University Press, 1983.
Rieff, P. *Freud: The Mind of the Moralist.* New York: Anchor Books, 1961.
Rimmon-Kenan, S., ed. *Discourse in Psychoanalysis and Literature.* London: Methuen, 1987.
Rosenzweig, F. *Naharayim* (Hebrew). Jerusalem: Mosad Bialik, 1977.
Rosen, G. *Madness in Society.* New York: Harper, 1969.
Rosen, S. *My Voice Will Go with You.* New York: W. W. Norton, 1982.
Rosenfeld, J. M. "Serving the Collective or the Individual? Lessons from the Wars of Israel." *Social Service Review* (June 1980):220-37.
Rossi, I. *From the Sociology of Symbols to the Sociology of Signs.* New York: Columbia University Press, 1983.
Rotenberg, B. *The Prophesy.* Unpublished manuscript. Jerusalem, 1987.
Rotenberg, M. *Damnation and Deviance.* New York: Free Press, 1978.
______. *Dialogue with Deviance.* Philadelphia: ISHI Publications, 1983.
______. *Re-biographing and Deviance.* New York: Praeger, 1987.
Rotenstreich, N. *Jews and German Philosophy.* New York: Schocken Books, 1984.
Rychlak, J. F. "The Multiple Meanings of 'Dialectic.'" In *Dialectic: Humanistic Rationale for Behavior and Development,* edited by J. F. Rychlak. Basel: S. Karger, 1976.
Sacks, O. *The Man Who Mistook His Wife for a Hat.* London: Picador, 1986.
Sandler, P. "Lebaayat Hapardes Vehashita Hamerubaat" (On the Problem of the Pardes and the Four Interpretation Method). In *Pirsumey Hachevra Lecheker Hamikra Beyisrael,* Vol. 1, edited by A. Biram. Jerusalem: Kiryat Sefer, 1955.
Sarbin, T. R. "The Concept of Hallucination." *Journal of Personality.* 35 (1967):359-80.
______. "Schizophrenic Thinking: A Role-Theoretical Analysis." *Journal of Personality* 37 (1969):190-209.
______. "On Self-Deception." *Annals of the New York Academy of Sciences* 364 (1981):220-35.
______. "The Narrative Quality in Action." Unpublished paper, 1989.
Schafer, R. *The Analytic Attitude.* New York: Basic Books, 1983.

______. "Self-Deception, Defense and Narration." *Psychoanalysis and Contemporary Thought* 10, no. 3 (1987):319-46.
Scholem, G. *Major Trends in Jewish Mysticism.* New York: Schocken Books, 1941.
______. *The Messianic Idea in Judaism.* New York: Schocken Books, 1972.
______. *Sabbatai Sevi: The Mystical Messiah.* Princeton, N.J.: Princeton University Press, 1973.
______. *Kabbalah.* Jerusalem: Keter, 1974.
______. *Elements of the Kabbalah and Its Symbolism* (Hebrew). Jerusalem: Mosad Bialik, 1977.
Schur, E. *The Awareness Trap.* New York: McGraw-Hill, 1977.
Schwaber, E. "Interpretation and the Therapeutic Action of Psycho-Analysis." *International Journal of Psycho-Analysis,* 71, part 2 (1990):229-40.
Schweid, E. *Mysticism and Judaism According to Gershom Scholem.* Jerusalem: Magnes Press, 1983.
Screech, M. A. *Erasmus, Ecstasy and the Praise of Folly.* London: Penguin Books, 1988.
Sheridan, A. *Michel Foucault: The Will to Truth.* London: Tavistock, 1982.
Shneurson, S. Z. *Maamarey Haadmor Hazaken* (The Sayings of the Old Rebbe). New York: Otzar Hachasidim, 1976.
Shopsin, B., ed. *Manic Illness.* New York: Raven Press, 1979.
Sica, A. *Weber, Irrationality and Social Order.* Berkeley: University of California Press, 1988.
Silverman, J. Shamans and Acute Schizophrenia. *American Anthropologist* 69 (1967):21-31.
Spence, D. *Narrative Truth and Historical Truth.* New York: W. W. Norton, 1982.
______. *The Freudian Metaphor.* New York: W. W. Norton, 1987.
Spiegel, J. *Transactions.* New York: Science House, 1971.
Stewart, K. "Dream Theory in Malaya." in *Altered States of Consciousness,* edited by C. Tart. New York: Wiley, 1969.
Strack, H. L. *Introduction to the Talmud and Midrash.* New York: Temple, 1969.
Suzuki, D. T. *An Introduction to Zen Buddhism.* New York: Grove Press, 1964.
Szasz, T. S. *The Myth of Mental Illness.* New York: Haeber, 1961.
Ten Houten, W. D. "Social Correlates of Cerebral Lateralization: A Neurosociological Approach." In *Language and Cognitive Styles: Patterns of Neurolinguistic and Psycholinguistic Development,* edited by R. N. St. Clair and W. Von Raffler-Engel. Amsterdam: Swetz & Zeitlinger B. V. Lisse, 1982.
Theunissen, M. *The Other.* Cambridge, MA: MIT Press, 1983.
Thompson, J. B. *Critical Hermeneutics.* Cambridge: Cambridge University Press, 1985.
Tishby, Y. *Mishnat Hazohar.* Jerusalem: Mosad Bialik, 1971.
Tulkin, S. R., and M. J. Konner. Alternative Conceptions of Intellectual Functioning." *Human Development* (1973):33-52.
Todorov, T. *Symbolism and Interpretation.* Ithaca, NY: Cornell University Press, 1982.
Uffenheimer, B. "Akdamot Lesheelat Haekstaza Hanevuit." In *Sefer Bar Ilan,* edited by M. Chalamish. Ramat Gan, Israel: Bar Ilan University Press, 1987.
Underhill, E. *Mysticism.* New York: New American Library, 1974.

Urbach, E. E. *The Sages: Their Concepts & Beliefs* (Hebrew). Jerusalem: Magnes Press, 1971.

van der Heide, A. "PARDES: Methodological Reflections on the Theory of the Four Senses." *Journal of Jewish Studies* 35, no. 2 (1983):147-59.

Watts, A. *Psychotherapy East and West.* New York: Vintage Books, 1975.

Watzlawick, P. *The Language of Change.* New York: Basic Books, 1978.

Weber, M. *The Protestant Ethic and the Spirit of Capitalism.* London: Unwin, 1970.

______. *The Sociology of Religion.* Boston: Beacon, 1967.

Weeks, G. R. "Toward a Dialectical Approach to Intervention." *Human Development* 20 (1977):277-92.

Weeks, G. R. and D. L. L'Abate. *Paradoxical Psychotherapy.* New York: Brunner/Mazel, 1982.

Weiss, J. G. *Studies in Braslav Hassidism.* Jerusalem: Bialik Institute, 1974.

Weiss-Halivni, D. *Peshat and Derash.* New York: Oxford University Press, 1990.

Witztum, E., J. T. Buchbinder, and O. Van Der Hart. "Summoning a Punishing Angel: The Treatment of a Depressive Patient with Dissociative Mystical Features." *Bulletin of the Menninger Clinic* 54, no. 4 (1990): 524-37.

Wolfson, E. "Left Contained in the Right: A Study in Zoharic Hermeneutics." *AJS Review* II, no. 1 (1986):27-52.

Wolfson, H. A. *Philo.* Vol. 2. Cambridge, MA: Harvard University Press, 1947.

Yaacov Yosef Hakohen. *Toldot Yaacov Yosef.* Jerusalem: Agudat Beit Vayelifaly, 1963.

Yaker, H. M. "The Schizophrenic Perception of Time." In *The Future of Time,* edited by H. M. Yaker, H. Osmond, and F. Cheek. New York: Andor Books, 1972.

Zax, M., and E. L. Cowen. *Abnormal Psychology.* New York: Holt, 1972.

Zilboorg, A. G. *A History of Medical Psychology.* New York: W. W. Norton, 1941.

Zipor, M. "Al Gilguleyhen shel derashot 'Al-tikrei.'" In *Yovel Sinai,* edited by Y. Refael. Jerusalem: Mosad Harav Kook, 1987.

Zunz, Y. L. *Haderashot Beyisrael.* Jerusalem: Mosad Bialik, 1974.

Index

For Product Safety Concerns and Information please contact our EU representative GPSR@taylorandfrancis.com
Taylor & Francis Verlag GmbH, Kaufingerstraße 24, 80331 München, Germany

www.ingramcontent.com/pod-product-compliance
Lightning Source LLC
Chambersburg PA
CBHW062357140725
29618CB00007B/344

9780765805836